d 2-

The Invention of Progress

The Invention of Progress

The Victorians and the Past

Peter J. Bowler

Basil Blackwell

First published 1989

Basil Blackwell Ltd
108 Cowley Road, Oxford, OX4 1JF, UK

Basil Blackwell, Inc.
3 Cambridge Center
Cambridge, Massachusetts 02142, USA

British Library Cataloguing in Publication Data

A CIP catalogue record for this book is available from the British Library.

Library of Congress Cataloging in Publication Data
Bowler, Peter J.
The invention of progress: the Victorians and the past / Peter J.
Bowler.
p. cm.
Bibliography: p.
Includes index.
1. Social evolution. 2. Progress. 3. Anthropology—History—19th
century. 4. Human evolution. I. Title.
GN360.B67 1990
303.44—dc20 89–36164
ISBN 0–631–16107–4

Typeset in 11 on 12pt Ehrhardt
by Hope Services, Abingdon
Printed in Great Britain by
Billings & Sons Ltd, Worcester

Contents

Preface

This book had its origins in a programme broadcast in London Weekend Television's series *The Making of Britain*. Lesley Smith, who was researching the series, decided to include a programme on the Victorians' fascination with the past. She soon realized that the topic could be extended beyond the bounds of 'modern' history to include prehistory and even the study of the fossil record. I was brought in on the strength of my interests in nineteenth-century evolutionism, and a programme was put together under the title 'The Invention of the Past'. This particular title was chosen to indicate that the Victorians created an image of the past which would fit in with their ideology of progress. Even at the time, I was aware that my knowledge of Victorian attitudes towards modern and classical history was, to say the least, rather sketchy, but I did my best to describe how the idea of progress served to unify what might otherwise have seemed to be quite separate debates in the areas of history, archaeology and biological evolutionism. I was pleased to find that I could correlate some of my own ideas on Victorian evolutionism with what other historians have been saying about contemporary attitudes towards the more recent past. Further reading soon convinced me that a useful book could be written around the theme of the conflict between two models of progress in the Victorian era – what I have called the continuous and the cyclic models of progress – as they were extended to cover the ever wider range of the past opened up by archaeology and geology. The project was taken up enthusiastically by Virginia Murphy and the editorial staff at Basil Blackwell, and the result lies before you.

By its very nature this is an interdisciplinary book, and I have tried to write at a level that will make the material comprehensible to nonspecialists in the various areas surveyed. Obviously, I write with more confidence on the topics of geology, palaeontology and evolution theory, since these are my primary fields of research. I hope that historians of science will find something of interest in my efforts to show that the models of the past used in these areas can be shown to reflect the same concerns as those underlying debates on human history. Conversely, I hope that readers more familiar with other aspects of Victorian culture will find it useful to have new avenues opened up by which they can approach the contemporary debates on evolution and mankind's place in nature. It will not escape the attention of historians of science that I have used this survey to promote my own rather unorthodox views on the emergence of evolutionism. I can only say in my defence that as I tried to extend my knowledge of the Victorians' attitudes towards the past, I became ever more strongly convinced of the violence that we do to the historiography of evolutionism by making the emergence of the theory of natural selection the centrepiece of the so-called 'Darwinian revolution'.

This is unashamedly a book on the history of ideas. I have made it quite clear that I see the two opposing theories of progress as having strong ideological overtones, but I have not engaged in the kind of minute sociological analysis that has become fashionable in the history of science. As far as I can tell, most of what I say is compatible with the new interpretations offered by these detailed studies, but I have been more interested in the possibility of building bridges between the history of science and other areas of Victorian studies. There is still room for fruitful generalization, especially when this can help to break down the barriers that exist between the history of science and other areas of the history of ideas. All too often, these barriers have been created by historians of science themselves insisting upon too close an adherence to what hindsight perceives to be the 'main line' of scientific development. Even when studying the wider impact of theories such as evolutionism, we have often allowed our work to be restricted by preconceived ideas about which issues were the most important.

As far as I am aware, this book offers the first serious attempt to link Victorian ideas on the past across such a broad spectrum. The fact that historians of geology and evolutionism have not, so far, thought to explore the links between history and the historical sciences is another symptom of the determining role played by hindsight. Because geology and palaeontology opened up a world beyond human history, we have tended to assume that scientists in these areas were free to create models of the past that did not relate to contemporary ideas on the development of society. If anyone should object that I have ignored the scientific dimension of geology, palaeontology or evolutionism, my only defence is that I have other fish to fry. The newly professionalized geology of the Victorian era was nevertheless a *historical* science, and its practitioners were often at pains to ensure that their ideas on the history of life on earth were compatible with their beliefs about the origin of mankind and the progress of civilization. The historical sciences, like the more rigorous study of human history that emerged in the same period, applied their methodology to the verification of theoretical models of the past that reflected the wider values of Victorian society. It is thus no coincidence that we can trace parallels between the models used to analyse the various levels of the past.

One final point: this book is subtitled *The Victorians and the Past*, but in fact it covers a somewhat broader timespan than the Victorian era itself. Many features of the mid-nineteenth-century debates were already beginning to emerge before Victoria came to the throne, and the Edwardian era certainly preserved and developed some aspects of late Victorian thought. As the epilogue suggests, the 'Victorian' ideal of progress survived into the early decades of the twentieth century, before collapsing in the face of accumulating social and philosophical pressures.

Peter J. Bowler
Belfast, 1988

List of Illustrations

Plates

Figures

Introduction:
Patterns of History

The nineteenth century saw an unprecedented acceleration in the
development of material civilization. As the century began, Britain
had just begun its industrialization. By the time Victoria came to the
throne in 1837 the railways had begun to spread across the landscape.
By the end of the century Europe and America were centres of
massive industrialization with the power to dominate the world – and
the world was girdled by a network of railways, steamship lines and
telegraph cables that allowed vast empires to be administered.
Europeans had achieved world domination through their pioneering
efforts to develop an industrial civilization. Yet this period of material
progress was also an age dominated by a fascination with the past.
History offered the preferred way of understanding how both human
society and the material world operated. The Victorians read learned
works on history and historical novels avidly, and the period saw
major advances in historical methodology based on a growing
awareness of the differences separating the characters of the various
epochs of social development. Immense publicity surrounded the
work of archaeologists who filled in the details of classical and biblical
history.

Why should an age of progress have been fascinated by the past? The
answer to this question lies in the tensions that rapid progress created
within Victorian culture. Technological change can itself be frightening
as well as fascinating: many early critics of the railways thought they
would harm both the countryside and the health of their passengers.
The growth of the factory system led to all the horrors associated with
overcrowded cities, and the resulting social tensions were all too

obvious. Britain had escaped the terrors of the French Revolution, but had to grapple with unrelenting demands for social reform, both from the captains of industry and from the lower ranks of the new industrial hierarchy. The nineteenth century saw itself as an age of transition from mediaeval to modern values – a transition that was often painful and that opened up massive uncertainties as to what modern values should be.

John Stuart Mill's series of articles on 'The Spirit of the Age' in 1831 reflected this general recognition that social change was taking place faster than ever before. The idea of comparing one's own age with the past, Mill argued, could only become popular at a time when everyone had become conscious of living in a changing world. Recognition of change inevitably generated a concern for the future: 'The conviction is already not far from being universal, that the times are pregnant with change; and that the nineteenth century will be known to posterity as the era of one of the greatest revolutions of which history has preserved the remembrance, in the human mind, and in the whole constitution of human society.'[1]

The practical question was how to predict the future course of society. Radical thinkers, including Mill, felt that the past was dead in the sense that it could no longer be looked upon as a source of authority. Ancient social and moral values might not be relevant in the modern world. Some thinkers adopted a totally ahistorical position, dismissing the past completely and advocating a reform of society based on a recognition of the underlying principles of human behaviour. The utilitarian school, personified by Jeremy Bentham, followed this course, believing that the individual's desire for happiness was the mainspring of social life and should be made the basis of all legislation.[2] Mill was well aware of this approach since his father, James Mill, was a prominent member of the Benthamite school. But when he wrote 'The Spirit of the Age' he was already familiar with other social programmes that paid more attention to history. He was in contact with the French followers of Saint-Simon, including the young Auguste Comte, who discerned a pattern in history which they believed would make sense of the current social changes.[3] One did not have to follow the past, but one could use it to see the general trend of social development and thus to predict the future. Of even greater influence in this direction were the writings of

[1] Mill, *Collected Works*, XXII, pp. 228–9 (full details of all works cited appear in the bibliography). 'The Spirit of the Age' appeared in five parts in the *Political Examiner*.

[2] On the utilitarians see Halévy, *The Growth of Philosophic Radicalism*.

[3] *The Autobiography of John Stuart Mill*, pp. 114–17.

German historians and Idealist philosophers, who saw development through time as the key to the understanding of the world. German thought was already percolating into Britain under the influence of Samuel Taylor Coleridge – a fact that Mill was later to acknowledge by classing Bentham and Coleridge as the twin centres around which nineteenth-century thought revolved.[4]

The Victorians' fascination with the past was thus the product of an age obsessed with change, desperately hoping that history itself might supply the reassurance that could no longer be derived from ancient beliefs. The search for the first principles of social organization did not lead to maxims that could be applied irrespective of time, because society developed through time and it was necessary to understand the pattern of development before any attempt could be made to predict or control the future. The Victorians sought reassurance through the belief that social evolution was moving in a purposeful direction. The idea of progress became central to their thinking precisely because it offered the hope that current changes might be part of a meaningful historical pattern.

Although the passion for history generated vast quantities of research and a new self-consciousness about the methodology of studying the past (stimulated largely by the Germans), the fact that history had a purpose for the Victorians ensured that the enterprise would be no mere fact-gathering exercise. As A. Dwight Culler has shown, they used the past as a mirror in which to view their own time.[5] The idea of progress was imposed upon history to create the sense of order that the Victorians craved. In a very real sense they *invented* the past, since all the factual discoveries of antiquaries and archaeologists had to be interpreted within a conceptual scheme that satisfied the cultural demands of the age. There was no unanimity over the character of progress, however, because different groups within Victorian society had different needs that could only be satisfied in different ways. The bold assertions of radical materialists and positivists were anathema to those who still wished to fit the rise and fall of ancient civilizations into a scheme reflecting the workings of divine providence. As we shall see, the Victorians invented not a single idea of progress, but several such ideas, each with its own religious, philosophical and ideological implications.

The Victorians' obsession with history was fuelled by an immense extension of the range of past events open to their investigation. The

---

[4] Mill's articles on Bentham and Coleridge (from the *Westminster Review*, 1838 and 1840) may be found in his *Collected Works*, X, pp. 76–163. On the influence of German thought in nineteenth-century Britain, see Ashton, *The German Idea*.
[5] Culler, *The Victorian Mirror of History*.

historical mode of thinking may have had its origins in an interest in the relationship between ancient and modern civilizations, but it could be applied to any sequence of events in time. The Victorians learnt more about the classical and biblical past through the development of archaeology – but they were also the first to confront the fact that an extension of the same techniques revealed a hitherto undreamt-of antiquity for the human race. Exploration of the 'stone age' added a whole new dimension to the study of how society developed, a dimension taken up eagerly by anthropologists seeking to understand the 'primitive' cultures still to be found in many parts of the world. The geologists and palaeontologists of the early nineteenth century created the first realistic outline of the history of the earth and its inhabitants based on the fossil record. Their discoveries, like those of the prehistorians, seemed to challenge the traditional biblical story of the creation upon which many still relied for a meaningful interpretation of human origins. We are used to thinking of the controversies surrounding geology and the theory of evolution as symptomatic of the emerging conflict between science and religion. But these were *historical* sciences, and their radical implications were enhanced by the fact that they dovetailed with more familiar areas of history where archaeologists and anthropologists were independently challenging existing ideas.

Modern scholars are certainly aware of the historical dimension to Victorian thought. As we shall see below, there is no shortage of material analysing the work of Victorian historians and historical novelists. Yet to a large extent this analysis has been conducted without reference to the extension of history into the remoter past.[6] The excitement surrounding the work of archaeologists excavating sites of classical or biblical interest has also been documented, but generally as an area separate from Victorian historical writing. The emergence of prehistoric archaeology and anthropology form separate areas yet again, usually the province of scholars with a specific interest in the origins of these disciplines. The debates centred on geology and evolution theory are also the province of specialized historians of science. Accounts of Victorian culture note the effects of the Darwinian revolution, but often show little appreciation of detailed modern research in this field. In turn, the 'Darwin industry' in the history of science has paid little attention to contemporary develop-

---

[6] An exception is Mandelbaum's account of nineteenth-century thought, *History, Man, and Reason*. Toulmin and Goodfield's *The Discovery of Time* surveys a broad range of historical studies, but concentrates mainly on geology and evolution theory in the period after 1800.

ments in archaeology and anthropology, let alone to the general
historical dimension of nineteenth-century thought.

The purpose of this book is to break down these barriers by
showing that there are common themes uniting the debates in history,
archaeology, anthropology, geology and biological evolutionism. I
shall argue that particular episodes such as the debate over Darwin's
theory were part of a comprehensive effort to explore the patterns
through which the past (and hence the present and future) could be
understood. The *Origin of Species* was controversial because it
symbolized the challenge to the biblical view of history that had
already been thrown down by the geologists and the advocates of
human progress. Evolution became a central theme of late-nineteenth-
century thought because it brought together parallel changes in
attitudes towards human history, human origins and the development
of life on earth. Only by looking across the whole field of Victorian
historical studies can we hope to understand what these debates were
really about.

The idea of progress was of central importance because it offered a
compromise between the old creationism and the more extreme
manifestations of the new materialism. By the middle of the century,
few educated people could escape the realization that the Genesis
story of mankind's creation by God offered at best only a symbol of
how and why we came into the world. If the universe was a dynamic
rather than a static system, how could one hold on to the belief that it
worked according to a rational and morally acceptable plan? The
concept of evolution supplied an answer to this question by
suggesting that all phases of the universe's development, from the
creation of life through to the expansion of European civilization
around the globe, were aspects of a general progressive scheme
designed to create order out of chaos.

An obvious, if limited, example of this tendency to view history as
the record of a purposeful development is the 'Whig interpretation' of
British history. Here the story of how the British constitution had
developed was rewritten to endorse the values of a particular party.
The Whigs (or Liberals, as they became) believed that freedom of
thought and of commercial enterprise were the foundations of
Britain's power. They thus made heroes of the historical figures who
seemed to have contributed to the enhancement of those liberties. As
W. E. H. Lecky wrote: 'We are Cavaliers or Roundheads before we
are Conservatives or Liberals.'[7] The Whigs' hero-worship of
Cromwell was all too obviously value-laden, but as Victorian Britain

---

[7] Lecky, *The Political Value of History*, p. 19.

Plate 1   William Frederick Yeames, *And When Did You Last See Your Father?* (1878).
Yeames shows a young Cavalier being interrogated by a group of Roundheads. The picture is clearly
intended to generate a romantic sympathy for the lost cause of the monarchy, overthrown by
colourless – and very ruthless – Puritans.

National Museums and Galleries on Merseyside, Walker Art Gallery

grew in power, the underlying values of Whiggism were increasingly taken for granted even by those who were not politically in the Liberal camp.[8] Modern historians hold up Whig history as an example of the dangers inherent in approaching the past with too strong a commitment to the present.[9] Indeed, we now use the term 'whiggism' to denote any form of history told in such a way as to make the present seem the inevitable outcome of a trend running through the past. The idea of continuous social progress was, in effect, Whig history on a cosmic scale, in which the development of society was portrayed as an inexorable ascent towards Victorian values. As we shall see, this faith in the inevitability of progress was to have its critics – and the attacks would become all the more vigorous when the idea was extended to other fields outside the realm of modern history.

The demand for reforms allowing greater freedom was aimed at giving the middle classes a level of political power that would match their economic role in a newly industrialized society. By claiming that all the progress of previous eras had flowed from the same trend, reform could be made to seem the inevitable outcome of the natural processes of social evolution. But the expansion of knowledge about the past allowed progressionism to be extended far beyond the confines of modern history. As philosophers such as Herbert Spencer began to think in more general terms about the development of society, they became convinced that even the earliest phases of human prehistory must have been governed by the same trend. Social evolutionism allowed certain aspects of the Whig interpretation of history to be painted on a much broader canvas. Archaeologists used the discovery of stone and bronze tools to back up the idea of technological and social progress, while anthropologists increasingly tended to see those technologically primitive races that had survived into the present as illustrations of how contemporary man's ancestors had lived back in the stone age.

The advent of biological evolutionism allowed this progressive scheme to be extended even further back in time. After some controversy, even the origin of the human race itself came to be interpreted as a development arising from ape-like ancestors, following a progressive trend that could be seen in the fossil record stretching upwards from the earliest forms of life. By stressing the progressive character of evolution, the followers of Darwin and Spencer were able to head off the claim that they had diminished the status of mankind. The human race might not be the direct creation

[8] See Burrow, *A Liberal Descent*.
[9] The classic critique is Butterfield's *The Whig Interpretation of History*.

of God, but it was now at the cutting edge of a universal trend towards higher things. More important, the whole process of development from the origins of life through to the emergence of industrial capitalism had been generated by the ongoing activities of individual organisms and individual people trying to conquer their environment. Evolution was the sum total of a vast multitude of individual progressive acts, allowing middle-class values to be seen as the driving force of an essentially purposeful system of nature. Some liberals were reluctant to speak of a divine plan underlying the ascent of life, because they were anxious not to compromise with the traditional belief that the social hierarchy was established by the Creator. Yet their insistence that progress advances towards a morally significant goal retained an element of cosmic teleology reminiscent of the older tradition.

There was also a darker side to the Victorian image of the past. The arrogance of the progressionists sparked off a distinct unease among those who viewed current social developments with a more jaundiced eye. The charge that evolutionism meant atheism and the loss of all moral values was difficult to sustain because the evolutionists did everything in their power to ensure that progress was seen to have a morally significant goal. But the fact that the charge could be made at all was symptomatic of the uncertainty created by the new developments. The opponents of simple progressionism tried to brand evolution as a theory in which everything is reduced to chance, and in which therefore there can be no goal towards which the whole system is moving. Very few Victorians could accept either cultural relativism or the view that nature is an undirected and essentially purposeless system. Many were worried by the loss of the old values and felt that the new idea of progress was not enough to restore the traditional sense of mankind's unique spiritual place in the world. They wanted to retain at least a modernized version of the belief that God played an active role in history. The emergence of the human race and of great civilizations must arise from something more than the summation of individual acts of selfishness. Perhaps there had been an overall progression, but these more conservative thinkers remained convinced that it was a more complex, and ultimately a more mysterious process than the liberals assumed.

From this more conservative position arose another vision of progress as a sequence of distinct episodes or cycles, with each species, race or civilization rising to new heights and then making room for its successor. The assumption that history is essentially repetitive or cyclic had once been more powerful than any form of directionalism − and it remains the orthodox viewpoint of most cultures outside the Judaeo-Christian tradition. Christianity had ensured that history would be seen as the record of a process with a beginning and an end, and the new progressionism was in this sense a continuation of this developmental vision under a new guise. Only a very few Victorians were able to see history as purely cyclic or nondirectional, but by synthesizing the cyclic and progressionist models it was possible to establish a compromise that seemed to preserve more of the traditional Christian viewpoint. If all the advances made during the history of life and the history of civilization led ultimately to stagnation and the need for renewal before a new episode of progress could begin, it would be obvious that something more than individual human effort was needed to initiate each upward step.

Any educated Victorian knew about the decline of classical civilization and was thus forced to confront the possibility that his own society might face a similar fate. As the harmful social effects of industrialization became more apparent, some critics longed for the supposed order and certainty of the mediaeval world. The pattern of development was not necessarily one of unidirectional progress, and could not be explained as the sum total of a myriad everyday events. The cyclic view of progress accepted that each race or civilization will rise and fall in its turn, each contributing something towards the eventual fulfilment of the divine plan. The origin of each new phase of development – and hence the origin of the human race itself – was not the predictable outcome of a universal trend running through the whole sequence. Human effort was meaningful only to the extent that it helped the nation to achieve its destiny; mere selfishness led to degeneration rather than progress. The origin of nations, like the origin of species, represented an essentially mysterious injection of creative power transcending the normal laws of nature and raising things on to a higher plane.

The thesis of this book is that the tension between the progressionist and the cyclic views of development enlivened the whole range of Victorian historical studies. In discussions of the growth of civilization or of the ascent of life displayed by the fossil record, each of these two alternatives was equally likely to emerge. The fact that similar alternatives were considered in all areas of historical thinking provided a unifying structure for debates on the difficult questions that had to be confronted when dealing with the major progressive steps in the ascent from the earliest forms of life to modern civilization. Only by recognizing the interplay between these two interpretations of the pattern of historical development shall we be able to understand the positions adopted by the Victorians who confronted issues such as the origin of mankind and the relationship between mind and nature.

One way of trying to understand the origin of these two alternatives is by unpacking the implications of the most common metaphor used by Victorians in discussing the process of historical development: a comparison with the life cycle of the individual. The term 'evolution' itself had originally been applied to the growth of the embryo, and took on its modern meaning only in the mid-nineteenth century through a deliberate extension into all areas of development.[10] Individuals, civilizations and even biological species were supposed to experience birth, growth and maturity. One of the most popular expressions of nineteenth-century evolutionism was the recapitulation theory – the claim that the past evolution of the species is displayed in the growth of the modern embryo. But this analogy was capable of being explored in two significantly different directions, thereby generating the tension between the two alternative patterns we wish to explore. The tension arises, quite simply, from the decision either to concentrate on the 'progressive' phase of growth through to maturity, or to admit that all growth cycles end in old age, death and replacement by the next generation. The nineteenth century had an essentially 'developmental' world view, but the idea of development formed only a loose framework for discussion because the analogy with growth could be explored in these two quite different forms.

The concept of a steady growth from birth through to maturity forms the most optimistic version of the developmental model. It finds its expression in the simplest version of progressionist evolutionism, still popular among many nonspecialists even today. The evolving entity is assumed to begin as a simple structure with the potential to develop steadily towards the full flowering of maturity. The embryologists of the early nineteenth century – many of them Germans – charted the growth of the human foetus from the fertilized ovum, providing a detailed model that could be used for all processes of development through time. The chief characteristic of such a model is that the stages of development are thought to succeed one another inexorably, driving the system on towards its fully developed state. Teleology – the assumption that development moves towards a purposeful goal – is built into the embryological analogy from the start. Once we begin to think of the history of civilization, or of life on earth, as following the same pattern as the growing embryo, we are locked into a model in which evolution is seen as the ascent of a ladder towards ever-higher states of development. Those who

[10] See Bowler, 'The Changing Meaning of "Evolution"'.

construct such an analogy almost invariably assume that their own species or culture represents the highest stage of development reached so far. The more self-confident Victorians certainly saw the spread of European power around the globe as an indication of their own cultural maturity.

The classic problem faced by exponents of this analogy is: why are there so many cultures or species which have not developed as far as possible up the scale? Why has Britain enjoyed a uniquely favoured constitutional development? Why has the white race progressed so much further than any other? Why are there still apes and other 'lower' animals apparently left behind by the march of evolution? The problem was most frequently resolved by treating all other cultures and species as merely immature versions of the highest. 'Primitive' tribes and apes represent lower rungs on the ladder by which Victorian Britain ascended to its pre-eminent status. This technique invokes the idea of parallel evolution, in which many different lines of development ascend the same scale but at different rates, the slower ones being left behind at levels corresponding to ancestral stages in the development of the highest. Victorian anthropologists assumed that contemporary 'primitive' tribes were exact equivalents of the Europeans' stone-age ancestors. Exactly the same model was used by biologists to explain the continued existence of the lower animals. Once parallelism is invoked, the only remaining question is that of why some lines have advanced up the scale faster than others. This was usually answered by an appeal to the more stimulating environment within which some lines were thought to have evolved.

The darker side of developmentalism can be expressed by pointing out that the analogy with the complete life cycle lends no support to the belief that the stages of development must inevitably ascend towards ever higher levels. After maturity come senility and death, with reproduction, i.e. the creation of a new, as yet immature individual as the only means of perpetuation. Aware of the decline of ancient civilizations, many Victorian historians preferred such a cyclic model. They saw each civilization making its own contribution and then passing the torch on to another while it faced its own inevitable end. Such a view could retain a long-range optimism while allowing for the eventual decline even of the Victorians' own culture. On this model there is still a 'main line' of ascent, yet the parallels between different episodes of cultural development are more subtle. Each race or culture has its own period of growth, maturity and decline superimposed on the overall ascent of civilization.

What is perhaps less well known is that geologists and biologists tracing out the development of life on earth frequently appealed to the same analogy. To them, the fossil record revealed *phases* of development, as the Age of Reptiles, for instance, was succeeded by the Age of Mammals. Later on, many palaeontologists thought they could trace the decline of groups such as the dinosaurs, as though the whole family entered an age of senility as the prelude to extinction. This cyclic model of evolution would allow one to argue that the appearance of mankind represented the start of an entirely new phase in the ascent of life, thereby evading some of the theological criticisms aimed at the assumption of a simple continuity between animal and human history.

How, then, does Darwin fit into all of this? A facetious answer would be 'with difficulty', for there is no doubt that the aspects of Darwin's theory most prized by modern biologists are distinctly nondevelopmental in character. I have argued elsewhere that the revival of Darwin's theory by modern biologists has encouraged historians of science to take a whiggish view of nineteenth-century evolutionism which conceals its developmental foundations.[11] Because we now think that natural selection (as synthesized with Mendelian genetics) represents a major contribution to evolution theory, we have assumed that Darwin's discovery and publication of his theory must represent the key steps in the development of evolutionary biology. There is no doubt that the *Origin of Species* played a major catalytic role in converting the scientific world to evolutionism, and this precipitated the synthesis of ideas on the animal and human phases of development. But natural selection remained peripheral to most biologists' views on the mechanism of evolution until well into the twentieth century. Late-nineteenth-century evolutionism remained emphatically developmental in character, and we should, perhaps, pay as much attention to the debate between the progressionist and cyclic viewpoints in this area as we normally do to the criticisms levelled against Darwin.

Some aspects of Darwin's thinking retained a developmental character, and he made sure that the *Origin of Species* could be interpreted as a contribution to progressionism. But in private he recognized that the chief thrust of his theory was a direct challenge to the developmental view of the history of life. By concentrating on how a species adapts to changes in its environment, Darwin undermined the whole logic of the analogy with stages of growth. His model of evolution was not a ladder of development but a branching tree in which there was no central 'trunk' running through to mankind as the goal of creation. A single species might divide into two, three or

---

[11] See Bowler, *The Non-Darwinian Revolution.*

even more 'daughter' species, if samples from the original population migrated to different localities. Each branch would adapt to its new environment as best it could, and there would be no reason for the biologist to rank the end-product of one line of evolution as being superior to or more mature than any other. The implications of this approach, dimly recognized by Darwin and only fully expounded by his modern followers, are that evolution has no main line and hence no particular goal. The human race is not the inevitable end-product of animal evolution, but an unusual species formed by a unique combination of circumstances forced upon its ancestors. In cultural evolution, the equivalent model is one in which each culture is accepted as an equally valid expression of mankind's potential. No culture is inherently superior to any other, and certainly none represents an ancestral stage though which another passed on the way to higher things.

Significantly, there were few Victorian historians or anthropologists who could adopt such an attitude of cultural relativism, just as there were few biologists who could accept that evolution did not lead inevitably towards the human level of intelligence. Developmentalism flourished because the Victorians were convinced of their own unique place in history, and were thus compelled to relate all other cultures and species to their own origins. Whether cyclic or progressive, the developmental approach denied the purely relativistic implications of the branching model of evolution. It could not admit others as equals, only assess their contribution to the main line of development – or dismiss them as living fossils. Acceptance of cultural relativism and of a truly divergent model of biological evolution only became possible in the twentieth century with the collapse of the optimistic attitude which had sustained Victorian progressionism. If we wish to understand the contributions of the nineteenth century, we must be prepared to recognize the central importance of the debates over the rival interpretations of development in all areas of history.

One final point must be made to clarify the broader implications of the progressionist and the cyclic models of development. It has long been fashionable to depict the late-Victorian era as a time dominated by a ruthless attitude of 'social Darwinism'. Struggle was the driving force of progress, and the elimination of the unfit was held to be necessary for both natural and social development. There should be no pity for those who failed to contribute. Darwin certainly popularized the phrase 'struggle for existence' and was accused by his critics of portraying nature as a totally amoral system. But in fact the use of 'Darwinian' language was frequently associated with progressionist interpretations of development, both linear and cyclic. In the liberal tradition, individual effort was the driving force of progress, while individual failure was rewarded by nature's punishment. Although Herbert Spencer coined the phrase 'survival of the fittest', he laid comparatively little emphasis on the elimination of the congenitally unfit. For him, the whole purpose of struggle was to encourage everyone to maximum effort: the natural penalties of failure were the best inducement to do better next time.

Even supporters of the cyclic model of development were inclined to use what looks like 'Darwinian' language when discussing the replacement of a worn-out race or civilization by its successor. Indeed, some of the most blatant exploitations of the struggle metaphor can be found in the writings of those who were advocating a cyclic model of development in opposition to Darwin and Spencer. The whole point of a progressionism designed to identify one's own society as the high point of development is that any individual, or any other society, that does not measure up to the required standards must be pushed aside to make room for further progress. A ruthless attitude towards failure was characteristic not so much of Darwin's theory of branching evolution, but of the Victorians' wider faith in their own superiority. 'Lower' races were stagnant failures, relics of earlier episodes in the history of mankind's ascent, with nothing further to contribute towards the march of progress. Darwin became a convenient symbol of this more ruthless attitude to failure, but his theory was in some respects only an aberrant product of the progressionism that was the true source of 'social Darwinism'.

Part I

The Development of Society

1

Progress and Civilization

The novels of Sir Walter Scott introduced many Victorians to a sense of history with their dramatization of past ages. Scott's ability to evoke the character of an earlier period may reflect the influence of Romanticism, but his interest in social development had been stimulated by the 'philosophical historians' who had flourished in eighteenth-century Scotland. Independently of the German revolution in historiography, these social philosophers created a model of history based on a hierarchy of developmental stages, with economic factors as the driving force of progress. Scott himself lost confidence in progress, but his readers saw the novels as illustration of how British society had modernized itself since the middle ages. Historians such as Macaulay popularized the claim that industrial progress had created a more advanced state of society. The Whig interpretation of history was designed to exalt the virtues of freedom and initiative essential to a *laissez-faire* economy. Anyone who had helped the cause of liberty was a hero, anyone who had opposed it, a villain. But underlying the Whig interpretation was the assumption that the present state of society was the inevitable outcome of past trends – the villains could check, but never reverse, the march of progress. As J. W. Burrow has shown, this essentially teleological view of Victorian society as the goal of progress came to be shared by a majority of historians as Britain rose to the status of a global power.[1]

To the extent that the Whig historians accepted the Scottish model of economic development, they were forced to concede that Britain

[1] Burrow, *A Liberal Descent.*

offered merely a special illustration of trends affecting European society as a whole. Britain might have been the first country to reach the threshold of the industrial revolution, but others must be making their way towards the same goal. Industrial development was the result of inventions made by individuals; and individuals worked best in a free-enterprise society. Economic necessity thus led all nations towards the liberal virtues of toleration and freedom. The claim that history reveals a general trend towards liberalism can be seen in W. E. H. Lecky's *History of the Rise and Influence of the Spirit of Rationalism in Europe*, published in 1865. Lecky saw the freedom of thought made possible by the Reformation as a characteristic of European civilization as a whole – although he conceded that there had been a corresponding loss of enthusiasm and the willingness to commit oneself to a cause.[2] Social philosophers such as Herbert Spencer treated the development of human society since the earliest time as a universal trend towards 'modern' values, thus generalizing the process that the Whig historians explored through the growth of British institutions.

The model of social development in which liberal values are the product of inevitable socio-economic trends enabled the commercial and professional classes of Victorian Britain to maintain that the society they were creating represented the goal to which all other nations must aspire. The laws of social development were inexorable, but they operated by summing up the results of individual efforts. *People* made progress possible – although they were not free to create whatever society they chose. The theory of economic determinism postulated only one ladder of development, to be climbed by all. In thus seeing social evolution as directed towards a single, morally significant goal, the individualist tradition retained a form of cosmic teleology. Its exponents may have been unwilling to stress the role of the Creator's guiding hand, since this would smack too strongly of the aristocracy's appeal to a divinely created social hierarchy. But it was hard to conceal the implication that nature – including human nature – was designed to achieve a moral purpose. As the concept of progressive evolution by natural forces was gradually extended to include the origins of the human race itself, some evolutionists found it convenient to stress this implication precisely because it allowed them to head off the claim that their theory undermined the moral character of mankind. If the human race arose from animal ancestors by the accumulated effects of individual effort, it became vital to argue that the process was at least indirectly the expression of an underlying divine purpose.

[2] Lecky, *History of . . . Rationalism in Europe*, II, pp. 408–9.

In this respect, if no other, the Whig approach to history and sociology mirrored the assumptions of its greatest rival. We shall see in chapter 2 below how more conservative thinkers adjusted to the idea of social change by postulating the existence of a divine plan of development. For them, societies evolved along lines predetermined by archetypical forces, their potential unfolding just as the embryo grows within the womb. The two interpretations differed over the driving force and the exact pattern of change, but were united in the faith that nothing could stop the march of society towards its goal. Both held that Victorian Britain was to play a key role in this stage of the world's history. Liberals and conservatives alike thus preferred a developmental model of social evolution in which change is directed toward a preconceived goal.

The European nations' industrial power gave them the ability to dominate the world, and the theory of progress held that they had the moral right to lead other branches of humanity into the light. Given such a view of European cultural maturity, it was inevitable that anthropologists studying less industrialized societies would regard them as being lower down the scale of development. This interpretation received a powerful boost when it was realized that Europe itself had once been inhabited by stone-age peoples whose way of life must have been as 'primitive' as that of the lowest modern savages. The cultural evolutionism of the mid-nineteenth century gave substance to the theory of social development proposed by the philosophical historians. It imposed a preconceived view of how societies must develop on to the data being gathered from all around the world. The earlier stages of Europe's social development could be seen preserved through to the present in those cultures which had advanced less far up the scale. There was no room here for a branching model of social development: to accept that other cultures were equally valid expressions of human nature would imply a relativization of values that most Victorians found unacceptable.

But why, then, had Europe – and more especially Britain – advanced so much more rapidly up the scale of social development? It was easy enough to claim that certain kinds of environment are more conducive to progress. The Whig historians had already argued that Britain's status as an island had preserved its liberties by protecting it from continental threats. But if this argument were taken too far, it might imply that the development of society was crucially dependent upon geographical factors – in which case the supposedly universal hierarchy of cultural stages might not be universal after all. Henry Buckle solved this problem by treating the great empires of warmer climates as abnormally overdeveloped forms of an early stage in the cultural and technological hierarchy. But an increasing number of historians and anthropologists eventually came to suspect that the various human races had become endowed with different capacities for intellectual development. This view became quite plausible once the theory of biological evolution became popular, and even some liberals adopted the view that races which evolved in a less stimulating environment acquired a less well developed mental capacity.

Whig History

The central plank of the Whig programme was an appeal to individual liberty at the expense of ancient aristocratic privileges. As J. W. Burrow has pointed out, however, such a policy could be justified in several different ways.[3] One could appeal directly to the rights of the individual, as established by philosophical analysis, bypassing history except as a record of unjust oppression. Sir Robert Walpole's supporters, for instance, had treated liberty as a purely modern acquisition established by the Glorious Revolution of 1688. But the Whigs soon began to look to the past for moral support, creating an image of the seventeenth century as a period of struggle between freedom-seeking Protestants and a repressive Stuart monarchy tainted with Catholicism. Thus the concept of modern liberties as the culmination of a historical trend began to emerge.

The thinkers of the eighteenth-century Enlightenment were generally on the side of liberty, and took a dim view of the middle ages as a period of religious overenthusiasm. They hoped that rational analysis would now reveal the true nature of mankind, thereby showing men how to construct the best form of society. Some radicals dismissed the past altogether and tried to define the rights of man which they hoped would be enshrined in future constitutions, if some 'enlightened despot' could perhaps be persuaded to adopt the philosophers' views. British thinkers were less inclined to rely on converting the existing rulers and hoped to force reforms on a reluctant government by popular pressure – a position sustained by Bentham and his supporters in the early nineteenth century.

Others suspected that liberty was not something that could be produced by the stroke of a pen, even if it were possible to discover the underlying principles of human nature. History was important because it revealed that society had developed through a series of stages towards its modern, potentially liberal form, driven by

[3] Burrow, *A Liberal Descent*, ch. 1.

inexorable economic pressures. Only by understanding the stages of development could the philosopher hope to predict the direction in which society should be moving. On the continent, the idea of progress was proclaimed in Condorcet's famous sketch of 1795.[4] But long before this, the Scottish philosophical historians had defined their own scheme of human progress. As the modern world grew in confidence, respect for the ancients decreased, and it became easier to believe that the trend of social change was towards greater material wealth and liberty. .

Adam Smith's *Wealth of Nations* expounded the economic philosophy of the commercial age: all men are selfish and seek to improve their position; but their efforts to better themselves invariably result in benefits to society as a whole. This was the principle of the 'natural identity of interests', with its teleological implication of an 'invisible hand' somehow ensuring that public benefits arose from individual selfishness. Left to themselves, individual human beings will increase not only their own wealth, but also the wealth of society as a whole, thus stimulating economic and social progress.

Smith's lectures on jurisprudence during the 1760s explicitly developed the claim that social progress, if not checked by climate or by repressive policies, follows an inevitable sequence of developmental stages leading towards free-enterprise capitalism. The implicit teleology of the system was extended to include the idea of a pre-ordained pattern of development that was, at least in principle, open to all societies. Smith postulated four stages of social development: the age of hunting was succeeded by the ages of herding, agriculture and commerce, the driving force of progress being the application of human ingenuity to the need to feed the expanding population.[5] Each mode of production had its own characteristic form of society, but at each level the efforts made by individuals to improve their lot generated a pressure towards the next stage of development. In primitive societies the individual's freedom to innovate was often restricted, but the degree of freedom expanded as society advanced. Freedom of enterprise became absolutely essential as the economy moved towards the industrial mode of production, where technical innovation became the order of the day. Similar views on the progress of society through stages defined by ever more complex economies

---

[4] Translated as *Sketch for a Historical Picture of the Progress of the Human Mind*. On the origins of the idea of progress, see Bury, *The Idea of Progress*, Pollard, *The Idea of Progress* and Nisbet, *History of the Idea of Progress*. The theme of this chapter corresponds roughly to Nisbet's chapter 6, 'Progress as Freedom'.

[5] Smith, *Lectures on Jurisprudence*, pp. 14–16. On the underlying principles of Smith's view of society see Halévy, *The Growth of Philosophic Radicalism*, ch. 3.

were expressed in Adam Ferguson's *Essay on the History of Civil Society* (1767) and John Millar's *Origin of the Distribution of Ranks* (1771).[6] Ferguson argued that progress was an essential human characteristic and drew a comparison with growth: 'Not only the individual advances from infancy to manhood, but the species itself from rudeness to civilization.'[7]

On this model, it would make no sense to look to the remote past for the source of modern liberties. If Britain enjoyed more freedom than other European countries, this was because it had advanced further from the agricultural, or feudal, state of society towards a commercial economy. But the philosophical historians' theory did, nevertheless, allow one to applaud the efforts of those members of the commercial classes who had striven for liberty in recent times. Not all Enlightenment thinkers agreed with this assessment, however. It was, in fact, another Scottish historian who challenged the original Whig interpretation of British history in which the struggle for liberty had been projected back on to the seventeenth century. David Hume was far better known in his own time as a historian than as a philosopher, and his *History of England* (originally published in 1754–61) had applied Enlightenment values in a way that demolished the Whigs' argument. As a sceptic, Hume had no sympathy for the religious fanaticism of the Puritans, so he defended the Stuart kings by claiming that there was no existing tradition of liberty for them to trample upon. When Sir John Dalrymple found evidence that two of the Whig heroes, Lord Russell and Algernon Sydney, had been in the pay of France, Hume's position seemed triumphantly vindicated. For the Whigs of the early nineteenth century, Hume remained the chief threat to the model of history in which British liberties were supposed to have a traditional foundation established by several centuries of struggle against an absolutist monarchy.

Hume did not deny progress; he merely denied that England could have established a tradition of liberty while still in the feudal or agricultural stage of social development. On the Scottish model, economic forces alone could generate social progress, and it would be the historians' task to identify the stages of social development underlying the political events of the last few centuries. This view of social development became enshrined in the historical novels of Sir Walter Scott. As a young man, Scott had absorbed the teachings of

---

[6] The third edition of Millar's book is reprinted in Lehmann, *John Millar of Glasgow*.

[7] Ferguson, *Essay on the History of Civil Society*, p. 1. In the last part of the book, Ferguson notes that luxury may lead to the decline of civilization.

the philosophical historians, and his genius enabled him to illustrate the stages of social development by highlighting the predicament of individuals caught up in the process.[8] Scotland was a useful setting because its social development had first been held up and then subsequently accelerated after the revolution of 1745. The Highlanders had preserved an ancient form of society which had then been destroyed by the forcible change of its economic base. As Scott wrote in the postscript to *Waverley*: 'The gradual influx of wealth, and extension of commerce, have since united to render the present people of Scotland as different from their grandfathers as the existing English are from those of Queen Elizabeth's time.'[9]

Whereas some historians had presented feudalism as a foreign system imposed on the English by the Norman invaders, Scott accepted that it represented a natural stage of social evolution.[10] *Ivanhoe* became his most popular novel because the Victorians could read it as a portrait of the British character emerging from the fusion of Saxon and Norman elements. Some later historians would see the Norman conquest as the imposition of an alien feudal system upon the English by foreign invaders, while others claimed that the process was necessary to temper the Saxons' love of freedom with the Normans' passion for organization. But Scott seems to have accepted the conquest as merely another example of the artificial acceleration of what was, in the end, a necessary transition to the next stage of social evolution. The feudal state of society was a step forward, whatever the harmful side-effects resulting from the unprincipled use of power. The spirit of chivalry was, in any case, already at work refining the more brutal aspects of aristocratic character. Eventually, nationalism would come to play the same civilizing role as society advanced towards a more modern form. At first Scott seems to have believed that the law should always be reformed to keep up with social progress, but he soon began to adopt a more conservative position, and *Ivanhoe* can also be read as a warning that order – even feudal order – is always preferable to anarchy.

In terms of the model suggested by Scott and the philosophical historians, the social development of Britain was only a slightly modified version of that to be expected in any country moving towards

[8] On Scott and the philosophical historians see Brown, *Walter Scott and the Historical Imagination*; Culler, *The Victorian Mirror of History*, ch. 2; Fleishman, *The English Historical Novel* and McMaster, *Scott and Society*.

[9] Scott, *Waverley, or 'tis Sixty Years Since (Waverley Novels*, I, p. 376).

[10] Scott expressed interest in reports of other societies which seemed to show that they followed the same pattern of development; see McMaster, *Scott and Society*, p. 66.

Plate 2   Sir John Everett Millais, *A Dream of the Past – Sir Isumbras at the Ford* (1857). Although the knight is depicted as a protector of the weak, this picture is more a product of Victorian nostalgia than an argument for chivalry as a force of social progress. It was originally exhibited along with mock-mediaeval verses which did little to elucidate its meaning. The children in Kipling's *Puck of Pook's Hill* had a print of Sir Isumbras in their room (see p. 36).

National Museums and Galleries on Merseyside, Lady Lever Art Gallery

a commercial economy. As Adam Smith explained, the transition to liberalism may have been accelerated by Britain's position as an island, since the absence of invasion threats allowed the country to leapfrog one step in the process of social development.[11] The first consequence of the move towards a commercial economy was that the king made use of his increased revenue to raise a professional army, thus gaining powers undreamt-of during the feudal period. This allowed the creation of a centralized state which attempted to manipulate commerce for its own ends. The commercial classes inevitably pressed for reforms that would give them greater freedom – and the French Revolution showed the explosive consequences that would follow if the monarchy resisted the trend. Britain had escaped the problems of social transition experienced by other European countries because its monarchs had no excuse for building up a standing army. In this sense, the inevitable triumph of liberalism was merely accelerated by an accident of geography.

The assumption that social development was driven by inexorable economic pressures was challenged by an alternative tradition in which the British constitution was seen as something precious, a gift of history expressing a unique national spirit. This almost mystical view of the nation's past was integral to the thinking of Edmund Burke, whose respect for tradition ran counter to the Whigs' demands for reform. For Burke, the constitution represented the natural unfolding of the people's innate desire for order and liberty, not a product of economic necessity. As the mediaeval historian Sir Francis Palgrave wrote in 1837: 'Our constitutional form of government has been produced by evolution. As the organs were needed, so did they arise.'[12] This is one of the earliest uses of the term 'evolution' to denote a process of social development, and it is clearly meant to imply the growth of a unique entity in response to a national sense of identity.

The Whig historians of the early nineteenth century sought to mediate between the rival models offered by the social philosophers and the Burkeans. They wanted to present the growth of British liberties as an inevitable trend towards the modern state of society, but they were also willing to concede that the constitution represented a uniquely suitable way of achieving the final goal. This tension can be seen in the historical writings of Thomas Babbington Macaulay.[13]

---

[11] Smith, *Lectures on Jurisprudence*, pp. 265–70.

[12] Palgrave, *Truths and Fictions of the Middle Ages*, p. 201.

[13] On Macaulay see Burrow, *A Liberal Descent*, part 1; and on his early career Clive, *Thomas Babbington Macaulay*. For a different interpretation of Macaulay's position see Hamburger, *Macaulay and the Whig Tradition*.

In his early, often polemical, essays and in his magisterial *History of England from the Accession of James the Second*, Macaulay walked a tightrope balancing between social evolutionism and the tradition of portraying Britain as the chief repository of liberalizing virtues. As a writer, he shared the novelists' ability to reconstruct the political debates of the past with sympathy for the 'spirit of the age', yet he was determined to evaluate historical figures in terms of their contributions to the liberalizing trend.[14]

Material progress was inevitable, but it was achieved through the enterprise of individuals, not the guiding hand of government. In his 1830 review of Southey's gloomy *Colloquies on Society* Macaulay wrote:

> History is full of the signs of this natural progress of society. We see in almost every part of the annals of mankind how the industry of individuals, struggling up against wars, taxes, famines, conflagrations, mischievous prohibitions, and more mischievous protections, creates faster than governments can squander, and repairs whatever invaders can destroy. We see the wealth of nations increasing, and all the arts of life approaching nearer and nearer to perfection, in spite of the grossest corruption and the wildest profusion on the part of rulers.[15]

Small wonder that Macaulay spoke in favour of the Reform Bill in 1832, even if this turned out to be only a symbolic step towards the ending of aristocratic privileges.

The implication of the claim that progress is decreed by natural law seems to be that nothing can stand in the way of the transition from an absolutist to a liberal form of government. Yet in his review of Hallam's *Constitutional History*, Macaulay acknowledged that the progress of civilization did not necessarily favour liberty. England had only narrowly escaped the slide into despotism promoted by the growth of standing armies elsewhere in Europe.[16] His own *History of England* developed the theme that the revolution of 1688 confirmed the liberties defended by Protestants through the reigns of the Stuart

---

[14] See for instance Macaulay, 'Sir James Mackintosh', *Critical and Historical Essays*, p. 326 (a review of Mackintosh's *History of the Revolution in England of 1688*).

[15] Macaulay, 'Southey's Colloquies', *Critical and Historical Essays*, p. 121. Robert Southey's *Sir Thomas More: Or Colloquies on the Progress and Prospects of Society* of 1829 argued that people had been better off in More's time.

[16] Macaulay, 'Hallam's Constitutional History', *Critical and Historical Essays*, pp. 71–2; see also *The History of England*, I, p. 43.

kings. Charles I was a bad influence, despite the fact that the theory of economic determinism held the transitional phase of absolutism to be inevitable. The famous sections of the *History* depicting social conditions were meant to substantiate the view that progress was, in the end, the result of economic pressures.

The bulk of Macaulay's analysis was relentlessly political, however. He was determined to show that the revolution of 1688 was not a new initiative, but a 'vindication of ancient rights'.[17] And yet there is a sense in which Macaulay was presenting Britain as a lucky but perfectly understandable exception to the normal rule of social evolution. The limited monarchies of the middle ages had conceded certain rights to their subjects, rights which had been eroded elsewhere in Europe but preserved in England thanks to its unique geographical position. The country had thus gained a head start in the transition to the next phase of social development, because modern liberals could build upon older liberties which had disappeared elsewhere. In effect Britain had leapfrogged the phase of absolutism that would normally intervene between limited feudal monarchy and modern liberalism. The constitution was precious because it was the guardian of those ancient rights which had been preserved by this accident of geography.

As a historian, Macaulay wished to understand the evolution of the British constitution, but his approach left open the possibility that there was an underlying law of progress for civilization as a whole. An increasing number of Victorians were prepared to accept the existence of such a law, thereby retaining the developmental model of the philosophical historians. The idea that history was subject to *law* helped to give meaning to what would otherwise be a bewildering array of facts. If that law could be seen to favour the growth of cherished values such as toleration and liberty, so much the better. The historians could concentrate on defining the especially favourable circumstances affecting Britain, while social scientists could try to elucidate the underlying law of progress. Since both enterprises shared the same set of values, the law of progress would turn out to be merely a generalization of the Whig interpretation of history.

An important intermediary between the historical and sociological approaches can be seen in Henry Buckle's *History of England*, the first volume of which appeared in 1857. In his introductory chapters,

[17] Macaulay, *The History of England*, II, p. 660. Magna Carta was the classic illustration of an English monarch conceding liberties to his subjects, although the nineteenth century saw a gradual recognition of the fact that the charter was a purely feudal document; see Pallister, *Magna Carta: The Heritage of Liberty*.

Buckle defended the claim that human activities are subject to natural law, and tried to define the causes which have shaped the growth of civilization. Buckle is best known for his efforts to show that climate and geography have a bearing on social development, but he manipulated these factors to support the Whig view that Britain was uniquely placed to enjoy rapid progress. He explicitly rejected the claim that the various races of mankind are endowed with different capacities, quoting John Stuart Mill's comment: 'Of all the vulgar modes of escaping from the consideration of the effect of social and moral influences on the human mind, the most vulgar is that of attributing the diversities of conduct and character to inherent national differences.'[18] Here Buckle and Mill reveal their continued reliance on the eighteenth-century concept of the universal identity of human nature. Whatever was special about Britain, it was not – as was so widely believed in the later nineteenth century – the inherent character of its people.

Buckle argued that the availability of food in a particular area influenced the character of that area's population and determined its level of social development. Once agriculture was established, a fertile soil led to a rapid expansion of the population, as in the early civilizations of Egypt, Mesopotamia and India. But in the hot countries food is so easily produced that labour remains cheap and a rigid distinction emerges between rich and poor. Such civilizations are invariably ruled by despots who stifle not only liberty but the further development of learning and skills.[19] Northerly areas, where food is harder to produce, saw civilization develop more slowly, but promoted a different social structure, less prone to fall under the yoke of tyrants. Labour was more valuable; the individual thus had more freedom and was better able to contribute to economic progress. Once the people of Europe had put their feet on the ladder of progress, they could ascend further than the inhabitants of hotter climes.

Buckle thus provided the Whig interpretation of history with a useful means of explaining why civilization had developed first in the warmer regions of the earth. The great empires of the past were an aberrant and ultimately sterile overdevelopment of a particular stage in the evolution of society. It was easier to get an agricultural civilization going in a warm climate, but the very factors which encouraged the start of agriculture also led to highly centralized

[18] Mill, *Principles of Political Philosophy*, in *Collected Works*, II, p. 319; see Buckle, *History of Civilization in England*, I, p. 40n. Buckle also insisted that a white child is born with no greater capacities than a savage; see ibid., p. 178.
[19] Buckle, *History of Civilization in England*, I, ch. 2, esp. pp. 70–81.

governments which stifled all further development. The inhabitants of northern regions found it more difficult to establish an agricultural economy (perhaps they actually needed the stimulus provided by contact with the early empires), but once they had reached this stage they were on the first rung of the ladder of progress that would lead inexorably towards industrialization. Buckle thus related the Whig interpretation of modern history to his readers' awareness of the great empires mentioned in the Bible. In explaining the static character of this kind of society, he also formed a link between the ancient empires and those still existing in warmer countries. The great monuments of India were produced by a social system equivalent to that of ancient Egypt. In conquering the native states of India, then, the British could feel confident that they were breaking an evolutionary deadlock in which the people of the sub-continent had been trapped by the accident of geography.

Buckle insisted that the progress towards industrialized society required no development of the moral sense, only the continued application of intellectual powers.[20] Social progress was an inevitable consequence of economic forces acting upon human ingenuity, at least in those parts of the world where the climate did not interfere. As European countries developed a commercial economy, the military became a separate class which soon declined in influence. Buckle insisted that 'in our country, a love of war is, as a national taste, utterly extinct.'[21] Political economy showed the futility of war and the advantages of free trade, thereby promoting the growth of a pacific spirit. Improvements in transportation were breaking down the barriers that led to disagreements among nations. This rejection of jingoism was typical of the liberals' hopes for social development, hopes that were, however, soon to be dashed by the rising tide of imperialism in the later Victorian era.

As far as Buckle was concerned, the advantages of the social and economic improvements taking place were shared by all European countries, and would soon be shared by the whole world. Britain was unique only in that its insular position had allowed its people's social development to proceed unhindered. Popular freedom had developed more rapidly because there was no threat of foreign invasion to serve as an excuse for governments seeking to control society.[22] Geography was important once again, but only to the extent that an island people

---

[20] Ibid., pp. 180–1.
[21] Ibid., p. 198. Buckle excused the Crimean War as a rupture between Russia and Turkey, the two most barbarous powers left in Europe.
[22] Ibid., p. 232.

was given a slight advantage in the transition from the feudal to the industrial level of social development. In the end, the move towards liberalization was inexorable in any northern climate. Thus Buckle firmly subordinated the Whigs' respect for the constitution to the general theory of social progress which had been implicit in at least some of Macaulay's work. The earlier Whig compromise with the Burkean notion of a unique spirit in the British constitution could not survive the transition to a commercial economy whose leaders hoped to spread their own values around the world. As the emphasis fell ever more heavily on the necessity of social evolution, the advantages enjoyed by Britain were demoted to a level equivalent to all the other environmental factors that had accelerated or retarded progress in various parts of the world. The historian might busy himself trying to uncover these accidental factors as they influenced the growth of a particular nation, but the real task of the student of society was to uncover the underlying laws of evolution.

Social Evolutionism

Buckle himself was as much a sociologist as a historian; his interests went beyond the unique aspects of British society to include the general laws of social development. For many Victorians, the elucidation of these laws was the main goal of research into history, and the histories of different nations or races became merely a source of information upon which to base their generalizations. Soon anthropologists' studies of modern 'primitives' were being called in to supplement written history in the elucidation of the earliest, i.e. prehistoric, phases of social development. But the link between social and intellectual development was preserved by all those thinkers who saw human effort as the driving force of progress. Environmental factors such as climate might determine how far up the scale a particular race might advance, but only by limiting the extent to which individual human beings were able to study and take control of the world around them.

The concept of necessary stages in the development of the human intellect had already been enshrined in the 'positivist' philosophy of Auguste Comte. Buckle himself thought highly of Comte, and John Stuart Mill wrote extensively on his philosophy, without, however, accepting the very narrow view of 'positive' science which Comte advocated for the highest level of understanding.[23] Comte distinguished

[23] Ibid., p. 5n. and Mill, *August Comte and Positivism*.

three phases in the progress of the human intellect as it strove to understand the natural world. In the first or religious phase, everything was attributed to the power of gods and spirits. The second or metaphysical stage saw the spirits replaced by mysterious underlying forces. Only in the final or positivist phase did mankind realize that true scientific knowledge consisted solely of an accurate description of phenomena. Many shared Mill's suspicions of Comte's hostility to theorization, but the general notion of a steady advance towards rational understanding fitted in well with the social philosophers' claim that society developed by means of individual efforts to understand and control nature. Comte's view that European culture was now moving into the positivist phase of knowledge dovetailed neatly with the claim that a commercial economy based on free enterprise was the highest state of society.

What, then, of the less developed societies? Buckle's appeal to climate as a factor that could limit social development shows that the philosophical historians recognized the need to grapple with this problem. Their theory had to be extended on to a global scale, if only to resist the claims of those traditionalists who still defended the biblical story of mankind's degeneration from a divinely inspired state of grace. The Scottish model of social progress implied that all societies began as groups of primitive hunters, but such a view was regarded as distinctly unorthodox throughout the first half of the nineteenth century. Primitive tribes were generally regarded as indications of just how low mankind could sink when the gift of divine revelation was lost completely. Comte and Buckle were clearly struggling to overthrow this biblical view of human history, but their efforts were to some extent blocked by the knowledge that civilizations such as those of ancient Egypt and China dated back to what many still regarded as the earliest days of mankind. The biblical view that mankind had been in existence for only a few thousand years did not begin to collapse until the 1860s, and only then did it become possible for the progressionists to invoke the remote human past as the period of initially primitive social organization from which all later developments had sprung.[24] The story of this re-evaluation of human antiquity will be told in part II of this book; our purpose here is to show how it enabled the anti-biblical forces to establish social evolutionism as the basis for a general model of human history.

The crucial question was the status of non-European peoples who

[24] The role of changing ideas on human antiquity in the emergence of cultural evolutionism is stressed by Stocking, *Victorian Anthropology* and by Trautmann, *Lewis Henry Morgan*.

seemed far removed from the commercial or industrial state of development. As European power spread around the globe, ethnologists were able to bring back information about a wide range of peoples at varying levels of technological development. It was India which posed the most immediate problem. The more enlightened British administrators felt that it was their duty to encourage the Indians to rise above the chaos which had allowed Europeans to conquer so much of the sub-continent. There was disagreement, however, over the true status of Indian culture. Some Europeans looked to the east as the source of spiritual enlightenment and argued that the underlying basis of Hindu culture was highly developed, even though it had degenerated somewhat in modern times. This claim was rejected by the liberals, who saw India's lack of economic development as an indication that Hindu society was still at a low stage of development. In his *History of British India*, James Mill dismissed stories of ancient grandeur as fables and declared that the Hindus had 'made but a few of the earliest steps in the progress of civilization.'[25] Great empires were not a sign of social progress in the tropics – a view echoed later by Buckle.

The debate over the relative standing of Indian society came to a head over the question of which language should be used for native education. The 'orientalists' argued that, since Sanskrit was the origin of all Indo-European languages, the natives should be educated in the vernacular. Liberals saw English as the best means of disseminating western values and thus of modernizing Indian society. This position was supported vigorously by Macaulay when he went out to India as Legal Member of Council in 1834.[26] He was convinced that Indian society was at a low state of development and had little respect for Indian culture. Yet he was certain that Indians could be introduced to western values through education, and could thus be artificially pulled up the ladder of progress. His famous Minute on Education of 1835 played an important role in implementing this policy. The claim that social evolution could be accelerated by imposing more advanced ideas on to the leaders of a backward society was now put to the test; but the hopes of Macaulay and the progressives were doomed to failure. The Brahmins would not acknowledge the superiority of European values, and the 1857 Mutiny convinced many Britons that India was a barbaric country that could only be civilized by force.

[25] James Mill, *History of British India*, II, p. 152.
[26] On Macaulay's period in India see Clive, *Thomas Babbington Macaulay*, chs. 11 and 12.

The failure of this attempt to modernize a 'backward' society placed liberal thinkers in a quandary. If social progress resulted from individual acts of intiative, then individual Indians should have been able to appreciate the benefits they were being offered and the whole society should soon have become Europeanized. The liberals had to explain this collective refusal to see the light, yet they shared Mill's reluctance to invoke a vulgar racism that would dismiss the Indians as mentally unfit to be civilized. Their solution was, as J. W. Burrow has pointed out, to acknowledge a limit on the extent to which an individual can transcend the bounds of the culture in which he has been raised.[27] The scale of social evolution was a rigid path defined by the very nature of human thought and behaviour; ascent of the scale could only be by small increments, and a lower society could not be modernized overnight by contact with a higher one. In this respect, at least, the liberals were forced to accept a central feature of the rival German model of social development, in qualifying the simple individualist view of society with the recognition that cultures have a unity and coherence of their own which imposes limits on the thinking of anyone raised within them.

The stages of development postulated by the philosophical historians now became something more than a by-product of economic forces, and it was necessary to analyse in much greater depth the mental and social factors determining the transition from one level to the next. Among the social evolutionists who took up this challenge in the 1860s were Sir Henry Maine, John McLennan, Edward B. Tylor, Sir John Lubbock and, in America, Lewis Henry Morgan. Between them they forged a linear model of cultural development defining the stages that must be traversed by any society advancing from savagery towards the high point of European civilization. Because there was only one conceivable line of social development, the diversity of cultures around the world was explained by assuming that each was characteristic of a particular state of development. Each society followed an independent line of evolution, but all were moving in parallel along the same scale of development. Some had advanced further than others, and the lowest societies thus exhibited exact equivalents of the stages through which the more advanced had passed in the distant past.

The anthropologists thus felt able to fill in the details of the lower stages of development postulated by the philosophical historians: modern 'savages' threw light on those remote areas of history not covered by written records. It was the archaeological evidence

[27] See Burrow, *Evolution and Society*.

suggesting that all societies had begun in a primitive 'stone age' which convinced many thinkers that progressionism offered the only alternative to the biblical world view. Lubbock played a major role in the development of prehistoric archaeology, and Tylor was in close contact with another archaeologist, Henry Christy (see part II below). At one time it was common for historians of anthropology to invoke the publication of Darwin's *Origin of Species* in 1859 as the key stimulus in the emergence of cultural evolutionism.[28] More recently, Burrow, Stocking and others have pointed out the peripheral nature of Darwin's theory: *cultural* evolutionism would almost certainly have become popular whether or not the theory of natural selection had appeared.[29] Perhaps the clearest evidence of this is that the linear character of the cultural evolutionists' model offers a distinctly non-Darwinian view of progress. Where Darwin used the metaphor of a branching tree as the image of evolution, the anthropologists retained a developmental 'stage theory' in which differences were explained in terms of varying speeds of ascent up a uniform ladder of progress.

Sir Henry Maine's *Ancient Law* of 1861 was the first of the new generation's attempts to reconstruct the early stages of social development. But Maine had no sense of the enormous implications opened up by the extension of human antiquity and confined his analysis to the Indo-European peoples which, he supposed, were offshoots of the more progressive Aryan race. Maine assumed that the earliest form of society consisted of well organized family groups, each controlled by a patriarch. The majority of anthropologists, however, thought that Maine had simply missed out the earliest stage of all. On the Scottish model, hunting came before agriculture, yet the earliest Sanskrit records showed that the Aryans were already agriculturalists and hence not representatives of the original stage of society. The new timescale opened up by archaeology implied an initial period of true savagery from which all social institutions, including those of the Aryans, would have had to develop.

It was widely assumed that in a true 'state of nature' humans would have had no permanent family ties and would have reproduced promiscuously. The family itself was an institution developed as the human race began to acquire a more settled life style through technological progress. This opinion seemed to be supported by the

---

[28] See for instance Penniman, *A Hundred Years of Anthropology*, p. 20.

[29] Burrow, *Evolution and Society*; Stocking, *Race, Culture and Evolution* and *Victorian Anthropology*. The non-Darwinian character of social evolutionism is also stressed in Nisbet, *Social Change and History*, ch. 5. Other works on the history of anthropology include Harris, *The Rise of Anthropological Theory* and Hatch, *Theories of Man and Culture*.

fact that many modern 'savages' had what the Victorians saw as very loose sexual habits. John F. McLennan's *Primitive Marriage* of 1865 expounded the view that in the original state of hunting and gathering, man's ancestors had lived as a 'promiscuous horde'.[30] The custom of a wife being 'abducted' by her husband was seen as a relic of the time when all women had been taken by violence because there were no social rules governing marriage.

Plate 3   Australian aboriginal marriage ceremony.
The picture shows a ceremony in which a young woman is 'captured' to be taken as a wife in another tribe. Lubbock and other anthropologists used such rites among modern 'savages' to illustrate what they assumed to be the primitive state of society from which all social evolution had begun.
From John Lubbock, *The Origin of Civilization and the Primitive Condition of Man*, frontispiece

John Lubbock supported the theory of ancient promiscuity in his *Origin and Development of Civilization* of 1870. He had already used the new stone-age archaeology to establish the primitive origins of mankind, and now studied the habits of modern savages for evidence of how our earliest ancestors had lived. His synthesis of archaeology and anthropology thus reveals the essence of what became known as the 'comparative method', which rested on the assumption that technologically primitive peoples represent exact equivalents of

[30] *Primitive Marriage* is reprinted in McLennan's *Studies in Ancient History*.

earlier stages in the development of more advanced societies. There was only one path of social progress, and those who had not advanced very far along it served as evidence from which their superiors could reconstruct the stages of their own and others' development.

The most complex model of social development from the level of promiscuous hunters was proposed by the American anthropologist Lewis Henry Morgan in his *Ancient Society* of 1877. Morgan defined three basic stages of savagery, barbarism and civilization, along with a host of subdivisions identified by technology and social habits. The stages formed a 'natural as well as a necessary sequence of progress', all but the lowest of which could still be seen in the modern world.[31] Morgan is remembered as an exponent of the view that economic factors determine social progress, but he also insisted that invention was guided by a 'natural logic which formed an essential attribute of the brain itself' and which gave uniform results wherever it was applied.[32] It was the interaction of economic forces and the human mind which yielded progress, and the whole system was pre-ordained to advance – wherever circumstances made it possible – towards the high point represented by modern western culture.

For other anthropologists, the growth of knowledge and beliefs was the chief focus of attention. Here the leading figure was Edward B. Tylor, whose *Researches into the Early History of Mankind* appeared in 1865. Again we find modern savages used to reconstruct the course of development, with Tylor paying particular attention to the growth of religion. His intention was to show that primitive beliefs in spirits and gods were understandable as early efforts by the human mind to grapple with puzzling phenomena such as dreams. The march towards civilization could thus be seen as a gradual refinement in the rational analysis of these phenomena. Tylor saw anthropology as a 'reformer's science' since it allowed one to detect and if necessary eradicate 'survivals' of ancient customs still embedded in modern society. But he shared the prevailing view that there was only one path of social and cultural development to be followed by all. He invoked the 'psychic unity' of the human race to explain the independent invention of similar tools and customs by all peoples at the same level of social evolution. If geographically separated tribes shared similar habits, this was a sign not of cultural transmission, but of each having independently made the same developments. Rather than invoke interactions between divergent cultures, Tylor preferred to assume

---

[31] Morgan, *Ancient Society*, p. 11. On Morgan see Kuper, 'The Development of Lewis Henry Morgan's Evolutionism', and Trautmann, *Lewis Henry Morgan*.
[32] Morgan, *Ancient Society*, p. 59.

parallel evolution up a single hierarchy of stages, thus preserving the Victorians' sense of their own cultural superiority.

One of the great exponents of Tylor's approach in later years was Sir J. G. Frazer, whose *Golden Bough* (first published in 1890) offered a massive account of how early magical and religious beliefs had evolved. In a later work, Frazer drew an explicit comparison between the growth of the individual mind and the evolution of culture: 'For by comparison with civilized man the savage represents an arrested or rather retarded stage of social development, and an examination of his customs and beliefs accordingly supplies the same sort of evidence of the evolution of the human mind that an examination of the embryo supplies of the evolution of the human body.'[33] This appeal to the recapitulation theory shows that the linear model of the philosophical historians had now become explicitly associated with the metaphor of organic growth. Through its extension into the area of religion, cultural anthropology had been forced to reconcile the economic bias of the philosophical historians with the metaphysical approach preferred by those who took their inspiration from Germany.

The analogy with individual growth already figured prominently in the social evolutionism of Herbert Spencer. As a political economist, Spencer had only a limited interest in anthropology, and he was too well aware of the possibility of degeneration to assume that 'primitive' societies were necessarily relics of ancestral steps in the evolution of civilization.[34] Nor did he share the Whig historians' respect for tradition: as far as Spencer was concerned, there was a duty to promote the transition to a free-enterprise society as quickly as possible. In 1851 his *Social Statistics* provided vigorous support for *laissez-faire* economics and predicted that western society would soon dominate the whole world. Like Buckle, Spencer assumed that the transition from a militaristic to a commercial society was inevitable. He thus shared the almost teleological view of those historians who saw modernism as the product of an inexorable social trend. But Spencer, to a far greater degree than Buckle, was concerned to identify the law of universal evolution. He adopted the theory of the transmutation of species long before Darwin published the *Origin of Species* and linked this with his social philosophy to create one of the nineteenth century's most comprehensive and influential expressions of evolutionism.

[33] Frazer, *Psyche's Task*, p. 162. On Frazer see Ackerman, *J. G. Frazer: His Life and Work.*

[34] Spencer, *Principles of Sociology*, I, p. 61 and p. 106. On Spencer's social philosophy, see Peel, *Herbert Spencer: The Evolution of a Sociologist.*

In theory, at least, Spencer realized that there was no single goal of evolution. Whereas the anthropologists adopted a linear model of growth towards maturity, Spencer saw that it was impossible to link all forms of life on a single ladder of progress. Each species represents the end-product of a particular line of specialization, so that one species can never represent an earlier stage in another's development. Growth must be growth towards complexity; and Spencer realized that there are many different ways in which either a biological organism or a society can become more complex. He thus adopted a branching rather than a linear model: 'Like other kinds of progress, social progress is not linear but divergent and re-divergent.'[35] One is left to assume that his faith in individualism allowed him to believe that one line of social evolution had permitted further progress than any of the others, thus effectively defining a 'main line' of development. Be that as it may, from the 1850s onwards Spencer advocated a universal progressionism linking biological, psychological and social evolution in a unified 'Synthetic Philosophy'. His essay 'Progress: its Law and Cause' appeared in 1857 and the *First Principles* of his philosophy in 1862.[36]

The fact that Spencer linked biological and social evolution, and saw free enterprise as essential for progress, has provoked charges that he led the move towards a ruthless 'social Darwinism'.[37] As with the anthropologists, though, the influence of Darwin's theory has been exaggerated. Although Spencer coined the term 'survival of the fittest' he did not accept natural selection as the chief mechanism of progress and did not see the elimination of the unfit as the sole purpose of a free-enterprise society. Freedom from government restraint and protection was invaluable mainly because it stimulated everyone to greater efforts. If suffering was the penalty for failure, all would learn nature's harsh lesson and would strive to do better in the future. Far from proposing an evolutionism based on the 'trial and error' elimination of random variation, Spencer shared the liberals' belief that individual effort and initiative formed the key to progress. The consequences would be harsh for the few who made mistakes,

[35] Spencer, *Principles of Sociology*, III, p. 325. Instead of the linear model of growth upon which the recapitulation theory is founded, Spencer adopted the embryological theory of K. E. von Baer, in which growth is a process of specialization (see part 3 below).

[36] 'Progress: Its Law and Cause' is reprinted in Spencer's *Essays*, I, pp. 1–60.

[37] See for instance Hofstadter, *Social Darwinism in American Thought*, ch. 2. For a different view see Bannister, *Social Darwinism* and Jones, *Social Darwinism and English Thought*.

but in the end everyone might hope to become perfectly adapted to the natural and social environment.

Among the social evolutionists, Spencer and Lubbock shared a common interest in the biological origins of humanity. In this respect they transcended the conceptual system within which the philosophical historians had formulated their theory of progress. Anthropologists such as Tylor and McLennan still retained the traditional faith in the unity and permanence of human nature, as had Buckle and Mill. They assumed that even in the most primitive social environment, a human being was still fully human. Indeed, it was to retain this belief that they invoked the theory of social evolution as a means of explaining why education could not raise a society too rapidly up the scale. Acceptance of biological evolution necessarily undermined this position, however, since it now became evident that our earliest ancestors must have been *mentally* as well as socially less advanced. Spencer's *Principles of Psychology*, first published in 1855, made it clear that the human mind adapted itself to its environment, so that individuals from different backgrounds do not have the same mentality. Lubbock and Spencer shared the view that savages are mentally inferior to white people because they have evolved in a less stimulating environment. Savages are fossilized relics of human evolution in the biological as well as the social sense: they illustrate the 'missing links' in the ascent of humankind. The advent of biological evolutionism was thus both an extension and a negation of the social progressionism of the early nineteenth century. For Spencer and Lubbock, *race* was vitally important in the modern world, since each race had evolved in a different environment and each had advanced to a different degree beyond the ancestral ape. Morgan too suspected that savages were mentally inferior to whites, and in his *Anthropology* of 1881 even Tylor succumbed to this belief.[38] The social evolutionists were thus drawn inexorably closer to a position that had long been advocated by their rivals, and in the later nineteenth century almost all interpretations of human history took race to be a crucial determinant of behaviour.

[38] Morgan, *Ancient Society*, pp. 38–40 and 59; Tylor, *Anthropology*, pp. 60, 73–4.

Interlude:

The Fascination of the Past

The Victorians certainly read a great deal about the past. Those who received a classical education were necessarily familiar with Greece and Rome, while everyone was expected to know the Bible. The multi-volumed histories of England by Macaulay and others had a wide readership among the educated; only later in the nineteenth century did a growing professionalism move academic history outside the realm of popular literature. Even then, historical novels continued to recreate the past in their readers' imaginations. Painters, too, created images of both great events and everyday life in earlier periods. Translated into prints, these images were used to illustrate the textbooks from which generations of schoolchildren learnt about the past. In depicting the more remote periods of history, a new level of realism was achieved by incorporating the discoveries made by archaeologists. Excavations of classical or biblical sites routinely generated newspaper headlines, and lengthy reports by excavators such as Layard and Schliemann became bestsellers. Eventually these reports began to undermine the more romantic image of the past created by some artists and writers.

Better knowledge of the past did not, by itself, generate more realistic images. Painters and novelists were unlikely to be sympathetic to the political economists' view of progress, and more often used their powers to evoke either a superficial or a nostalgic impression of earlier periods. It was easy to fall into the trap of portraying figures from the past as exhibiting Victorian attitudes in an exotic setting. The 'mediaeval revival' of the early nineteenth century and the classicism which replaced it exerted immense influence on Victorian tastes, but often only at a superficial level.[1] Edward Bulwer-Lytton's *Last Days of Pompeii* of 1834 made frequent references to archaeological excavations, but set a love story against the background of early Christianity in order to show that 'THE AFFECTIONS ARE IMMORTAL!'[2] Tennyson's *Idylls of the King* can also be seen as the expression of eternal myths against a superficially mediaeval background. To the extent that these works created a Victorianized image of the past, they tended to promote not a progressionist, but a cyclic view of history. Human passions and problems would remain the same, whatever the social background.

Those who followed the German technique of looking for the spiritual foundations of earlier eras were committed to a more realistic approach. Yet even here, there was a strong temptation to use the past as a standard against which to judge Victorian society. Thomas Carlyle's *Past and Present* was typical of the attempt to use an idealized picture of the middle ages as a means of criticizing modern industrial society. The mediaeval world was orderly and wholesome because everyone knew his place in the hierarchy – exactly the reverse of the thrusting, individualistic rat-race promoted by the liberals. Later on in the century, the Roman era would be used to evoke the atmosphere of imperial splendour and security that the British empire hoped to re-establish. By their very nature, such accounts of the past were artificial constructs used to make points about the present. Even Carlyle's version of the middle ages had been criticized as historically deficient, a device used to promote its author's appeal for strong leadership in the modern era.[3] It was difficult realistically to evoke the values and behaviour-patterns of a bygone age, and in the end no one was to improve on Scott's efforts in this direction. Perhaps the best Victorian novels with a historical dimension were those which dealt with the very recent past as a means of highlighting the changes with which everyone was familiar.

The novels of Charles Kingsley show how history could be used to convey a message of relevance for the present. *Hereward the Wake* and *Westward Ho!* both celebrate ancestral virtues that had become part of the heritage of imperial Britain. If Hereward exhibited the uncontrolled passion of the Saxon, he also revealed how the love of liberty had

---

[1] On mediaevalism see Chandler, *A Dream of Order* and Culler, *The Victorian Mirror of History*, ch. 7; see also Jenkyns, *The Victorians and Ancient Greece* and Frank Turner, *The Greek Heritage in Victorian Britain*.

[2] Bulwer-Lytton, *The Last Days of Pompeii*, p. 167. On historical novels see Fleishman, *The English Historical Novel* and Sanders, *The Victorian Historical Novel, 1840–1880*.

[3] See Culler, *The Victorian Mirror of History*, ch. 3.

become so deeply ingrained that the Normans had been unable to stamp it out. Amyas Leigh's crusade against the Spanish in *Westward Ho!* illustrated not only the Englishman's hatred of tyranny but also the adventurous spirit that had carried English values around the globe.

For Kingsley, though, there was more to freedom than the liberals' demand for the dismantling of commercial restrictions. In *Hypatia* he turned to the Alexandria of the fifth century AD to expose the wickedness of religious dogmatism as it was to become embodied in the Catholic Church. The conclusion states Kingsley's intentions quite plainly:

> I have shown you New Foes under an old face – your own
> likeness in toga and tunic, instead of coat and bonnet. One
> word before we part. The same devil who tempted those
> old Egyptians tempts you. The same God who would have
> saved those old Egyptians, if they had willed, will save you,
> if you will. Their sins are yours, their errors yours, their
> doom yours, their deliverance yours. There is nothing new
> under the sun. The thing that has been, it is that which shall
> be.[4]

Kingsley's was not an ahistorical view of the world's development, as we shall see in chapter 2 below, but he saw the process as the unfolding of a divine plan which expressed an eternal truth. The love of freedom was an integral part of that truth, and when Christians turned to dogmatism and intolerance they were betraying the underlying values of their faith and blocking the path that would lead to better expressions of the Creator's purpose. Not surprisingly, Kingsley's attack on Catholicism called forth a rejoinder in the form of John Henry Newman's *Callista*, where the central theme was the Church's fight against paganism.

Although fewer historical novels were published in the late nineteenth century than in earlier decades, the existing ones continued to be reprinted. In Edwardian times the themes expressed by Kingsley and others resurfaced in children's literature intended to reinforce imperial values. The adventure stories of G. A. Henty were frequently given a historical setting which allowed the empire to be seen as the product of a developing national spirit. Every period of history received attention. In *By England's Aid; or the Freeing of the Netherlands (1585–1604)* Henty charted the early stages of the

---

[4] Kingsley, *Hypatia*, p. 485.

Elizabethan Protestants' reaction to the power and cruelty of Spain. Other books covered the expansion of the empire in Ireland, North America, India and Africa, each location becoming the scene for an adventure that would encourage British boys to think of their nation's destiny abroad. At a more enduring level, the stories in Rudyard Kipling's *Puck of Pook's Hill* also reflect the continuity of British history through to the present. The stories lack the explicit jingoism visible elsewhere in Kipling's writings and convey an almost mystical sense of the land itself as the foundation of the nation's spirit. Each new element of the population – whatever its original ambitions – is absorbed into the slowly developing character of the British people.

Victorian painters often tried to recreate scenes from the past, although there were waves of fashion governing which eras were of most interest. British history was always popular, especially its more romantic figures such as Mary, Queen of Scots.[5] By focusing on individual acts of tragedy or heroism, paintings could generate a romantic image of the past; but they could also identify those individuals who had done most to guarantee future liberties. The Civil War, for instance, could be used to evoke images of either reforming zeal or the traditional virtues of chivalry. Scenes from everyday life in the past might occasionally be used to convey the misery resulting from outdated social practices, but more often the genre painter found it more congenial to romanticize the conditions of earlier periods. In the mid-century, many painters contributed to the nostalgic vision of the mediaeval period as a time of social harmony based on a natural hierarchy.

Art history itself was important to some, the pre-Raphaelite movement in particular seeking a return to the 'more truthful' representation of nature practised by mediaeval artists.[6] John Ruskin endorsed the pre-Raphaelites' artistic aspirations and explicitly connected the virtues of mediaeval painting with the wider values of a society imbued with religious faith rather than selfishness. For Ruskin, the Renaissance was an artistic and philosophical disaster, introducing a new world based on inferior moral values. He attacked the belief that culture had been developing towards maturity: the transition from the middle ages to the Renaissance was equivalent not to the growth of a child into a man, but to the metamorphosis of a caterpillar into a butterfly – although in this case the new creature was inferior to the old.[7]

[5] See Strong, *And When Did You Last See Your Father?*
[6] There are many accounts of the movement; see for instance Wood, *The Pre-Raphaelites* and, more generally, Reynolds, *Victorian Painting*.
[7] Ruskin, *Lectures on Architecture and Painting*, pp. 185–9.

Ruskin's fulminations against post-mediaeval developments in culture were typical of those who advocated a return to a more orderly society based on religious belief. The liberals were, of course, his chief target, but they were seldom interested in defending themselves by an appeal to modern artistic standards. The Renaissance eventually came back into fashion as British writers began to appreciate the work of continental historians such as Jules Michelet and Jacob Burckhardt.[8] In J. A. Symonds' *Renaissance in Italy* (originally published 1875–86), the period was fitted into a progressionist account of history as the key era in which a sense of human freedom emerged. Writers such as Matthew Arnold and Walter Pater saw distinctively 'modern' characteristics in Renaissance art and thought. Not all Renaissance enthusiasts were progressionists, however: Burckhardt saw it as a glorious interlude before the rise of the modern state began to stifle freedom, while Pater adopted a cultural relativism which looked for something of value in the art of all eras and appealed to changing cultural values to explain why certain art-forms were most active at certain times. Unperplexed Hellenic humanism had encouraged sculpture, the mysticism of the middle ages had expressed itself in painting, but the modern world looked to literature to give a sense of freedom within the complex, law-bound world revealed by science.[9]

The fact that a classical education was still *de rigueur* for a gentleman ensured that many Victorians retained a deep interest in the ancient world. The men who governed an expanding empire based on modern industry were nevertheless imbued with values imposed upon them by close study of both the Bible and the classics of Greece and Rome. Even those such as Macaulay who called for the modernization of education could not escape the legacy of their own upbringing. This fascination with the ancient world is not as strange as it might seem, since the Victorians were able to create images of the past which matched their own requirements. George Grote's *History of Greece* (originally published in 1846) appealed to liberal tastes by creating an idealized view of Athenian democracy under Pericles. Macaulay's *Lays of Ancient Rome* highlighted the virtues of those who founded the Roman republic. Imperial Rome was, however, more to the taste of the later generation which sought an ancient parallel to the Pax Britannica. The great empires of Egypt, Assyria and Babylon were also a focus of attention because of their biblical connections. These ancient empires were often glamourized

[8] See Culler, *The Victorian Mirror of History*, ch. 10.
[9] Pater, *The Renaissance*, pp. 184–5.

Plate 4   John Martin, *Belshazzar's Feast* (mezzotint, 1826).
The original painting was exhibited with great success in 1821 and was reproduced extensively, often as a Bible illustration. Martin's apocalyptic vision of the past also extended to spectacular reconstructions of dinosaurs and other extinct species revealed by the fossil record. By the 1840s, the work of 'Mad Martin' was being ridiculed as tasteless overdramatization.

to emphasize how religious values had to be created independently of material splendour.

Many nineteenth-century painters tried to recreate the atmosphere of the ancient civilizations. In the 1820s and the 1830s, John Martin's depictions of Old Testament scenes had enjoyed wide popularity both as paintings and as prints in illustrated Bibles.[10] Martin's grandiose reconstructions of palaces credited the ancients with architectural powers greater than those of the nineteenth century itself (they are thought to have inspired the epics of twentieth-century film makers). Yet Martin's apocalyptic visions were soon dismissed as the products of a deranged mind, suggesting that the Victorians were developing a more realistic impression of the ancient world. At the very least, they were no longer willing to glamourize it as a period of greater opulence than their own. A painting such as Sir Edward Poynter's *The Catapult* depicts Roman warfare with an intensity that could only highlight the brutality of the era (see plate 6 below). Yet in many cases, painters still turned to the ancient world as a source of mythological fantasy or as a means of drawing attention to the luxuries enjoyed by the wealthier classes in all ages. In the classical revival of the late nineteenth century, painters such as Alma-Tadema sought to reconstruct the world of ancient Greece and Rome with a new realism.[11] But by concentrating on the life of the leisured classes, they presented the ancients very much as 'Victorians in togas' and thus promoted an almost cyclic vision of history. At best, such paintings served to highlight the luxuries available only to an imperial power.

The artists and writers who tried to create a realistic image of the ancient world could take advantage of the increased level of knowledge made available by archaeology. The late eighteenth century had seen a revival of interest in classical sculpture, and the excavations at Pompeii had thrown light on the everyday life of the Roman era. Napoleon's expedition to Egypt helped to reveal the splendours of that ancient civilization. In the early nineteenth century, however, Egypt was the only biblical nation known from its actual monuments. Only in the 1840s did Mesopotamia begin to yield up its secrets, as travellers such as Henry Layard began to excavate the mounds covering the cities of the Assyrians.[12] Layard became a celebrity, his book, *Nineveh and its Remains*, published in 1849, a bestseller. Intense excitement surrounded the arrival of two colossal

[10] See Feaver, *The Art of John Martin.*
[11] See Wood, *Olympian Dreamers.*
[12] See Waterfield, *Layard of Nineveh* and, more generally, Lloyd, *Foundations in the Dust.*

Plate 5 Lowering the great winged bull of Nineveh.
Layard stands on the top of the mound, supervising the first
stage in the transportation of the massive Assyrian statues to the
British Museum.
From Austen Henry Layard, *Nineveh and its Remains*, frontispiece

winged bulls for display at the British Museum. The Assyrian palaces
were certainly impressive structures, even if they did not measure up
to the grandiose visions of Martin. But the bas-reliefs brought back
by Layard and others created a clear impression of an empire that was
powerful yet brutal, sounding a note of realism that fitted in well with
the progressionist interpretation of the ancient world. Whatever the
opulence of classical Rome, the earlier empires of the east had been
based solely on the drive for military glory by a handful of powerful
leaders.

Great interest was also expressed in Heinrich Schliemann's
excavations at Troy and other pre-classical sites. Homer's poems
were, of course, familiar to any educated person, but the story of the
Trojan war had been widely dismissed as a myth of no historical
value. Historians such as Grote passed over the pre-classical era as a
barbaric prelude to later glories. Yet others were determined to
establish the historical reality of Troy and Mycenae. W. E. Gladstone
conducted a lifelong campaign to vindicate the Homeric stories.
Schliemann was a self-made man who defied academic opinion by
suggesting that excavation at the appropriate sites would uncover the
real world that had formed the backdrop for Homer's epics. In the

1870s he explored the ruins of what he triumphantly claimed to be Troy itself, before moving on to contemporary sites in Greece. Schliemann's reports routinely generated newspaper headlines and the extended accounts of his work were widely read. Gladstone himself wrote the preface to Schliemann's *Mycenae* of 1875. Modern historians have begun to suspect that Schliemann was little more than a charlatan, but there can be no doubt that his 'discoveries' exerted a deep influence on the Victorian imagination.[13]

If the excavations revealed that Troy was a real city, they also showed that Homer's picture of it was greatly exaggerated. The city that had supposedly withstood a siege by a hundred and ten thousand Greeks was in fact a small town capable of holding three thousand people. Schliemann himself wrote: 'I am extremely disappointed at being obliged to give so small a plan of Troy; nay, I had wished to be able to make it a thousand times larger, but I value truth above everything, and I rejoice that my three years' excavations have laid open the Homeric Troy, even though on a diminished scale, and that I have proved the *Iliad* to be based upon real facts.'[14] Once again, archaeology had a direct impact on how the Victorians could visualize the past. The great empires of the ancient world were real enough, but they had been built upon primitive bronze- or early iron-age technologies that fitted neatly into the progressionist scheme. One could admire the Homeric Greeks' imagination, but not their level of material culture. At one point, Schliemann thought he had dug down through the bronze-age deposits to the underlying level of the stone age.[15] He soon had to abandon this possibility, but by the time he wrote *Troy and its Remains*, everyone was aware of the fact that the earliest human remains were those of stone-age 'savages'. A new kind of archaeology had emerged, dealing with a past so ancient that it was completely prehistoric (see part II below). This would reinforce the growing belief that the earliest human civilizations had grown from savage origins. Popular surveys such as Winwood Reade's *Martyrdom of Man* helped to create a new image of the ancient world as a period in which mankind had struggled to rise above the baser instincts. In the end, for all the efforts made by artists to glamourize the past, the Victorians were forced to acknowledge that the overall thrust of human history represented a rise from savagery, just as the anthropologists claimed.

[13] See Calder and Trail, eds, *Myth, Scandal and History: The Heinrich Schliemann Controversy*. For a more conventional account of Schliemann see Cottrell, *The Bull of Minos*.

[14] Schliemann, *Troy and its Remains*, p. 344.

[15] Ibid., p. 83.

2

Rise and Fall

The Whig view of progress saw the emergence of individual freedom as both cause and consequence of economic development. But there were other forces at work within Victorian culture which could generate a very different concept of progress. It was becoming increasingly clear that British scholars had fallen behind continental historians, especially the Germans, in creating a new framework for understanding the past. As German standards were imported, so was the cultural matrix within which this new approach had been generated. Here was a tradition in which individualism was dismissed as a shopkeepers' mentality: real history studied the development of the larger social units within which individuals found the meaning of their lives. Progress meant the gradual unfolding of the spiritual potential latent within these larger units, what Robert Nisbet has called 'Progress as Power' as opposed to 'Progress as Freedom'.[1] When imported into Britain, this continental approach became the basis for what has been called the 'liberal Anglican' view of history.[2] Its practitioners were deeply religious men such as Thomas Arnold. They saw the need to accept the concept of a changing world, but were determined not to let the radicals get away with the claim that progress led only towards the elimination of ancient social constraints. Societies were organic wholes, and their history was governed by potentials that could only be explained as gifts from their Creator.

Because the liberal Anglican view saw society as an organic unit, it

---

[1] Nisbet, *History of the Idea of Progress*, chs. 6 and 7.
[2] Forbes, *The Liberal Anglican Idea of History*.

was inherently drawn towards the analogy between progress and the individual's growth to maturity. A powerful evocation of this analogy can be found in Frederick Temple's essay on 'The Education of the World', which appeared in the controversial theological collection *Essays and Reviews* in 1860:

> We may, then, rightly speak of a childhood, a youth, and a manhood of the world. The men of the earliest ages were, in many respects, still children as compared with ourselves, with all the blessings and with all the disadvantages that belong to childhood. We reap the fruits of their toil, and bear in our characters the impress of their cultivation. Our characters have grown out of their history, as the character of the man grows out of the history of the child.[3]

Progress is the unfolding of God's plan through humanity's ever more mature appreciation of His intentions. To many conservatives, the claim that divine revelation would have to be reinterpreted by successive generations was deeply disturbing. *Essays and Reviews* was violently condemned as an attempt to undermine the authority of the Bible. The critics preferred the traditional view in which mankind was supposed to have degenerated from a divine state of grace. But men like Arnold and Temple were determined to define a compromise that would accept the spiritual growth of the human race through time while allowing them to retain the belief that – just like individual development – the process represented the unfolding of a divine plan toward its goal.

We have already seen that the analogy with growth towards maturity was employed by progressionists in the individualist–rationalist tradition. But some exponents of progress as the inexorable product of social forces were suspicious of the analogy for the very good reason that, if carried too far, it led one to suppose that development may be followed by degeneration into senility and death. By its very nature, the analogy with growth can be exploited in two ways: one can concentrate solely on the phase leading through to maturity, or one can include the complete life cycle and accept that it ends with an inevitable decline. The liberal Anglicans were prepared to admit the complete cycle because the concept of decline posed no problem for them. Since they postulated inbuilt potentials rather than

---

[3] Temple, 'The Education of the World', in *Essays and Reviews*, p. 4. On the reception of *Essays and Reviews* see Willey, *More Nineteenth-Century Studies*, ch. 4.

an inexorable economic force as the motor of progress, they could accept that the overall development of humanity's potential might unfold through a series of distinct contributions. Each nation in turn might add its quota to the store of mankind's spiritual knowledge and then pass the torch on to another, while itself undergoing a decline. The cycle of the growth and decay of nations could be imposed on the overall pattern of humanity's development.

Everyone knew that decline was possible, with the fall of Rome as the classic example. Macaulay himself had celebrated the civic virtues of the earliest Romans in his *Lays of Ancient Rome*. Gibbon's immense account of the empire's collapse was known to all educated men, and the whole episode had been used by some eighteenth-century thinkers as the basis for a cyclic view of history. Adam Ferguson had accepted that a civilized society could be corrupted by luxury – although Gibbon hoped that modern technology would ensure that the European nations could not be overrun by a new wave of barbarians. The theory of inevitable progress had obvious difficulties with the phenomenon of degeneration. It could appeal to economic factors to explain why progress was slower, but ultimately more effective, in a demanding climate, but it was hard pressed to account for the collapse of a European power such as Rome.

The liberal Anglicans had no problems in this area: they could accept the cyclic pulse of history, seeing each episode as an element within God's overall plan. The Teutonic barbarians who destroyed Rome contained the seeds of Europe's later greatness. They took over the legacy of the ancient world preserved by the Church and exploited it in a new way made possible by their love of freedom and respect for the family. This claim struck a chord in the sympathies of many British historians, because it was widely believed that the constitutional liberties developed in later centuries had their origins in earlier times. The philosophical historians might see limited freedom as the by-product of a feudal economy, but others saw liberty as a precious inheritance from the Saxons who had founded the English nation. The Saxons were clearly Teutonic in origin, and it was thus possible to see both the British constitution and European civilization as natural products of racial character. Philology, the study of languages, suggested that Teutons, Romans and Greeks were all branches of the same Aryan stock. The colonial empires of the nineteenth century could thus be seen as an expression of the European race's potential for world domination in this era of mankind's development. What Mill dismissed as 'vulgar' racism was to become a dominant theme in the writings of many Victorian historians.

The Pulse of History

On the continent, individualism had been swept away by the sense of national identity created in the Napoleonic period. The old Enlightenment dream of individual freedom was no longer the goal of social progress. Comte's theory of intellectual development may have sounded attractive to British liberals, but Comte himself adopted a thoroughly authoritarian view of how the human race should be governed. Meanwhile, among Prussian thinkers the state had become the chief vehicle through which the growing maturity of the human spirit should be expressed. In the hands of Johann Gottlieb Fichte, Kant's respect for the individual's moral awareness was translated into an idealist concept of the state as an expression of the divine will. When developed by G. W. F. Hegel, this idealism became the basis of an immensely influential philosophy of historical development. For Hegel, history displayed the progress of the human spirit, which could be seen to advance in a series of waves or surges, each mounting higher than the last. The driving force of each upward surge was the emergence of a new national spirit. The concept of the dialectic was based upon the assumption that historical progress is not continuous: the driving force of each epoch necessarily generated its spiritual opposite and thus paved the way for the synthesis that would replace it.

Marx and Engels were to take this discontinuous model of progress and integrate it with the theory of economic determinism which, by itself, had generated a more gradualistic approach to social change. It is one of the ironies of history that Marx was impressed by L. H. Morgan's outline of the stages in social development, a classic product of the gradualist school. Everyone wanted stages of development, but the nineteenth century produced two different models of how the stages succeed one another. Marx and Engels found one way of synthesizing the two models, but we shall see that the idea of a racial hierarchy provided an alternative that proved far more popular at the time.

The German view of society encouraged a new attitude towards history based on the intensive use of written sources as the basis for a sympathetic reconstruction of the spirit underlying each episode in humanity's development. Particularly influential was Barthold Niebuhr's history of Rome (1811–12), which identified stages of development within Roman culture. It was to Niebuhr that Thomas Arnold turned in 1824 when he became aware that continental techniques had transcended anything available in Britain.[4] Arnold was a product of the 'Germano-Coleridgian' school which sought an alternative to radical individualism through the preservation of traditional pillars of the national spirit such as the Church. He accepted the reality of social change, but far from welcoming industrialization with open arms he saw man's unrestrained application of his rational powers as a threat. Christianity in the form of the Anglican Church offered an alternative vehicle for accepting and channelling social change as an expression of God's purpose. As headmaster of Rugby school, Arnold was in a position to direct the education of the natural leaders who would govern the country's future evolution. One of his chief goals was to instil a new respect for the traditional foundations of western culture. This included not only the creation of a new and more vigorous approach to Christianity, but also a revolution in the teaching of the classics.

Arnold's own *History of Rome* made clear the development of Roman society from the early stages revealed by ancient legends. But he was equally interested in Greece, and the most succinct expression of his philosophy of history can be seen in the essay usually called 'The Social Progress of States' which appeared as an appendix to his edition of Thucydides in 1835. What struck Arnold most forcibly was that in spite of the great differences which could be seen between ancient and modern civilizations, there were nevertheless parallels which seemed to indicate that both had gone through a similar cycle of development. We can recognize the essential characteristics of the modern age – yet there were periods in the history of Greece and Rome which seemed 'modern' beause they reflected a similar stage of cultural development. A completely cyclic theory of history would negate the belief that God has an ultimate purpose for mankind, but if the cycles represented phases in the overall development of the human spirit, the result would be a non-materialistic theory of progress. Arnold was not indifferent to economic forces, since he held that these were important for controlling the speed at which a nation advanced through its life cycle. Nations began as aristocracies, but the ruling class was eventually overthrown as the commons acquired wealth through trade.[5] Various factors, especially foreign threats, could interfere with the natural cycle of development, and

[4] See Forbes, *The Liberal Anglican Idea of History* and Culler, *The Victorian Mirror of History*, ch. 5. See also *The Life and Correspondence of Thomas Arnold*.
[5] See Arnold's edition of Thucydides, *History of the Peloponnesian War*, I, appendix 1, pp. 621–2.

Plate 6   Sir Edward Poynter, *The Catapult* (1868).
Poynter shows a catapult in use at the siege of Carthage in 146 BC,
suggesting the power of Rome in its period of youthful
expansion. The mechanism of the catapult is depicted in
considerable detail, and the painting was originally bought by an
engineering tycoon. Prints of *The Catapult* were often used to
illustrate school history textbooks.
From the collection of the Laing Art Gallery, Newcastle upon Tyne.
Reproduced by permission of Tyne and Wear Museums Service

here Arnold echoed the Whig view that Britain had been fortunate in escaping entanglement in foreign wars.[6]

If undisturbed, the sequence of stages in the history of each nation succeeded one another inevitably, just as they did in the growth of the individual. One could identify 'a natural period in history, marking the transition of every country from what I may call a state of

[6] Ibid., pp. 626–8.

childhood to manhood.'[7] But the length of time spent in each stage varied according to the conditions, and some nations had never matured. Again Arnold echoed the Whig view by declaring that the vast areas of Asia and Africa prevented social development, while Europe benefited from the proximity of the sea.[8] In this essay Arnold avoided the topic of national senility, but it is clear that he saw each nation contributing something to mankind's development before it declined. This was brought out more clearly in his *Introductory Lectures on Modern History*, where he argued that the modern period showed 'a fuller development of the human race, a richer combination of its most remarkable elements.'[9] The modern European race was Teutonic in origin and had no affinity with the peoples of Greece and Rome, yet it had inherited much of moral significance from the earlier civilizations. Greece was the source of the intellect, Rome of the law and, indirectly, of the moral thinking of Christianity. Where, then, lay the future course of human development? Unless the Slavic races had the potential to take over the direction of mankind's spiritual growth, it was up to Europe: 'If our existing nations are the last resources of the world, its fate may be said to be in their hands – God's work on earth will be left undone if they do not do it.'[10]

Arnold's death in 1842 robbed the liberal Anglicans of their chief spokesman, but various themes outlined in his work continued to be explored in later decades. German ideas of universal development went on exerting a direct influence, notably through the writings of the Prussian minister in London, Baron Christian Bunsen. Bunsen saw Christianity as vitally important for mankind's spiritual growth and held that nations disappear after having prepared the way for others to solve new and higher moral problems.[11] Significantly, it was Bunsen who encouraged the young Max Müller to promote the new science of language in Britain, and we shall see below how philology shaped ideas on the contributions made by ancient races. In a book dedicated to Müller, the philologist F. W. Farrar (better known as the author of the school-story *Eric, or Little by Little*) echoed the theme that several races had contributed in turn to God's great plan of development for humanity. The Egyptians had created order out of chaos, the Semites had explored the heights of religious inspiration, while the Aryans contributed the more active virtues. 'It is to the

[7] Ibid., p. 615.
[8] Ibid., p. 637.
[9] Arnold, *Introductory Lectures on Modern History*, p. 26.
[10] Ibid., p. 31.
[11] Bunsen, *Christianity and Mankind*, III, pp. 35–7.

result of their *combined* work – to the science and strength of the Aryan inspired and ennobled by the religious thoughts that were revealed to the Semite – that the immediate future of the world belongs.'[12]

It was left for Charles Kingsley to expand Arnold's thesis in detail. In the preface to his historical novel *Hypatia* (1853) and in a series of lectures at Cambridge published as *The Roman and the Teuton* (1864), Kingsley unpicked the delicate network of events that had to unfold in order that God's plan should be fulfilled. Rome contributed law and order, but only by establishing a brutal tyranny. Freedom was a heritage from the Teutonic peoples who had destroyed Rome, yet it was vital to the divine plan that the barbarians should not conquer the eastern empire, since there the metaphysical subtleties of Christianity would be worked out. The Teutons could not have done this themselves since they were essentially childish at the time. 'For good or evil they were great boys; very noble boys; very often very naughty boys – as boys with the strength of men might be . . .'[13] This was no metaphor, since 'races, like individuals . . . may have their childhood, their youth, their manhood, their old age, and natural death.'[14] But the Europeans' youthful ancestors were capable of absorbing and benefiting from the thought of the Church fathers. 'Our duty is, instead of sneering at them as pedantic dreamers, to thank heaven that men were found, just at the time they were needed, to do for us what we could never have done for ourselves; to leave us, as a precious heirloom . . . a metaphysic at once Christian and scientific.'[15] The Church eventually fell under the spell of the empire's thirst for domination – this is the real subject of *Hypatia* – but only after its spiritual message had been passed on to enlighten the freedom-loving Teutons and pave the way for modern Christianity.

It became fashionable to sneer at Kingsley as history became more academic, but his lectures and books were immensely popular and helped to create an image of European culture as a civilizing force in the modern world. The expansion of European power could thus be seen as part of God's plan, a necessary step in the spiritual education of the whole world. Such an attitude could easily take on a nationalistic slant as Britain became more conscious of its imperial destiny in the later years of the century. Kingsley's own *Westward Ho!*

[12] Farrar, *Families of Speech*, p. 186.

[13] Kingsley, *The Roman and the Teuton*, p. 5. On Kingsley's life and thought see *Charles Kingsley: His Letters and Memories of his Life* and Thorp, *Charles Kingsley, 1819–1875.*

[14] Kingsley, *The Roman and the Teuton*, p. 6.

[15] Kingsley, *Hypatia*, p. xvi.

focused on the Elizabethan seamen as a liberating force striving against the tyranny of Spain. Since Britain was the purest expression of European development, it was her duty to lead the way in controlling as much of the world's population as possible. The world would be saved not by economic necessity but by men acting under the inspiration of a historically constructed national spirit.

This idealistic interpretation of imperialism was developed by J. A. Cramb in a series of lectures in 1900 published as *The Origins and Destiny of Imperial Britain*. Cramb saw the World Spirit manifesting itself as 'the unseen force from within the race itself.'[16] Britain had become conscious of its destiny now that the war in South Africa had forced it to assert its right to develop a new kind of empire based on freedom and toleration. War was a permanent condition of human life, since the striving for conquest was a manifestation of the World Spirit and was justified when it resulted in the expansion of a morally enlightened power.[17] Far from being an expression of materialistic social Darwinism, this glorification of struggle had its origins in the idealist philosophy of the state against which liberals such as Darwin and Spencer struggled in the name of individualism.

For Cramb, each empire of the past represented a distinct ideal: Greece expressed beauty, Rome power and Egypt mystery. The British empire arose from a synthesis of metaphysical speculation and practical application which highlighted the 'world-historic significance of the English reformation'.[18] Although Cramb criticized the simplistic analogy between the life cycle of the nation and that of the individual, he accepted that there was a cyclic rhythm to history analogous to the seasons of the year. Empires did not decay by accident, but because 'each imperial race starts its career dowered with a vital capacity of definite range.' Thus it was clear that 'regret or surprise at the passing of empires is like regret or surprise at the passing of youth.'[19] Yet the cycles were cumulative: 'The form perishes, nation, city, empire; but the creative thought, the soul of the state endures.' It endures because it is absorbed into the spirit of the next imperial race. 'Rome was the synthesis of the empires of the past, of Hellas, of Egypt, of Assyria. In her purposes, their purposes lived . . . In Britain the spirit of Empire receives a new incarnation. The form decays, the divine ideal remains, the creative spirit gliding from this to that, indestructible.'[20]

[16] Cramb, *The Origins and Destiny of Imperial Britain*, p. 5.
[17] Ibid., pp. 144–5.
[18] Ibid., p. 68.
[19] Ibid., pp. 195 and 175.
[20] Ibid., pp. 179 and 186–7.

Among the authorities cited by Cramb to support his cyclic theory of imperialism were Ruskin and Carlyle, although neither would have shared his optimistic hopes for the future. Ruskin certainly opted for a cyclic model of history, and in his study of Greek art defined clear stages of development and corruption spanning almost a millenium.[21] The rise of mediaeval Christian art represented a new cycle, but Ruskin was convinced that the path of modern culture since the Renaissance led inexorably downward. Carlyle had a more positive view based on a different version of the cyclic model in which periods of belief and unbelief alternated in the growth of the human spirit. Life in an age of unbelief was depressing, but such eras were necessary to clear the way for the next creative synthesis. Having himself escaped from the 'everlasting No' of materialism, Carlyle hoped to inspire the leaders of his own generation with a new sense of purpose that would divert the industrialists' energy into more spiritually profitable channels. The moral force of strong personalities was always needed to generate meaningful activity in the population at large, and the secret of reconciling despotism and freedom was to ensure that the despotism was just.[22]

Matthew Arnold shared a similar cyclic view of historical development, inspired both by his father, Thomas, and by Carlyle. In his inaugural lecture as Professor of Poetry at Oxford in 1857, Arnold recalled the theme of his father's teaching in history, arguing that the characteristics of a 'modern' age can be seen at various points in the development of the human spirit.[23] History was thus a cyclic process, and although at first oppressed with the fear that the present was a period of degeneration, Arnold eventually moved on to a more optimistic belief that a new age of cultural development was dawning. From Goethe he borrowed the notion of the *Zeitgeist* or Time-Spirit which develops and carries with it the ideas of individual thinkers.[24] In later writings such as *Culture and Anarchy* Arnold argued that culture develops through the tension between two antagonistic forces, Hebraism and Hellenism.[25] Religious intensity and artistic creativity are both important, but each epoch has seen one or the other become the dominant force of the time. The cycles of cultural development are thus formed by the swings from one side to the other in a creative

[21] Ruskin, *Arata Pentelici*, p. 126.

[22] Carlyle, *Past and Present*, pp. 241–2.

[23] Arnold, 'On the Modern Element in Literature', *Complete Prose Works*, I, pp. 18–37.

[24] Arnold, 'Dr Stanley's Lectures on the Jewish Church', in *Essays in Criticism*; see Arnold, *Complete Prose Works*, II, p. 77.

[25] Arnold, *Culture and Anarchy*, ch. 5. In *Complete Prose Works*, V.

process for which both are essential. Puritanism was a natural product of the Hebraic spirit, and its role in the English Reformation had blinded many to the wider Hellenizing influence of the Renaissance. In his own time, Arnold saw his chief goal as softening the puritanical element in Victorian culture without opening the floodgates of anarchy.

The Myth of Race

Kingsley's writings carried a strong suggestion that the cycles of development were linked not merely to nations but to races. In the later nineteenth century, an increasing number of historians began to accept that racial background played a major role in shaping a nation's character. Those who saw Britain as a leading force in civilizing the world were attracted to the view that the British people – thanks to their unique environment and history – expressed the superior potential of the Teutonic race in a particularly effective way. With varying degrees of intensity, historians evoked the logic of racial superiority sketched out in Sir Charles Dilke's *Greater Britain* of 1869, in which a survey of the empire revealed how the 'cheaper' races were being displaced by European and especially British colonists. Although no historian, Dilke saw the rise of Greater Britain (by which he meant the British empire) as the triumph of 'Saxondom'. He proclaimed that the Americans 'are run into an English mould: Alfred's laws and Chaucer's tongue are theirs whether they would or no.'[26]

Not everyone succumbed to the myth of racial destiny, of course. Kingsley's successor as professor of modern history at Cambridge, Sir John Seeley, retained the belief that history reveals a purposeful trend in the nation's development; but his *Expansion of England* (1883) supported imperialism without resorting to a claim for white superiority. Britain should spread its influence by accepting the colonies as parts of itself, not as mere possessions; the conquest of India was made possible by better discipline and 'says nothing of any natural superiority on the part of the English.'[27] To the vast majority of those who accepted Seeley's expansionist rhetoric, however, it seemed obvious that the growing power of Britain flowed from an inherent racial advantage.

[26] Dilke, *Greater Britain*, preface and p. 572.
[27] Seeley, *The Expansion of England*, p. 233. See Wormell, *Sir John Seeley and the Uses of History*.

With hindsight it is all too easy to see where this conviction of racial superiority would lead. But there was a slightly less sinister side to the investigation of racial origins which arose from the ease with which it was synthesized with the liberal tradition. As J. W. Burrow has shown, many of the later Victorian historians were 'liberal' in the sense that they saw British history as a process by which the individual gained greater power to influence the nation's destiny, and it was easy enough to assume that only members of the white race had personalities strong enough to benefit from such a trend.[28] Once again, the German influence was paramount. To create their own sense of national identity the Germans had naturally turned to their Teutonic origins, evoking an almost mystical sense of the independent, saga-loving barbarians who destroyed Rome to establish the foundations upon which northern European culture would be built. Britain could share this heritage because the Saxons were clearly of Teutonic descent. Instead of tracing the constitutional origins of liberty back merely to the feudal epoch, one could argue that British liberties had a more ancient origin. The Norman conquest was necessary to unify the nation, but in the long run it consolidated the framework within which ancient Teutonic liberties would be expanded into modern democracy. In this interpretation of constitutional history, kings and their ministers were less important than the local assemblies that had kept racial customs alive through into the period in which a strong national spirit was established.

At the beginning of the century, Sharon Turner's *History of the Anglo-Saxons* (1799–1805) had created an image of the Saxons as a crude but freedom-loving people. Their assembly of nobles or Witena-Gemot was suggested as the foundation upon which the modern parliamentary system was to be built.[29] For Turner, the Anglo-Saxons had preserved ancient freedoms more effectively than any other Teutonic people, which was why 'the provisions of Magna Carta were not claimed as innovations, but as the ancient rights and privileges of the nation.'[30] The Saxon nobles had been so independent that they would have torn the nation apart, had not the Norman conquest tightened the bands of unity. Similar views were expressed in John Mitchell Kemble's *The Saxons in England* of 1849, a work dedicated to the Queen as a 'history of the principles which have given her empire its pre-eminence among the nations of Europe'.

[28] Burrow, *A Liberal Descent*. The theme of racial origins is explored more explicitly in MacDougall, *Racial Myth in English History*.
[29] Sharon Turner, *History of the Anglo-Saxons*, III, ch. 4.
[30] Ibid., III, p. 229.

Kemble saw British liberties as stemming from 'our Anglo-Saxon forefathers' and presented his book as 'the history of the childhood of our own age; – the explanation of its manhood'.[31]

We have already seen how Kingsley stressed the importance of the Teutons' love of freedom, and the same theme was developed at a more academic level by the Regius Professor of Modern History at Oxford, William Stubbs. In his *Constitutional History of England* Stubbs portrayed the growth of the modern constitution as the natural outgrowth of ancient liberties. He insisted that we must break the 'charm' of the mediaeval period and recognize it as a dark time in our history when traditional freedoms were almost destroyed. Were it not for his conviction that good would triumph in the end, Stubbs felt, the historian of the middle ages would lay down his pen with a heavy heart.[32] The true source of our liberty was the Saxon character: 'The German element is the paternal element in our system, natural and political.'[33] Here the seeds of future developments were planted, surviving not as laws but as customs that were never quite stamped out by the Normans. England struck a balance between centralized France and divided Germany, retaining its national unity thanks to the Normans, but preserving the old traditions at the local level until they could flourish again in modern times.[34]

The precise relationship between the Saxons and the Normans was explored in Edward A. Freeman's *History of the Norman Conquest* (1867–76). Freeman had studied under Thomas Arnold and sneered at Kingsley's 'Teutonism' – yet he too shared the view that the Saxons' love of freedom had laid the foundations of modern democracy. The Norman conquest was a great turning point, he insisted, but it had frequently been misunderstood: it was not the beginning of modern Britain but a necessary shaking-up of ancient traditions. The infusion of foreign blood and customs was only temporary, since 'in a few generations we led captive our conquerors; England was England once again, and the descendants of the Norman invaders were found to be among the truest of Englishmen.'[35] Freeman saw the Normans – who were, of course, of Scandinavian origin – as Teutonic brothers crossing the channel to be liberated from the autocratic attitudes they had acquired in France. Freeman was no simple progressionist, however. The influence of Arnold

---

[31] Kemble, *The Saxons in England*, p. v.
[32] Stubbs, *Constitutional History*, II, p. 613.
[33] Ibid., I, p. 11.
[34] Ibid., I, pp. 230–4.
[35] Freeman, *History of the Norman Conquest*, I, p. 2.

Plate 7   Ford Maddox Brown, *The Body of Harold brought before
William the Conqueror* (1844–61).
The Normans are, of course, elated, but William looks pensive,
as though aware of the future significance of his victory.
Manchester City Art Gallery

shows forth in occasional references to the ebb and flow of events, as
when he noted that the lack of unity in modern Europe had 'by one of
the strange cycles of history' brought us back to a state resembling the
pre-Roman era.[36]

The most aggressive use of the racial theme in British history came
in the work of a historian whom Freeman detested, James Anthony
Froude. At the start of his career, Froude had shocked polite society
with his *Nemesis of Faith* (1849), which charted his disillusionment
with Christianity after an experience with J. H. Newman and the
Tractarians.[37] Under the influence of Kingsley, he soon returned to

[36] Freeman, *The Chief Periods of European History*, p. 176.
[37] On this episode in Froude's career see Willey, *More Nineteenth-Century Studies*,
ch. 3. More generally, see Dunn, *James Anthony Froude* and Rowse, *Froude the
Historian*.

the fold, however, and began to develop the theme that the English Reformation was an event of paramount importance in the emergence of the modern world. He shared Kingsley's belief that England's expansion had been made possible by a national character created through the absorption of Roman values by a freedom-loving Anglo-Saxon people. But where Stubbs and Freeman studied the earlier phases in the survival of Anglo-Saxon values, Froude turned to the Reformation as the modern outburst of the spirit of freedom. His early writings on the sixteenth-century seamens' battles with Spain helped to inspire Kingsley's *Westward Ho!* Froude's *History of England* (1856–70) turned aside from the constitution to focus on the reigns of Henry VIII and Elizabeth as the critical period in which traditional freedoms were preserved from the threat posed by European centralization.

The *History* breaks off with the Armada, since with its defeat the power of Spain was broken and the way prepared for the expansion of modern Britain. Our spiritual independence was now guaranteed, although problems remained to be solved – and *were* solved on the scaffold in Whitehall, and in 1688.[38] Froude stressed the balance between individual action and the chances of history: Drake and the other sailors had fought as much against Elizabeth's vacillation as against Philip of Spain, and had they failed the emancipation of Europe would have been delayed indefinitely.[39] Froude's *English Seamen in the Sixteenth Century* developed this point at a more popular level.

Like Carlyle, whom he greatly admired, Froude preferred strong leaders, and he violated the Whig tradition by praising the oppressive measures used by Henry VIII to preserve the break with Rome. Strength of will was necessary to get anything done in this world, although Froude was prepared to admit that more often it was strong groups rather than strong individuals who succeeded. The seamen of the sixteenth century were a classic example: they represented a Protestant minority that had won the day because it was prepared to fight while the majority was not. 'The true right to rule in any nation lies with those who are best and bravest, whether their numbers are large or small . . .'[40] By the further efforts of their descendants, England had expanded its power around the globe. Froude was an ardent imperialist, and his lack of any sense of necessary progress made him all the more concerned about the empire's future. The

---

[38] Froude, *History of England*, XII, p. 562.
[39] Ibid, XII, pp. 532–8.
[40] Froude, *English Seamen*, p. 158.

Plate 8   Sir John Everett Millais, *The Boyhood of Raleigh* (1870).
Millais's picture of the young Raleigh being told of the wonders
that lie beyond the seas is a perfect expression of the Victorians'
attitude towards their Elizabethan ancestors who had begun the
world expansion of British power.
Tate Gallery, London

'progress' of modern industry threatened to destroy the nation by
concentrating the population in the cities, thus uprooting the peasantry
that were the heart of any nation's spirit. The empire was necessary to
relieve the overcrowding by providing space into which English
families could expand without losing their identity.[41]

Froude made it clear that strength of will and love of freedom were
racial characteristics which gave the English a right to dominate
others. He had a prejudice against the Irish, the remnants of a Celtic
stock who were brave but undisciplined, 'the spendthrift sister of the
Aryan race.'[42] He also justified the slave trade of the sixteenth century

[41] See Froude, *Short Studies on Great Subjects*, II: 'England and her Colonies' (pp.
180–216) and 'On Progress' (pp. 350–96). See also Froude's *Oceana*.
[42] Froude, *The English in Ireland*, I, p. 24. The role of Anglo-Saxonism in
fomenting anti-Irish prejudice is explored by Curtis, *Anglo-Saxons and Celts*.

on racial lines. The American Indians had died rather than be enslaved by the conquering whites, but the blacks of Africa lived in a natural state of barbarism and 'would domesticate like sheep or oxen . . .'[43] Other races clearly did not share the desire for freedom that was so characteristic of the Anglo-Saxon. The Europeans' ability to use their own initiative ensured that the expansion of the white race around the globe was inevitable; but Britain would have to be willing to fight if it wanted to retain its share of the available territory.

The thesis defended by Stubbs, Freeman and others was that the Saxons in England had – through the accidents of history and geography – preserved the heritage of freedom established by the Teutonic people who had invaded Europe at the fall of Rome. But the liberal Anglican view established by Thomas Arnold required more than race-spirit to ensure that God's plan would be fulfilled. As both Arnold and Kingsley made clear, the character of European civilization was an amalgam of the free spirit of the Teutons with the legacies of Judaism, classical Greece and Rome. The Hebraic spirit, as Matthew Arnold called it, was clearly imported from another race, but it had been made available to the Teutons via the synthesis with classical learning worked out in Rome's eastern empire. Was it possible, though, that a wider historical unity could be forged by recognizing an underlying relationship between the dominant races of ancient and modern Europe? Thomas Arnold had seen no such racial unity, but by 1850 it was becoming recognized that the contributions of Greece and Rome might have been made by peoples who shared kinship with the Teutons as branches of common root.

Freeman developed this theme quite explicitly in his *Comparative Politics* of 1873. He acknowledged that the Greeks, Romans and Teutons were 'the three great historic races, the races which have played the foremost part among mankind, the races whose history really makes up the political history of man.'[44] All three were, in fact, branches of the great Aryan stock which had divided into northern and southern families when it entered Europe. The southern family had become civilized more quickly, but the Greeks' development of cities had prevented them ever becoming a nation. Rome came closer to being a nation in the modern sense, but it was reserved for the Teutons, who never founded cities by themselves, to inherit and build upon this primitive foundation. The northern swarm had bided its time, husbanding its strength for when its tribes would gather themselves into the nations of Germany, Scandinavia and England.

[43] Froude, *English Seamen*, p. 38.
[44] Freeman, *Comparative Politics*, p. 35.

Freeman was quite clear as to the source of the information that allowed the historian to recognize this underlying unity: it was philology, the science of language, which showed that Greek, Latin and the Teutonic languages were derived from a common stock. By offering fresh insights into the state of prehistoric Europe, philology thus allowed the racial interpretation of British history to establish links with a wider myth of racial unity in the overall development of European civilization.[45]

Philology originated in Sir William Jones's suggestion in 1786 that the ancient Indian language of Sanskrit could be linked to Persian, Greek, Latin and the Germanic languages. In the early nineteenth century, German scholars such as Franz Bopp and Jacob Grimm began to explore these links in detail, constructing, in effect, an evolutionary tree of 'Indo-European' languages and elucidating the processes by which words tend to change through time. Sanskrit was, if not the actual root-language, certainly very closely related to it. Eventually the term 'Aryan' was coined to denote this whole family of languages (from the Sanskrit *arya*, a noble). In 1846 a young student of Bopp named Max Müller came to England at the suggestion of Baron Christian Bunsen, the Prussian minister who was doing much to promote German ideas on universal history. Müller's aim was to study ancient Indian texts collected by the East India Company, and he soon settled down at Oxford to become a permanent feature of the British academic establishment. Müller's 1861 *Lectures on the Science of Language* (originally delivered at the Royal Institution) helped to popularize the findings of the new discipline.

At a time when prehistoric archaeology was still in its infancy, philology seemed to offer an important clue as to the early history of the Indo-European people. If language was anything to go by, the diverse nations of Europe were not only linked to one another in the remote past, but had originally sprung from a homeland somewhere in Asia. Greek, Roman and Teuton shared a common cultural heritage, and it was perhaps inevitable that many would assume a common racial origin. Müller himself endorsed this assumption in his *Lectures* when he wrote that the first ancestors of the Indians, Persians, Greeks, Romans, Slavs, Celts and Germans 'were living together within the same enclosures, nay under the same roof.'[46] The

---

[45] On the link between history and philology see MacDougall, *Racial Myth in English History*, and Burrow, 'The Uses of Philology in Victorian England'.

[46] Müller, *Lectures on the Science of Language*, p. 198. Müller subsequently tried to distance himself from the identification of race by language, arguing that the Aryan descendants were unified by a common culture, not a common racial origin; see his *Biographies of Words*, pp. 89–90.

western branches of the Aryan stock had, of course, been deeply influenced by religious ideas transmitted from the distinct Semitic races. Together, the progressive race and the deep ideas made a powerful combination. As F. W. Farrar wrote in 1869, we can recognize

> the two great races to whose existence is due all, or nearly all, which makes man distinctively man; – the stately, thoughtful Semitic race, to which belong within but a few days' journey such volcanic centres of religious enthusiasm as Mecca, Sinai, and Jerusalem, and to which was given to express for ever the most unfathomable depths of religious emotion, and the loftiest heights of holy inspiration; – and the noble, ever-progressive Aryan race, the progenitor of Persian and Pelasgian, and Celt and Teuton, the discoverer of well-nigh everything which is great and beneficent in the arts of war and peace, the race from whose bosom came Charlemagne and Alfred, Dante and Shakespeare, M. Angelo and Raphael, Newton and Descartes, – the parent in the modern world of the metaphysical subtlety of Germany, and the vital intelligence of France, and the imperial energy of England, the parent in the ancient world of the lofty spiritualism of India, 'of the glory that was Greece, and the grandeur that was Rome'.[47]

As Farrar's comments suggest, the teachings of philology dovetailed neatly with the liberal Anglican view of history and the belief in Aryan or Teutonic supremacy. The link was hardly accidental, since both had their origins in Germanic influences. Arnold's and Kingsley's vision of a divine plan operating through the rise and fall of empires drew upon the idealist philosophy of universal development promoted by Germans such as Bunsen. Philology had been created by scholars who shared the same view of history. Theirs was no theory of necessary progress, but a mystical search for common origins in a past state that may have been simple, but which already contained all the seeds of future development. Just as the Bible taught the common origin of the races separated after the tower of Babel, so philology saw Aryan as a powerful root-language expressing a truly spiritual culture. If one went far enough back, perhaps the Aryan, Semitic and other families would be found to be products of a single original tongue – Müller certainly thought so, although he admitted that he could not prove it. In the meantime, philology's task was to uncover the unity of

[47] Farrar, *Families of Speech*, pp. 4–5.

development within each family. At this level, it seemed that all the races which had participated in the rise of European civilization shared a common heritage that had given each in turn the stimulus to make its mark in the world.

In principle, philology provided a major alternative to the linear model of social progress expounded by the philosophical historians and the anthropologists. It advocated not a hierarchy of developmental stages, but a pattern of divergence from a common ancestry – a branching tree rather than a ladder. Müller set out a 'Genealogical Table of the Aryan Family of Languages' in which the divergence is evident, while the model of a branching tree was followed quite explicitly in a diagram used by Farrar and others.[48] The striking feature of Farrar's diagram is that the tree has no central trunk; no philologist would have dared to single out one European language as the 'main line' of Aryan evolution. British historians might favour the English as having best preserved the ancient Teutonic liberties, but in the long run they shared the philologists' view that many races had contributed to the overall pattern.

Such a model of branching development had, at least potentially, the ability to undermine the teleology inherent in the progressionist assumption that all social development tends toward a single goal. Darwin – who also used a branching tree to illustrate the divergent evolution of biological species – saw a close parallel between his theory and the process of change revealed by philology. As we shall see in part III below, Darwin tried unsuccessfully to switch the idea of biological evolution from simple progressionism to a less teleological branching model. The philologists had no intention of following Darwin, however, since they remained loyal to an alternative form of teleology more in tune with the biblical view of human origins. The goal-directed character of history was evident not in the ascent towards a predictable future, but in the underlying potential which unified all developments arising from a particular source. Since Darwin himself had to depend upon a progressionist account of the origin of human faculties, including speech, Müller was able to use philology as an argument against human evolution, despite their agreement on the branching character of historical development.

Müller always claimed to have been an 'evolutionist' long before Darwin published the *Origin of Species*,[49] but his definition of evolution was designed to avoid exactly those materialistic implications

---

[48] Müller, *Lectures on the Science of Language*, p. 380; Farrar, *Families of Speech*, p. 79.
[49] Müller, *The Science of Thought*, pp. xi and 89.

that Darwin built into the theory. There was no open-ended, haphazard chaos of developments, as Darwin would have us believe.
Instead, Müller argued that the development of languages had been
constrained to move along certain predetermined 'broad lines' which
allowed us to recognize distinct families of speech: 'The theory of
evolution to which I hold, and which seems to me confirmed more
and more by every discovery that has lately been made in the growth
of nature and the growth of the human mind as represented in
language, is this, that evolution in both starts from distinct beginnings
and leads to distinct ends.'[50] Evolution was not linear, but it *was*
predetermined, representing the unpacking of certain potentials built
into language at its very beginning, presumably by the Creator.
Müller argued repeatedly against the Darwinians' claim that language
could have evolved from the noises made by animals: it was a divine
gift which forever separated the human mind from the level of the
brutes.

Müller also recognized aspects of language evolution that were
degenerative rather than progressive. For him, the Aryan root-
language had a clarity and simplicity which ensured that any future
changes were bound to run the risk of clouding the original purity. In
particular, he believed that myths were a 'disease of language' caused
when the descendants of the Aryans forgot that some words had
originally been used in a metaphorical fashion. They thus began to
think that the sun, for instance, was a god, rather than merely a
symbol of the divine. Myths were not, as in Tylor's view, a confused
attempt to rationalize genuine phenomena, but a product of the laws
governing the way people use language.[51] This approach necessarily
denied that there was anything 'primitive' about the Aryan language.

Another phenomenon used to suggest degeneration was the
assumed decline in the rate of language evolution. Drawing on the
work of James Cowles Prichard, the noted philosopher of science
William Whewell insisted that the really fundamental divisions into
language groups had occurred long ago, while in more recent times
there had been only trivial developments within those groups.[52] The
development of language was thus gradually slowing down. Whewell's
claim is significant because it indicates a failure to appreciate the
implications of a branching model of evolution. In such a model,
branches have necessarily moved further apart the longer they have

[50] Ibid., pp. 93–4. On Müller's conflict with Darwin see Knoll, 'The Science of
Language and the Evolution of Mind'.
[51] See Schrempp, 'The Re-education of Friedrich Max Müller'.
[52] Whewell, *Philosophy of the Inductive Sciences*, I, pp. 677–9.

been separated, even at a constant rate of change. The recent changes only appear trivial because the branches have not had time to diverge further apart.

Various aspects of the philologists' position thus stood in stark contrast to the progressionism of the philosophical historians and the evolutionary anthropologists. From the latters' viewpoint, the ancient Aryans were already civilized and could not be treated as the starting point of cultural development. Müller himself at first tried to bridge the gap between the two positions by arguing that one could correlate the stages of language evolution with the stages of social development. Perhaps there was a more primitive language from which the Aryan, Semitic and other roots had evolved, originating in a time when all humans were mere hunter–gatherers. The deep origin of language would then lie in an 'antediluvian' period before the appearance of family groups or the herding of animals.[53] Here the divergence within the language groups is superimposed on a developmental stage-theory of the increasing sophistication of language types. This was consistent with Müller's hope that all languages would turn out to have a common origin, but he soon abandoned his attempt to compromise with progressionism. His later work stressed the uniqueness of language to mankind and the archetypical role of Aryan and the other roots as the foundations of modern languages.

In its mature form, then, Müller's system provided clear support for those who preferred idealist and racist theories of history. Writers who stressed the progressive character of the white race could use the Aryan myth to show that Greeks, Romans and Teutons were all branches of the same stock. The implication that language evolution was the unpacking of inbuilt potentialities fitted in neatly with the liberal Anglican belief that the successive contributions of each branch of the Aryan stock were part of a divine plan. The fusion of philology with the liberal Anglican tradition provided a comprehensive alternative to the simple progressionism of the philosophical historians and the cultural anthropologists. History was shaped by divine providence, not by the laws of political economy and rational thought. Both sides might appeal to individual effort as the driving force of change, but for the liberal Anglicans the individual's highest aspiration must be to uphold the cultural traditions that have enabled his race to make its contribution to the divine plan.

[53] See the diagram from Müller's account of the origin of language in Bunsen's *Outlines of Philosophy of Universal History*, reproduced in Kuper, 'The Development of Lewis Henry Morgan's Evolutionism', p. 9 and in Trautmann, *Lewis Henry Morgan*, p. 219.

Unfortunately for Müller, his attempt to provide the theory of racial destiny with a foundation in prehistory was doomed to failure. The concept of an Aryan archetype was plausible as long as the traditional biblical timescale of human history remained intact. In the 1860s, however, archaeologists began dramatically to extend their estimates of human antiquity. It became clear that the Aryans, if they existed, were a comparatively recent and quite civilized people. Behind them stretched the untold millenia of the stone age, in which the whole human race had lived in a state of savagery. The anthropologists, as we saw in chapter 1, now turned to the study of modern 'primitives' in an effort to reconstruct the earliest stages of social progress. Progressionism thus began to dominate late-nineteenth-century thought about human origins. Only the racial element of the liberal Anglican tradition survived, transmuted into a search for the evolutionary ancestry of the various races, low or high, which had survived into the modern world.

As we move to consider these developments in the study of prehistory, it is worth remembering that our survey of the cyclic and racial interpretations of modern history has shown that the image of struggle and conflict was not confined to the ideology of competitive individualism. The idealists who saw history as the unfolding of a divine plan had their own very different image of progress, and their own belief that the race which loses its place as the active participant in history must be displaced by its successor. If the supporters of *laissez-faire* individualism stressed competition within society, their rivals were equally willing to acknowledge the struggle between races or nations. Far from being a product of late-nineteenth-century 'social Darwinism', the image of races battling for supremacy has its origins in the idealist view of history. The concept of the 'survival of the fittest' was to be used by many thinkers who had little or no sympathy with Darwin's mechanism of biological evolution.

Part II

The Evolution of Mankind

3

The Antiquity of Man

We have seen that the Victorians' interpretation of their own immediate past was inseparable from their view of prehistory. The liberal Anglican view of history allowed conservative thinkers to argue that divine providence, not human effort, was the driving force of history. If the rise and fall of civilizations were controlled by God's great plan, then traditional religion should continue to influence the now-dominant European races as they played their part in world history. Respect for cultural roots should not be swept away by the demand for greater freedom: liberty meant the freedom to play a role in the nation's efforts to fulfil its destiny, not the mere exercise of selfishness. Through its link with philology, this approach offered a view of prehistory in line with the traditional biblical story in which mankind was taught the arts of civilization by its Creator. The claim that the Aryan race had already been civilized before it split up into the discrete peoples of classical and modern Europe was compatible with the biblical story, and with the belief that mankind had only existed on the earth for a few thousand years.

The alternative Whig interpretation derived much of its inspiration from the philosophical historians' thesis that economic factors drive all societies along a scale of complexity towards a commercial or industrial means of production and hence towards an individualist ideology. The Whigs respected the constitution as an evolving entity, but they could hardly conceal their feeling that its ultimate purpose was to allow the dismantling of traditional institutions in the name of free enterprise. To substantiate this view, they presented social evolution as an inevitable outcome of the forces governing the interaction of human beings with their environment. The implication of this was that the highly developed societies of both the classical world and modern Europe had sprung from primitive hunter–gatherers. Cultural anthropologists such as Tylor eventually began to use modern savages to illustrate the prehistoric phase of European development. To do this, however, they were forced to challenge the biblical view of human origins endorsed by the philologists.

By implication, the philosophical historians of the eighteenth century had already challenged the biblical story of creation by supposing that mankind acquired civilization gradually under the working of natural law. Social philosophers postulated a 'state of nature' before the emergence of the social contract, although not everyone agreed with Thomas Hobbes's claim that life in this original state had been 'nasty, brutish, and short'. The concept of a state of nature was, in any case, a convenient fiction for social analysis: no one could take it seriously as the original state of the human race so long as the traditional timescale of history remained unchallenged. If mankind was only a few thousand years old, the great empires recorded in the Bible coincided with the earliest days of the race. By the early nineteenth century, geologists had shown that the earth was much older than allowed for by the traditional date of creation (4004 BC according to the estimate of Archbishop James Ussher). Yet the old timescale of human history remained intact; it was still an article of faith to suppose that the human race only appeared after the earth was given its modern form in the last great geological catastrophe. For archaeologists and anthropologists to connect modern 'savages' with the earliest state of all humans, the timescale would have to be extended so that the biblical empires and the Aryans could be seen as comparatively recent products of a longstanding progressive trend.

The first part of this chapter tells the story of how archaeologists broke down the barrier that had inhibited the emergence of a modern view of prehistory. The transition was rapid – perhaps because it had been delayed for so long – and within a few years anthropologists had finalized the theory of cultural evolution in which modern 'primitives' were used to flesh out the philosophical historians' view of society's origins. The 1860s thus saw a revolution in archaeology and anthropology which coincided with, but in many respects occurred independently of, the Darwinian revolution in biology. The *Origin of Species* appeared in 1859 and its message was soon applied to human origins. Since evolution was supposed to be a very slow affair, a Darwinian account of human origins certainly required that our ancestors should have been recognizably human for a long period of time. But the revolution in archaeology would probably have taken place without Darwin, and by itself would have tipped the balance in favour of a progressionist account of the origin of society.

What Darwinism added was the possibility that our savage ancestors might have been biologically as well as culturally primitive, intermediates in the process by which the human faculties emerged from animal origins. From the image of our distant ancestors as brutal savages, it was a short step toward seeing them as 'ape-men'. Many thinkers were at first deeply disturbed by the prospect of an ape ancestry for mankind, but historians have now begun to realize that the great debate over human origins was over by the 1870s. Evolution was accepted, and the progressionist view was hailed as the only way of salvaging the belief that the operations of natural law fulfilled a divine purpose. The cyclic model of history survived among those who still saw each race as having a brief spell as the standard-bearer of progress before being eclipsed by a later, more highly evolved type.

The Origin of Society

Systematic investigation of human prehistory began in early-nineteenth-century Scandinavia, when scholars such as J. J. A. Worsaae and Christian Thomsen began to excavate ancient barrows and middens in search of information about the area's earliest inhabitants. Their motive was frankly nationalistic: as Worsaae noted, a nation which values its independence must know its own history, and Scandinavia had most to offer in the area of prehistory.[1] A pattern soon emerged from the excavations, allowing the archaeologists to propose a 'three-age system' in which the inhabitants of northern Europe had made use successively of stone, bronze and finally iron tools. The life style of the earliest Europeans certainly seemed to have been very primitive. By the middle of the century, the Scandinavian results were widely known – Worsaae's *Primeval Antiquities of Denmark* was translated in 1849 – and the three-age system was being recognized as a pattern valid for the whole of Europe.

The three-age system might have been seen as support for the progressionist view of social development, with the increasing sophistication of tools witnessing the response of human ingenuity to the problem of feeding a growing population. But this was not the interpretation put on their findings by Worsaae and his colleagues.

---

[1] Worsaae, *The Primeval Antiquities of Denmark*, p. 1. See Daniel, *A Hundred and Fifty Years of Archaeology*, pp. 38–54 and *Towards a History of Archaeology*. For a brief survey see also Bowler, *Theories of Human Evolution*, ch. 1.

They were convinced that each new level of culture was introduced not by invention but by the invasion of a more civilized people from the east. The bronze-age people were probably a Gothic tribe, and were certainly different from the stone-age inhabitants they displaced.[2] In a later book, Worsaae insisted that no native European race had developed a bronze technology – the metal had invariably been introduced by a dominant race from Asia, probably from India.[3] He thus endorsed the philologists' theory of Aryan invaders bringing a higher level of culture with them. The oldest inhabitants of Europe were not a progressive race, but degenerates waiting to be swept away by superiors who already existed to the east.

The archaeologists also wanted to reconcile their findings with the traditional timespan of human history based on the Bible. There was no suggestion in their work that the stone-age peoples of Europe should be associated with a long span of prehistory antedating the higher cultures of the East. Europe was merely a backwater inhabited by a race which had been pushed outside the pale of civilization. To put a progressionist interpretation on their discoveries it would be necessary to recognize that stone-age Europe was not merely contemporary with the civilizations of the ancient world; the stone age would have to be seen as the original state of society across the whole world, stretching back to a time long before the biblical empires had been founded. More time was certainly available, since even the most conservative geologists now admitted that the earth itself was much older than the biblical creation story implied. What was needed was evidence that stone-age humans had lived many thousands of years ago, at a time when the earth had still not taken on the form we know today.

Throughout the early nineteenth century there were occasional reports of human artefacts being found in geological deposits so old that they contained the bones of animals now extinct. Superficial deposits of gravel or boulder-clay were often called 'diluvium' and interpreted as the remains of Noah's flood, the last great geological catastrophe. Some geologists pointed out that if this was their origin, we should expect the deposits to contain human remains. But the majority preferred to believe that there could be no link between the geological and human timescales; that mankind only appeared *after* the last catastrophe. Reports of apparently ancient human remains were thus dismissed as the result of deliberate burial or, if found in caves, of the natural mixing of deposits. In 1822 the geologist William

[2] Worsaae, *The Primeval Antiquities of Denmark*, pp. 126 and 144.
[3] Worsaae, *The Pre-History of the North*, pp. 51–5.

Buckland visited Paviland cave near Swansea and found a human skeleton in deposits also containing the bones of extinct mammals. In his *Reliquiae Diluvianae*, however, he insisted that the 'red lady of Paviland' was a burial from Roman times.[4] The Reverend John MacEnery found a similar combination of human and extinct animal remains in Kent's cavern, on the south coast of Devon, but was persuaded to deny the antiquity of the human specimens.

In France, too, the majority of scientists were opposed to the extension of human antiquity and vigorously resisted the efforts of a minority who wished to take the new discoveries seriously. One of the most persistent excavators was Jacques Boucher des Perthes, an amateur who worked in the gravel beds of the Somme valley. These beds were clearly stratified and were undisturbed, yet Boucher des Perthes found numerous flint tools alongside the bones of extinct animals. When he published his findings, however, he insisted that the antediluvian toolmakers were an intelligent but nonhuman race, now extinct. This made it easy for sceptical experts to dismiss his findings as illusions or even outright frauds.

The revolution which broke down the barriers against acceptance of human antiquity began in 1858 when two reputable geologists, William Pengelly and Hugh Falconer, began to excavate at Brixham cave, near Torquay.[5] They too found stone tools and the bones of extinct animals in close proximity, and became convinced that human toolmakers must have lived in the remote past. More geologists came to the cave, including the highly respected Charles Lyell, and all were convinced by the evidence. The years 1859 and 1860 saw the publication of a number of papers supporting the view that the human race was of a much greater antiquity than had been previously supposed. British geologists went to France and confirmed that Boucher des Perthes' discoveries were genuine. Soon palaeontologists such as Edouard Lartet had begun a campaign to convert the French scientific community and to begin exploration of the many prehistoric sites in the south of their country. Much of the new evidence was summed up in Lyell's widely read *Geological Evidences of the Antiquity of Man* of 1863.[6]

Lyell himself held up modern savages as illustration of the lives of our prehistoric ancestors, but for some archaeologists the link with

[4] Buckland, *Reliquiae Diluvianae*, p. 90. See Grayson, *The Establishment of Human Antiquity*, ch. 5.

[5] See Grayson, *The Establishment of Human Antiquity*, and Gruber, 'Brixham Cave and the Antiquity of Man'.

[6] Note, however, that many experts dismissed Lyell's book as derivative; see Bynum, 'Charles Lyell's *Antiquity of Man* and its Critics'.

Plate 9   Prehistoric lake dwellings.
The reconstruction of this village, built on piles discovered in a
Swiss lake, was based partly on contemporary structures
observed by explorers in New Guinea, illustrating the Victorians'
tendency to see modern 'savages' as relics of early stages in
European prehistory.
From Charles Lyell, *Geological Evidences of the Antiquity of Man*,
frontispiece

anthropology was even more important. The anthropologists too depended on archaeology to support their claim that all societies had evolved from primitive origins. Edward B. Tylor worked with Henry Christy, an archaeologist studying the extensive prehistoric sites of Aquitaine. It was John Lubbock who produced the most comprehensive synthesis of the new developments in anthropology and archaeology. His *Prehistoric Times* of 1865 followed Lyell in surveying the evidence for the deep antiquity of mankind, but also devoted several chapters to a study of modern primitives. Lubbock noted that Christy and others had found bone tools in France which suggested that some early humans had lived very much as contemporary Eskomos did.[7] This fitted in with the newly popular theory of the ice ages, now being used to explain many of the geological phenomena originally attributed to the great flood. The Australian aborigines were an even better example of a 'living fossil' in the area of culture, as useful to the antiquary as was the sloth or the opossum to the palaeontologist.[8]

Lubbock spared no effort to paint a depressing picture of savage – and hence of prehistoric – life. Modern primitives were dirty, they had little religion, few morals, and no respect for women or the aged.

[7] Lubbock, *Prehistoric Times*, p. 256 and ch. XII.
[8] Ibid., p. 336.

Yet our own ancestors had lived like that for untold millenia as they gradually mounted the scale of social progress. Lubbock ended his book with a hymn of praise to progress, but unlike Lyell and Tylor he was prepared to extend the progressionist scheme to include the ascent of mankind from an animal ancestry. The ongoing progress of civilization was a continuation of the process by which the human species had risen from the apes. Man's stone-age ancestors, like modern savages, were both culturally and mentally inferior to the modern white race. They had poor tools and poorer morals because they had not yet developed the mental powers that would allow them to do better. Savages were thus both biological and cultural relics of the past. Monkeys use simple tools, Lubbock insisted, thus illustrating how our earliest, still brutish ancestors had taken the first steps of the road to greater intelligence and modern civilization.[9] No one could doubt that the level of happiness had increased through time as mankind gained greater control over nature, and Lubbock offered modern science as the source of unlimited future improvements that would benefit the human race.

In thus using archaeology and anthropology to create an image of initial human bestiality, Lubbock was directly challenging the biblical concept of degeneration from an original state of grace. At the 1868 meeting of the British Association he confronted Archbishop Richard Whately of Dublin on this issue and used the archaeological evidence to dispose of any lingering hope that the earliest humans might have received the gift of civilization directly from the Creator. A more persistent opponent was the Duke of Argyll, an amateur naturalist, whose *Primeval Man* of 1869 made the point that the archaeological record could prove only technological, not moral progress.[10] The evolutionist simply assumed that the makers of primitive stone tools had the moral characters of the most degraded modern savages; but there was no necessary link between the invention of better tools and moral development. According to Argyll, it was possible that our distant ancestors had spiritual capacities equivalent to our own, despite their lack of a sophisticated technology. His argument illustrated the extent to which evolutionary anthropology rested upon an assumption about the integral nature of economic and moral development. It also seems to anticipate the twentieth-century fear that humankind is not mature enough to deal with its ever-expanding military technology.

Whatever the validity of Argyll's warnings, his position became

[9] Ibid., p. 473.
[10] See Gillespie, 'The Duke of Argyll, Evolutionary Anthropology, and the Art of Scientific Controversy'.

increasingly isolated as evolutionism became the dominant metaphor of late-nineteenth-century thought. The success of Lubbock's campaign depended not just on the huge extension of prehistoric time, but also on the increasing evidence for the progressive development of an ever more sophisticated form of society. The 'stone age' was not a simple unit: it soon became evident that toolmaking skills (and presumably social organization) had developed over a vast period of time. The stone age of the Scandinavian archaeologists was established through the discovery of sophisticated tools of polished stone, but the new evidence suggested a much earlier and more extensive period in which primitive tools of chipped stone had been used. Lubbock coined the terms 'Neolithic' and 'Palaeolithic' to denote the ages of polished and chipped tools – the New and the Old stone ages.[11] The Palaeolithic was clearly of immense extent, and the discoveries of French archaeologists soon confirmed that there had been a succession of different toolmaking cultures occupying Europe through a period stretching back into the ice ages. Prehistoric sites could be analysed by the stratigraphic techniques already familiar to geologists, since in a series of layered deposits the upper layers are always more recent than the lower. It thus became possible to sketch in a historical sequence for European prehistory, extending the stages of social development back into a past so remote that the evolutionists could easily claim that the earliest relics were made by 'ape-men' more primitive than even the lowest modern savage.

There was at first some doubt about how best to classify the various Palaeolithic cultures, although from the start it was considered a first priority to arrange them into a historical sequence. The French palaeontologist Lartet suggested that sites should be dated by the animal remains associated with the stone tools. As the climate of Europe changed, so would the animals hunted by our ancestors. But other archaeologists pointed out that geographical factors would also affect the choice of animals hunted, rendering dating by this method highly suspect. The most obvious alternative was to identify sites by the actual technique used to make the stone tools. There were clear differences in style of manufacture between various levels at the same site, if that site had been occupied over a long period of time. Did this indicate bands of people with different toolmaking habits migrating back and forth across Europe, or was there a universally valid sequence corresponding to the order in which the techniques had been invented? Perhaps inevitably, the evolutionists opted for the

[11] Lubbock, *Prehistoric Times*, pp. 1–2.

latter alternative. The earliest tools certainly seemed to be the most primitive, and on this foundation they built a progressive sequence in which all toolmaking cultures were assigned a position in the scale ascending from the most basic chipped stone tools up to the sophisticated polished stone of the Neolithic.

The pioneer of this technique was the French archaeologist Gabriel de Mortillet. At the Paris Exposition of 1867 and later in his *Le Préhistorique* of 1883, de Mortillet identified a sequence of cultures named after characteristic sites and ranked into what he considered to be a natural progressive sequence. The oldest tools or 'eoliths' ('dawn stones') were of considerable geological antiquity, but were dismissed by some authorities as naturally fractured pebbles. Of the undoubted tools, the oldest and most primitive formed the Chellean culture, including the massive stone hand-axes found by Boucher des Perthes. This was followed by the Mousterian, in which the tools were made from flakes struck off from a flint core. Next came the Solutrean, using beautifully shaped blades of flint, and finally the Magdalenian, where stone was frequently replaced by bone. De Mortillet insisted that the sequence represented the natural progression which resulted from the invention of increasingly sophisticated techniques by the peoples of Europe. There were no invasions of higher cultures from elsewhere, except perhaps at the transition to the Neolithic.[12] When extended in the later decades of the century, the system revealed the broad panorama of human development depicted in figure 1. De Mortillet's system was thus a perfect counterpart to the linear progressionism of the anthropologists. It assumed that all peoples tended to evolve in parallel along the same sequence of cultural development. Modern savages such as the Australian aborigines had simply become stuck at a point corresponding to the late Palaeolithic of Europe.

De Mortillet was certainly aware of the ideological implications of his system. He was a prominent socialist, and saw evolutionary progressionism as the perfect foundation on which to build an argument for the inevitability of future reform. In his account of the display at the 1867 Exposition he claimed to have demonstrated the validity of the following propositions:

> The Law of the Progress of Humanity
> The Law of Similar Development
> The High Antiquity of Mankind.[13]

[12] De Mortillet, *Le Préhistorique*, p. 374.
[13] De Mortillet, 'Promenades préhistoriques à l'exposition universelle', p. 368. See Hammond, 'Anthropology as a Weapon of Social Combat'.

IRON AGE
BRONZE AGE
STONE AGE   NEOLITHIC
                 PALAEOLITHIC   Azilian
                                     Magdalenian   Time
                                     Solutrean
                                     Aurignacian
                                     Mousterian
                                     Acheulian
                                     Chellean (Abbevillian)
                                     Prechellean *or* eoliths

Figure 1   De Mortillet's sequence of prehistoric toolmaking cultures, as
extended by late-nineteenth-century archaeologists

De Mortillet's socialism would not have endeared him to English
readers, but his system fitted in so neatly with the assumptions of
evolutionary anthropology (and, increasingly, of evolutionary biology)
that it soon became the dominant interpretation of the Palaeolithic
throughout the English-speaking world. Thus John Evans, who
merely noted de Mortillet's scheme in the first edition of his *Ancient
Stone Implements* (1872), conceded in his second edition of 1897 that
it had become almost universally accepted.[14] Most surveys published
in the late nineteenth and early twentieth centuries routinely based
their account on de Mortillet's sequence of cultures. Along with the
sequence they implicitly accepted the assumption that progress is
inevitable and that there is a natural sequence through which all
cultures must pass as they ascend the evolutionary scale. Those races
which had not progressed as fast as the triumphant whites were
assigned to a lower position on the scale and dismissed as 'living
fossils' who would be swept away by the pressures of the modern
world.

The Emergence of Mind

The supposition that early humans had been culturally primitive did
not necessarily entail acceptance of an evolutionary account of how
the human race originated. Tylor had invoked the scale of cultural
development to preserve his belief in the uniformity of human nature;
he was never happy with the idea that the human mind could have

[14] Evans, *Ancient Stone Implements*, pp. 434–5 and 2nd edn, p. 483.

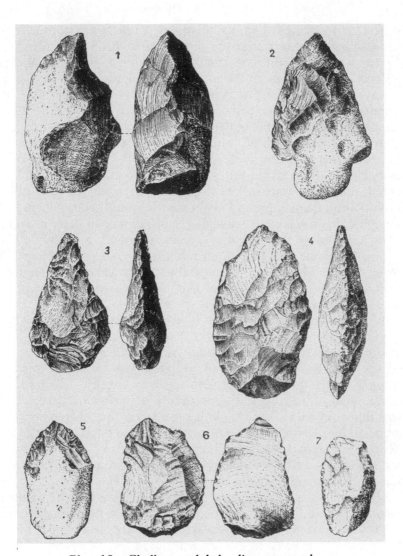

Plate 10   Chellean and Acheulian stone tools.
Left centre is the typical Chellean stone hand-axe, right centre
the more rounded Acheulian form. Apart from disputed
'eoliths', these were the oldest stone tools known in the
nineteenth century and formed the lowest stages of de
Mortillet's evolutionary sequence.
From Marcellin Boule, *Fossil Men*, p. 141

arisen gradually out of animal mentality. Lyell was disturbed by the prospect of an animal ancestry for mankind throughout his career. Yet as we saw in the conclusion of chapter 1 above, even Tylor succumbed eventually to the increasingly popular belief that savage races have retained a primitive level of culture because they have inferior mental powers. From this position it was but a short step to the claim that the people of the early Palaeolithic were less intelligent than ourselves, which in turn allowed them to be portrayed as intermediates in a line of development by which civilized mankind had emerged from an ape ancestry. The theory of biological evolution could thus be presented as a natural extension of the cultural evolutionism gaining ground in anthropology and archaeology. Some accepted this implication willingly. Lubbock was an early convert to Darwinism after the *Origin of Species* appeared in 1859, and de Mortillet was one of the first French scientists to support transformism, or evolution. The theory of cultural progress was thus extended to include an earlier phase in which primitive humans had evolved from an animal ancestry.

We traditionally associate the debate over human origins with the appearance of Darwin's theory. Everyone knows about T. H. Huxley's clash with Bishop Samuel Wilberforce at the 1860 meeting of the British Association, and everyone has heard of Disraeli's response to the question 'Is man an ape or an angel?' – 'My lord, I am on the side of the angels.'[15] The debate over *Man's Place in Nature* (the title of Huxley's 1863 book) is regarded as the centrepiece to any study of the Darwinian revolution.[16] This is not the place for another detailed survey of these events, but we are now in a position to see that far more was going on than the traditional concentration on the impact of Darwinism might imply.

Historians have, in fact, already begun to suggest that the traditional picture is in need of revision. Huxley's demolition of Wilberforce may not have been as effective as was once supposed, and Huxley himself has been revealed as only a lukewarm supporter of Darwin's detailed theory.[17] While there was a lot of heart-searching over human origins, it is now recognized that the dust of debate settled fairly quickly as a compromise was worked out in which the idea of progress was used to make evolution acceptable. Divine creation could be replaced by

[15] Monypenny and Buckle, *Life of Benjamin Disraeli*, II, p. 108.

[16] See, for instance, Greene, *The Death of Adam* and, more recently, Moore, *The Post-Darwinian Controversies* and Young, *Darwin's Metaphor*.

[17] See Jensen, 'Return to the Wilberforce–Huxley Debate' and di Gregorio, *T. H. Huxley's Place in Natural Science*.

natural evolution if the process was seen to embody the Creator's purpose by advancing inexorably towards a morally significant goal. In view of these revisions it is now possible to argue that the materialistic implications of Darwin's theory that are so attractive to modern biologists were largely evaded in his own time.[18] Darwin called his own account of human origins *The Descent of Man*, but most people's view of evolution was reflected more accurately in the title of the Scottish theologian Henry Drummond's *Ascent of Man* of 1894.

In the light of the developments reviewed above we can now see that ideas on human origins were inevitably conditioned not just by the confrontation between the Darwinists and the theologians, but also by contemporary studies in anthropology and archaeology – which were themselves integrated into the Victorians' view of history in general. If it were to be accepted that the origin of mankind was a natural process, theories about the nature of that process would almost certainly be modelled on available ideas about how societies and races originated. The evolutionists' main task was to show that the higher intellectual and moral faculties of the human mind could have emerged from the mentality of animals. More important, they had to thwart the objections of those who saw the human mind as something 'higher' than brute nature by showing that the evolutionary process was *intended* to achieve this goal. A theory of inevitable progress was the ideal basis upon which to argue that mental evolution up to and including mankind was part of God's plan for generating higher levels of awareness in the material universe. In effect, the developmental sequence of mental and social evolution postulated by the anthropologists would be extended back down the scale to include the intermediate phase in which the human race emerged from its animal ancestry.

The evolutionists thus conceived their task as the construction of a hierarchy of mental states forming a plausible bridge between the animal and human levels. The archaeological record suggested a steadily increasing level of technological sophistication which was widely, if unjustifiably, treated as evidence for an increasing level of intelligence in the course of the Palaeolithic. But as Argyll and other critics pointed out, better technology did not necessarily mean a more advanced moral character. It was for this reason that the evolutionists had to go beyond the archaeological record to reconstruct how early humans had lived and thought. The analogy with modern savages was useful precisely because it reinforced the claim that primitive humans were both less intelligent and less morally advanced than civilized

[18] See Bowler, *The Non-Darwinian Revolution*.

whites. If only a few more layers of mental development were stripped away, one would be dealing with creatures that were genuinely intermediate between apes and humans. Speculations along these lines allowed one to hypothesize the sequence of mental developments leading up to modern humanity, and it was then a relatively simple matter to explain how the advance had occurred. Since progress had been inevitable during the later phases of history, it seemed obvious that the same tendency had been operating, if more slowly, throughout the ascent of mankind from its animal ancestry. At every stage, new faculties had been added because they were an advantage in creatures trying to cope with the problem of getting a living in a natural environment. On this model, those races exposed to the most challenging environments would be expected to have advanced the furthest along the scale of development.

The prospect of an ape ancestry for mankind had already been introduced as part of the evolutionary theory proposed by the French naturalist J. B. Lamarck in his *Zoological Philosophy* of 1809. Historians used to assume that Lamarck's ideas were routinely dismissed by his contemporaries, but thanks to the work of Adrian Desmond we now know that the conservatives who attacked transformism were responding to a deliberate challenge by intellectuals who saw the theory as an integral part of their materialist ideology.[19] Radicals such as Robert E. Grant were well aware of the implications that could be drawn from a link between mankind and the animals. To suppose that man had evolved from the apes would threaten the concept of the immortal soul and would undermine the traditional foundations of morality and the social order. Throughout the 1820s and 1830s, political radicals and medical men trying to establish themselves on the fringes of the established profession used evolutionary ideas as part of their campaign against orthodoxy. When the senior figures of the establishment rejected evolution, they did so because its threatening implications were being actively pointed out to them by the radicals.

Another powerful weapon in the radicals' hands was phrenology, the theory that mental faculties are controlled not by the soul but by the physical structure of the brain. Phrenology was eventually dismissed as a pseudo-science, easily ridiculed in its supposition that a person's character could be read from bumps on the skull.[20] But this

[19] Desmond, 'Robert E. Grant: The Social Predicament of a Pre-Darwinian Evolutionist'; 'Artisan Resistance and Evolution in Britain, 1819–1848' and *The Politics of Evolution.*

[20] On the reception of phrenology see Cooter, *The Cultural Meaning of Popular Science.*

claim had its roots in the much more serious belief that each of our mental faculties is controlled by a particular area of the brain, which in turn rested on the assumption that it is the material substance of the brain which generates the mental functions. The materialist implications of this are obvious enough, and phrenology, like evolutionism, was incorporated into a philosophy in which everything – including the human mind – is held to work according to natural law rather than divine providence. The Edinburgh phrenologist George Combe wrote his *Of the Constitution of Man* of 1828 to promote such a radical alternative as part of a more general campaign for social reform.

In effect, phrenology added a materialist gloss to the theory of law-governed human behaviour already promoted by Enlightenment thinkers, including the philosophical historians. The liberal thinkers who followed the philosophical historians' model of social development could function within polite society because their talk of progress generated by economic and social laws was never extended to include the supposition that these laws were reducible to the laws of physics. The mind was still an autonomous, if law-governed, entity. But transformism and phrenology threatened this compromise by pro-claiming an outright materialism: the laws of the mind and of social behaviour *were* the laws of physics. In such a philosophy, the laws governing the progress of society could be exactly the same as those which had created the human mind through the process of biological evolution. The mind itself became a product of the laws of progress because increased intelligence and moral sense were inevitable consequences of an increase in the size of the brain. Long before archaeologists even confirmed the primitive status of early humans, radical thinkers were sketching in the outline of a theory which could explain how man's mental powers had arisen from lower origins.

These radical ideas were openly discussed in Scotland, although the conservative scientific establishment south of the border effectively closed ranks against the new materialism. The possibility that the progressionist viewpoint might be extended to include human origins was dismissed. In 1844, however, the topic was introduced abruptly to the general reading public by an anonymous work, *Vestiges of the Natural History of Creation*. Historians of the Darwinian revolution have always acknowledged that *Vestiges* began to popularize the general idea of evolution fifteen years before the *Origin of Species*, but all too often the book has been dismissed as a mere prelude to Darwinism. It is now becoming more widely appreciated that *Vestiges* offered a progressionist and largely non-Darwinian approach to evolutionism that almost certainly preconditioned the way in which the *Origin of Species* would be understood. Its author, the Edinburgh publisher Robert Chambers, drew explicitly on phrenology and other radical notions, and was quite out of touch with the kind of biogeographical considerations that were shaping Darwin's views. Thanks to the work of James Secord, we now know far more about the origins of Chambers's book and can see how it extended the progressionist view of historical development to lay the foundations for a reappraisal of human origins.[21]

It may be significant that Chambers had an early interest in Scottish history and was encouraged as a young man by Sir Walter Scott. By the 1830s he had become politically quite radical and had abandoned Christianity in favour of a deism in which the Creator was merely a remote lawgiver. His popular *Chambers's Edinburgh Journal* promoted the idea of progress through natural law, often by explaining the origin of races and societies in terms of historical progress. *Vestiges* used the theme of progress to link the development of life on earth, the origins of mankind, and the history of society into a single, unified subject. The model of growth or development towards maturity was appealed to over and over again as a means of promoting the view that the universe advances inexorably towards a higher state. On the question of human origins, Chambers invoked phrenology as an integral part of his campaign to show that behaviour – including moral behaviour – is subject to natural law and hence can have evolved from primitive levels. As the brain expanded in the course of progressive biological evolution, so did the mental and moral capacities, until at last something approaching the human mind appeared.

In this chapter on 'The Early History of Mankind' Chambers used philology to argue for the single origin of the human species, probably somewhere in Asia. He vigorously attacked those scholars who denied the primitive origins of human society. Long before the general acceptance of human antiquity, he followed the assumption of the philosophical historians that all societies began from a primitive state of hunting and gathering. Anticipating the views of the evolutionary anthropologists, he suggested that the impulse to develop a more advanced way of life was at work throughout mankind, resulting in the independent origin of civilization in many parts of the globe.[22] Whenever the density of population increased so that a few people had the leisure to think and invent, civilization grew – although it

[21] Secord, 'Behind the Veil: Robert Chambers and the Genesis of the *Vestiges of Creation*'. For further discussion of Chambers's evolutionary theory see ch. 5 below.
[22] Chambers, *Vestiges of the Natural History of Creation*, pp. 298–9.

was often threatened and undermined by the surrounding barbarians. The human races themselves indicated that 'development'
was the law governing history, since the lower races were, in effect,
merely immature versions of the more advanced, i.e. the white,
race.[23]

Vestiges was greeted by a howl of protest from conservative
scientists and theologians, but the book sold well and almost certainly
helped to ensure that evolutionism would be seen in a progressionist
light once Darwin had made the idea respectable. In one respect,
though, Chambers had failed to grasp the full potential of the social
progressionism already used to explain human history. He offered no
real explanation of how progress occurred: there was a law of
development built into nature by a remote Creator, but no suggestion
that His ends might be achieved through the accumulated efforts of
generations of individual organisms. Chambers explained human
progress by supposing that the law of development was always tending
to throw up the occasional genius whose inventions will advance
civilization, but he did not follow the individualist model in which the
collective activity of the whole population is the driving force of social
progress. He certainly refused to accept that animal evolution might
be the result of individual organisms striving to cope with their
environment. There was thus a hiatus in his theory; he had extended
the concept of developmental stages beyond society to include the
origin of mankind from animals, but he had missed the central theme
of the Whig approach which assumes that the law of progress always
works through the collective effects of individual effort.

During the 1850s the concept of development by natural law
became increasingly respectable, thus paving the way for both
evolutionary anthropology and the advent of Darwinism. The
problem of working out a plausible mechanism for both biological and
social evolution was solved during this decade by the philosopher who
was to become – along with Darwin – the veritable symbol of late-
nineteenth-century evolutionism: Herbert Spencer. We saw in the
conclusion of chapter 1 above how Spencer extended the logic of
laissez-faire individualism so characteristic of the Whig tradition into a
general mechanism of social evolution. Instead of concentrating on
the British constitution as a vehicle for promoting liberalism, Spencer
argued that all societies are governed by a law of progress in which
the economic pressure of feeding an expanding population encourages
the trend toward free enterprise. The gradual elimination of state
control is essential if all members of the population are to experience

[23] Ibid., pp. 306–9.

the full rigour of economic necessity needed to stimulate their initiative and force them to participate in economic development.

It was Spencer who realized that the mechanism of economic necessity can be extended to the animal kingdom in a way that will make effort and initiative the driving forces of biological as well as social evolution. Almost from the start of his career, Spencer had supported biological evolutionism on the grounds that, whatever the scientific problems, the alternative of divine creation was even more unlikely. He was thus predisposed to accept the development of humanity from a lower form and, of course, the primitive state of the earliest societies. Precisely because he was an evolutionist, though, Spencer was aware of the need to integrate his views on the biological and the social levels of development. Primitive societies would have begun to emerge even before our ancestors were fully human in the modern sense of the term, so it was possible to argue that the later phases of mental evolution and the earliest steps of social development had overlapped. Mental and social evolution could thus interact and reinforce one another. As Spencer wrote in his *Principles of Sociology* in 1876: 'Development of the higher intellectual faculties has gone on *pari passu* with social advance, alike as cause and consequence.'[24]

Spencer's *Principles of Psychology*, first appearing in 1855, had already developed the theme that the human mind is shaped not only by its own experiences, but also by the inherited effects of experience upon ancestral generations. The individual's response to the stimulus of the environment shapes not only his or her individual development but can also be imprinted on future generations by heredity and thus can shape the evolution of the race. Spencer thus accepted the evolutionary mechanism proposed by Lamarck at the beginning of the century: the inheritance of acquired characteristics. Although now discredited by modern genetics, Lamarckism played a major role in nineteenth-century evolutionism because – unlike Darwin's natural selection of random variation – it allowed the effects of individual effort and initiative to play a role in evolution.[25] In the most famous example, the ancestors of the giraffe saw a new source of food in the trees and began stretching their necks to reach it. The cumulative effects of their neck-stretching, inherited over many generations, have produced the giraffe we know today. Applied to mental evolution, Lamarckism allowed the benefits of experience to accumulate in the form of increased intelligence and social instincts.[26]

[24] Spencer, *Principles of Sociology*, I, p. 104.
[25] See Bowler, *The Eclipse of Darwinism*, chs. 4 and 6.
[26] For a recent survey of nineteenth-century views on the evolution of the mind see Richards, *Darwin and the Emergence of Evolutionary Theories of Mind and Behavior*.

According to such a theory, the appearance of a human level of mental activity is the inevitable outcome of the laws of nature, just as the appearance of an industrialized society is the inevitable outcome of social laws. Intelligence would naturally increase in the course of animal evolution, more especially in those species exposed to a more demanding and hence a more stimulating environment. Among creatures living in groups, social instincts and the ability to communicate would also be developed. At some point in evolution the interaction between expanding intelligence and the need to communicate with others would generate the origins of articulate language and hence of conceptual thought. From this point on a kind of feedback loop would be established; increased intelligence would allow more complex social behaviour, which would in turn stimulate greater intelligence. The introduction and gradual improvement of tools would be an inevitable by-product of applying intelligence to the problems of survival. The appearance of language serves as the crucial threshold to an accelerated phase of mental evolution, allowing the first species to reach that threshold to surge ahead of all rivals. Nevertheless, the forces at work after the emergence of society are merely extensions of those guiding the general process of evolution. The trend of modern history in the more advanced races of humanity is an inevitable continuation of the process which has created the human race itself.

Unlike Chambers, Spencer made no effort to depict the laws of evolution as a divine institution, and spoke only of an 'Unknowable' lying behind the reality perceived by our senses. Yet Spencer's system did not call for the complete rejection of traditional values. It applied materialism in a way that preserved and promoted the traditional middle-class virtues of thrift and enterprise, offering a future state of perfection in this world rather than the next. Small wonder that his philosophy was seized upon by liberal Protestants looking for a compromise with the new evolutionary sciences.[27] The concept of a hierarchy of developmental stages had been extended from social into mental and biological evolution, but the image of an inevitable ascent towards a higher state was retained so that more cautious thinkers could see the whole system of universal law as having a moral goal. The fact that Spencer coined the term 'survival of the fittest' to denote Darwin's mechanism of natural selection has led some

[27] See Moore, *The Post-Darwinian Controversies* and 'Herbert Spencer's Henchmen'. The claim that nineteenth-century evolutionism had a moral foundation also runs through Richards's *Darwin and the Emergence of Evolutionary Theories of Mind and Behavior*.

historians to dismiss his philosophy as an amoral 'social Darwinism' endorsing a ruthless ideology of indifference to the weak. But this was not how his contemporaries saw it: for them, the vision of evolution driven by the individual's efforts to better himself offered a way of reconciling the new sciences with values they were desperately anxious to retain.

Like the anthropologists' linear progressionism, Spencer's philosophy of evolution was already being formulated when the *Origin of Species* was published. Whatever the differences between natural selection and Spencer's Lamarckism (and those differences were all too easily slurred over), Darwin's success made it impossible for anyone to ignore Spencer's claim that social evolution would have to be extended to include the origin of human faculties. The biological evolutionists did remarkably little, however, to shape the Victorian concept of mental development. A. R. Wallace, the co-discoverer of natural selection, shared Lyell's fears about the origin of the human spirit and opted for supernatural intervention in this area.[28] Huxley's *Man's Place in Nature* of 1863 discussed the evidence for an evolutionary link between mankind and the apes, but said very little about how the transformation had been brought about. Darwin's 1871 *Descent of Man* was certainly a major contribution to the debate, but by the time it appeared the anthropological and sociological versions of evolutionism were already established, allowing Darwin to draw heavily upon the progressionist approach to substantiate his own views on primitive human origins. With one notable exception (discussed below), Darwin's view of human evolution was conditioned by the progressionism of his age. In this area, at least, he needed the idea of a steady progress from simple origins to explain how mankind had advanced so far beyond the animals. Like most of his contemporaries, Darwin saw European civilization and the white race as the highest products of social and mental evolution, and dismissed 'lower' races as branches of the human species which had not advanced so far up the scale of development.

Most evolutionists thought that the problem of human origins would be solved if they could specify a sequence of developments by which an ape's mentality could be boosted to the human level. Almost everyone assumed that social life and especially the emergence of language had played the vital role in stimulating the growth of human mental and moral powers beyond the animal level. Language marked the threshold at which the development of mind was suddenly

[28] See Kottler, 'Alfred Russel Wallace, the Origin of Man, and Spiritualism' and Frank M. Turner, *Between Science and Religion*.

boosted by the feedback between mental and social evolution (which explains why Müller's objections to an evolutionary origin of language were so important). The developmental approach was explored in detail by Darwin's heir-apparent in the field, George John Romanes. Strongly influenced by Spencer, Romanes turned increasingly to a theological view of evolution in his later career. In his *Mental Evolution in Animals* (1883) and *Mental Evolution in Man* (1888), he constructed an elaborate framework of evolutionary stages to bridge the gap between the two levels, each stage being related to a period in the development of the child from birth.[29] Bodily evolution was largely irrelevant, he declared, since our ancestors were already human in form, and were probably already making tools, before the crucial developments in mental evolution began. Social interaction alone stimulated the invention of language and the emergence of the human mind.

Like most Victorian evolutionists, Romanes had little or no interest in the question of why only one species, our own, had made the last crucial development. He saw no reason to depict the origin of the human race as a unique event depending on an unlikely combination of circumstances that might be unrepeatable. The implication of his analysis is that the advanced level of mentality is theoretically available to any species which can climb the scale of evolution to the threshold of language. The uniqueness of mankind lies solely in the fact that our ancestors reached the threshold first. If we had not done so, then some other form would have got there eventually and taken off along the same accelerated path of development. At one point Romanes speculated that the apes may have been unable to participate because they lacked suitable vocal organs for speech, although even this speculation implied that the apes *could* have become human if their advance had not been blocked by this one impediment.[30]

The air of inevitability which characterizes such accounts of human origins is typical of the historicism lying at the heart of Victorian evolutionism. Progress was assumed to be inevitable because it was possible to specify a single scale of development which must be followed whenever the stimulus of the environment drives organisms to advance themselves. Yet this principle of inevitable progress was not compatible with the theory of evolution that Darwin proposed. In his model of branching, divergent evolution, each species undergoes

[29] See the chart included as the frontispiece to Romanes, *Mental Evolution in Animals.*

[30] Ibid., pp. 154–5.

its own unique sequence of changes depending on the new environments it encounters in its migrations around the globe. One cannot predict the course of evolution because one cannot foresee the pattern of future migrations in an ever-changing world. It thus becomes meaningless to use the characteristics developed by one branch of life as a scale by which to measure the progress of others. In such a theory it became difficult to see the appearance of human mentality as inevitable. There is no single scale of development to be automatically ascended, and it should become a matter of crucial concern to identify the factors which led our ancestors to embark upon a line of evolution which separated them so effectively from the apes.

For all that he absorbed the progressionism of his contemporaries, Darwin appreciated this consequence of his theory, and in the *Descent of Man* he made a serious effort to ask why our ancestors had followed a unique evolutionary path. He realized that both our ancestors and the apes had always lived in social groups, so it was impossible to treat increased socialization as the cause of the differentiation. Our moral values emerged because an increased level of intelligence was applied to the rationalization of our social instincts. So the separation of humans from apes was a matter of increased intelligence, and the cause of separation would have to specify some activity in which only our ancestors could participate. Darwin's solution was to point to the upright posture of mankind as a unique adaptation to a different way of life outside the ancestral forests. This adaptation had the unexpected side-effect of freeing the hands for the making of tools, an activity denied to the apes by their continued use of the hand for locomotion. It was the hand, not the voice, which marked man's ancestors off from those of the apes and which stimulated the growth of human intelligence.[31] No other species will ever follow the same course, because no other species is ever likely to be exposed to the same improbable combination of circumstances in the course of its history. In Darwin's particular theory of evolution, mankind turned out to be unique after all, since his appearance could not be predicted as the inevitable outcome of a progressive trend.

It is significant that Darwin's suggestion was almost universally ignored by his contemporaries. The Victorians were not ready for the

---

[31] This idea occurs in the chapter of Darwin's *Descent of Man* entitled 'On the Manner of Development of Man from some Lower Form'; in the first edition this is chapter 4 (see I, pp. 138–45) and in the second edition, chapter 2 (see pp. 49–51). On the question of defining the key step in human evolution see Bowler, *Theories of Human Evolution*, especially ch. 7.

suggestion that the acquisition of an upright posture, not the achievement of a threshold in mental development, was the key step in human origins. Even when discussion of this idea began in the last decade of the century, the majority of palaeoanthropologists managed to subvert the logic of Darwinism by assuming that the upright posture was a consequence of increased intelligence. The nineteenth century's efforts to grapple with the problem of human origins were conditioned not by those aspects of Darwin's theory which have been retained by modern biology, but by the prevailing faith in the inevitability of progress to which even Darwin himself frequently succumbed. The assumption of a universal scale of mental and social development, along which species and races are driven by environmental and economic factors, had its origins in the work of the philosophical historians. It was extended by the anthropologists and archaeologists of the mid-nineteenth century in a way that allowed it to define the issues seen to be crucial when the scale was extended to include biological as well as social evolution. Evolution meant progress along a predictable course towards modern civilization as its inevitable goal. The fact that the goal was both predictable and morally significant allowed most Victorians to evade the more disturbing implications of the link between the human and animal scales of development. Extending the reign of law to include the origins of mankind as well as the origins of civilization was acceptable if the laws could be seen as the Creator's way of achieving His purposes in nature. Against the logic of this system, Darwin's effort to portray evolution as a haphazard process with no single goal was doomed to failure.

Interlude:
Missing Links

The evolutionists who extended the scale of social development to include the progressive appearance of human mental faculties were faced with the major problem of finding hard evidence to support their position. They had to base their reconstruction of the stages of mental development almost completely on assumptions about how the mentality of the higher animals would have to be boosted to reach the human level. Archaeology revealed the primitive state of early human technology, and it was often assumed on this basis that our early Palaeolithic ancestors must have been less intelligent than ourselves. Modern 'savages' were depicted as having less intelligence than Europeans, and were then used to illustrate the supposed appearance and behaviour of the Europeans' stone-age ancestors. But critics such as the Duke of Argyll were suspicious of the claim that the earliest humans were mentally degraded. They argued that the archaeological record proves only that our distant ancestors had not yet invented more sophisticated tools – not that they were too stupid to think of anything better than chipped stone. The only hope of testing the evolutionists' predictions would be to find the fossilized remains of the people who had made the stone tools. If early Palaeolithic skeletons were found, they should – according to the evolutionists – reveal a form of humanity with a brain-capacity smaller than that of modern Europeans.

Even this kind of evidence would not satisfy a critic who insisted that mental powers are derived from the immortal soul and not from the activity of the brain. The growing materialism of the late nineteenth century is illustrated by the fact that the assumed link between brain size and mental faculties was increasingly taken for granted in the evolutionary debates. In the early part of the century phrenology had been excluded from the ranks of the sciences for claiming that mental functions were generated by the brain. But in later decades it was routinely accepted that an increase in brain size would, at least in the long run, correspond to an increase in the level of mental activity. The theory of progressive evolution thus predicted that human fossils would show a steady increase in cranial capacity during the Palaeolithic. In fact, the discovery of ancient human remains was invariably surrounded by controversy, and some of the finds were incompatible with the simple progressionist assumption.

Beyond the hope of substantiating an increase in the level of human intelligence during the Palaeolithic lay the even more fundamental question of the link between humans and apes. Theories of mental evolution were based on a plausible reconstruction of the stages by which the higher mental powers had been generated. Such reconstructions were impossible to test directly, but here too confirmation of an increase in brain size would at least help to support the evolutionists' position. In popular terminology, the evolutionists needed to find the 'missing link' – a fossil (or, better still, a series of fossils) showing that there really had been creatures intermediate in brain size and physical appearance between apes and the lowest modern humans. Perhaps early Palaeolithic man would turn out not only to have a smaller brain, but also to retain some physical traces of his recent emergence from the apes. Earlier still, in the Pleistocene – the last geological epoch before the earth took on its modern form – one might hope to find genuine intermediates, more intelligent than apes yet still not human enough to have developed a recognizable technology. Here again it was difficult to find reliable fossil evidence. Nevertheless, by the end of the century the evolutionists had taken the extremely fragmentary fossil record and used it to construct a linear sequence which appeared to bridge the crucial gap between humans and apes.

The popular imagination, encouraged by a host of cartoons, had seized upon the great apes as the living embodiment of what our animal ancestors would have looked like. Up to a point this impression was justified.[1] T. H. Huxley's *Man's Place in Nature* developed the theme of the similarities between ape and human anatomies in an attempt to show that an evolutionary link was not implausible. The more conservative naturalist Richard Owen tried to

[1] On the problem of relating humans to apes see Bowler, *Theories of Human Evolution*, ch. 3.

argue that the human brain contains an organ not found in the ape – this was the *hippocampus minor*, caricatured as the 'hippopotamus minor' in Kingsley's *Water Babies*. Huxley successfully demolished Owen's claim, but he could do no more than minimize the anatomical gap. He could not prove an evolutionary link between humans and apes on anatomical grounds, and indeed it was not even clear what kind of link the evolutionists were looking for. In Darwin's theory of branching evolution, the living great apes could not be treated as relics of an early stage in mankind's ancestry, since they too must have evolved to some extent since the two families diverged on to separate paths. In any case, there were, and are, three species of great apes still alive in the world: the gorilla, the chimpanzee and the orang-utan. There was considerable debate as to which of these might be closest to the hypothetical ancestor of man. Owen's disciple, the anatomist St George Jackson Mivart, wrote his *Man and Apes* (1873) to argue that the relations between humans and apes are so complex that no evolutionary hierarchy can be discerned. In theory the Darwinists predicted that the ancestor of mankind would have been a more generalized ape, lacking the extreme characteristics of the modern great apes. Such creatures were known from the fossil record, but all too often even the scientists preferred to treat the gorilla or the chimpanzee as the starting point for their reconstructions of human ancestry.

The evolutionists realized that the fossil record was unlikely to reveal a complete sequence linking mankind back to a common ancestor with the apes. Darwin wrote a whole chapter of the *Origin of Species* to emphasize the 'imperfection of the geological record' and to argue that the detailed reconstruction of genealogies was likely to prove impossible. But any human remains from the distant past were inevitably going to attract a great deal of attention both from the evolutionists and from critics anxious to discredit their case. Unfortunately for the evolutionists, the first undisputed specimen of Palaeolithic man turned out to be nothing like the brutalized ancestor they were expecting. In 1868 human remains were found alongside tools of the Aurignacian culture at the rock shelter of Cro Magnon in the Dordogne. The 'old man' of Cro Magnon was described by Paul Broca and Armand de Quatrefages and became the type specimen for a race of early humans whose remains were soon found throughout Europe.[2] The Cro-Magnons were a tall, well built race with fine features and a large cranial capacity – ancestors of whom anyone could be proud and hardly the brutal savages predicted by the theory

[2] See de Quatrefages, *The Human Species*, ch. 27.

of progressive evolution. Other late Palaeolithic types soon came to light and formed the basis of much speculation about the origins of the modern human races (see chapter 4 below).

Far more promising from the evolutionists' point of view was an earlier but more controversial specimen unearthed in the Neander valley (Neanderthal) near Düsseldorf in 1857. A complete skeleton had been found by workmen, but many of the bones were destroyed before the remains were rescued by a local schoolteacher. These remains were described by Professor Schaafhausen, who noted their brutish appearance but did not suspect their true age. An English translation of Schaafhausen's paper contained additional notes by George Busk drawing attention to the ape-like features of the skull, especially its heavy supraorbital or brow ridges.[3] Immense controversy surrounded the find, especially since the bones had been removed from their surroundings and could not be dated. The eminent pathologist Rudolph Virchow dismissed the skeleton as that of a relatively modern individual who had suffered from congenital idiocy and rickets. This became the standard position of anti-evolutionists anxious to discredit the Neanderthal type as a candidate for mankind's brutal ancestry. Even Huxley found it impossible to accept the specimen as the crucial link between humans and apes. He devoted a considerable portion of his *Man's Place in Nature* to the remains, emphasizing their ape-like character but admitting that the capacity of the cranium suggested a brain size equivalent to that of modern humans.[4] Despite its apparent retention of features indicating an ape ancestry, then, the Neanderthal specimen failed on the most important criterion of all to match the prediction of an evolutionary intermediate. Huxley conceded that the individual probably fell within the range of variation possible in modern humanity.

Other authorities disagreed. In 1864 William King argued that the differences between the Neanderthal specimen and any modern human were so great that it would have to be counted as a distinct species of humanity, *Homo neanderthalensis*.[5] As long as the original discovery remained an isolated case, this opinion remained suspect, but the sceptics were at last confounded by the unearthing in 1886 of several Neanderthal-type skeletons at Spy in Belgium. These not only confirmed the existence of a distinct race or species with ape-like characteristics, but also provided an accurate dating since they were

---

[3] See Schaafhausen, 'On the Crania of the Most Ancient Races of Man'. On the Neanderthal discoveries see Reader, *Missing Links*, ch. 1.

[4] Huxley, *Man's Place in Nature*, ch. 3.

[5] King, 'The Reputed Fossil Man of the Neanderthal'.

found with stone tools of the Mousterian culture. By the end of the century the Neanderthal type was established on the basis of numerous discoveries and was widely regarded as the earliest form of humanity, clear evidence that the makers of early Palaeolithic tools had but recently evolved from the apes. The relatively large skull capacity was discounted on the grounds that the brain appeared to have been shaped quite differently to that of a modern human. The sloping forehead of the Neanderthals indicated that their brains lacked development in the crucial frontal region where the higher intellectual faculties were supposed to reside.

The interpretation of the Neanderthals as a stage in human evolution from the apes was boosted during the 1890s by the discovery of an even older human fossil. This was 'Java man' or *Pithecanthropus erectus*, discovered by Eugene Dubois in 1891–2.[6] Dubois had gone to the Dutch East Indies in search of early human remains, inspired by the belief that Asia rather than Africa might have been the centre of origin. Darwin had favoured Africa, but the existence of the orang-utan in south-east Asia helped to keep open the possibility of an Asian origin. The prominent German evolutionist Ernst Haeckel endorsed the case for Asia, and it can hardly be doubted that the old belief in Asia as the centre of Aryan dispersal was translated into a hope that this continent might turn out to be the cradle of the human race. Dubois was rewarded by the discovery of a skull fragment and thighbone in the Pleistocene deposits of the Solo river in Java. The skull had brow ridges like the Neanderthals but a much smaller capacity, approximately half-way between the ape and modern human levels. This allowed Dubois to present *Pithecanthropus* as an evolutionary intermediate, although the thighbone indicated a completely erect posture and thus helped to focus some attention on Darwin's long-neglected prediction that man's ancestors had walked upright before the great expansion of the brain took place.

Dubois's find sparked off another round of controversy, with some critics dismissing *Pithecanthropus* as an ape while others thought it was fully human – a disagreement that Dubois himself was able to exploit in his campaign to establish it as a true intermediate. He was forced to concede that the comparatively late date of the specimen indicated that it was probably not on the direct line leading to modern humanity. Perhaps the Java population was an isolated race which had retained primitive characteristics into a later period while evolution was advancing to greater heights elsewhere in the world. This, of course, was the standard explanation of how modern 'primitives' such

---

[6] See Reader, *Missing Links*, ch. 2.

as the Australian aborigines had survived. At the International Congress of Zoology held at Cambridge in 1898, Dubois insisted that even if *Pithecanthropus* was only our uncle rather than our grandfather, it was nevertheless 'a venerable ape-man, representing a stage in our phylogeny'. [7] His views were endorsed by Haeckel in a book translated as *The Last Link*, in which *Pithecanthropus* and the Neanderthals were presented as the main intermediate stages between the great apes and ourselves.

Eventually Dubois himself became so frustrated by the controversy surrounding his work that he turned his back on the scientific community and even abandoned his claim that *Pithecanthropus* was the missing link. Haeckel's support shows, however, that the older generation of evolutionists found *Pithecanthropus* to be exactly the kind of intermediate they needed to bridge the most crucial of all the gaps in the fossil record. In their anxiety to link mankind back to the most obvious point of origin in the animal kingdom, they were instinctively drawn to the idea of a linear hierarchy of developmental stages which paralleled the model already established by archaeologists, anthropologists and students of mental evolution. The sequence ape–*Pithecanthropus*–Neanderthal–savage–white man was both the simplest possible interpretation of the available evidence and a confirmation of the progressionist thesis. Palaeontology and comparative anatomy thus endorsed the linear model of evolutionary development established in the human sciences.

Haeckel's interpretation of Dubois's discovery was expanded by his disciple, the anatomist Gustav Schwalbe, in a series of books published at the turn of the century.[8] Although approaching the subject from the viewpoint of the anatomist rather than that of the psychologist or the anthropologist, Schwalbe shared the prevailing view that the origin of mankind would be explained once the evolutionist had constructed a plausible sequence of intermediate stages linking the ape to the human levels of development. Like Dubois, he admitted that the specimens of *Pithecanthropus* and the Neanderthals that had actually been discovered might not be on the main line of evolution, because they might be survivals of primitive types lingering on in isolated parts of the world. But it was not necessary to discover the physical remains of our true ancestors: the

[7] Dubois, 'Remarks on the Brain-Cast of *Pithecanthropus erectus*', p. 95.

[8] Schwalbe provided an account of his views in English for the volume published to mark the fiftieth anniversary of the *Origin of Species* in 1909; see his 'The Descent of Man'. On the establishment of the linear model of human origins, see Bowler, *Theories of Human Evolution*, chs. 3 and 4.

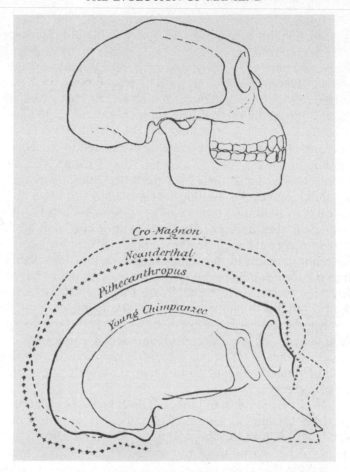

Plate 11   The skull of *Pithecanthropus* and a comparison with
the skulls of a Cro-Magnon, a Neanderthal and a chimpanzee.
Haeckel superimposes the outlines of the skulls to give an
impression of the steady expansion of the brain from the ape
through the *Pithecanthropus* and Neanderthal stages to the
modern human form.
From Ernst Haeckel, *The Last Link*, p. 25

fossils already found were enough to illustrate the stages through
which the line of development must have passed in the ascent from
the apes. The concept of a predetermined and universally valid line of
progressive development was thus retained.

This linear pattern of development was accepted by the young
Arthur Keith in his first comprehensive account of human origins in

1911.[9] Within a few years, however, Keith had dramatically altered his position to become a leading advocate of the claim that neither *Pithecanthropus* nor the Neanderthals had any connection with the ancestry of the modern human race. They were not even primitive survivals, but independent lines of hominid evolution unrelated to our own. Nature had produced many types of man, of which only one had survived into the present, exterminating all its rivals. The neat linear sequence of development erected in the late nineteenth century broke down in a welter of conflicting claims about parallel lines of evolution, racial migrations and the extinction of lower by higher types. This approach fitted the more belligerent attitudes which began to flourish in the age of imperialism preceding the outbreak of the Great War, but it also represented the application to human evolution of a rival conceptual scheme which had been explored in opposition to simple progressionism. The cyclic model of history, which saw the rise and fall of each race as a distant episode in the ascent of man, had not disappeared with the advent of evolutionism. It had been reconstructed as a theory of racial origins that would ultimately prove to be more enduring than the linear progressionism of the late nineteenth century.

---

[9] Keith, *Ancient Types of Man.*

4

The Origin of Races

The evolutionary anthropologists extended the philosophical historians' linear scheme of socio-economic development to include the primitive savages that mid-nineteenth-century archaeologists had begun to interpret as relics of the stone age. Once the idea of biological evolution had been introduced, a primitive level of culture could be taken as a sign of retarded development in the ascent from the apes. Nonwhite races were thus dismissed as having a lower intelligence than their European conquerors. Their subjection was an inevitable consequence of interaction with their superiors on the evolutionary scale. The most primitive savages became, in effect, the 'missing links' in human evolution, only one step higher than the ape-like Neanderthals. Evolutionism did not create this sense of a racial hierarchy, of course, but it provided a convenient justification for attitudes that had already emerged as a consequence of white imperialism.

In accommodating themselves to the Europeans' sense of racial superiority, the progressionists had been forced to abandon liberal attitudes that had originally supported a quite different view of humanity. The philosophical historians had shared the Enlightenment's faith in the uniformity of human nature, and it was only gradually that anthropologists such as Tylor were persuaded to accept that all races do not have the same capacity for cultural development. Even when turned into an explanation of the racial hierarchy, the liberal form of progressionism still accepted that all the races had been trying to ascend towards the same goal, albeit at different rates. The original sense of the uniformity of human character was reinforced in the

early decades of the nineteenth century by respect for the biblical
story of human origins, which presented all races as descendants of a
single creation. James Cowles Prichard's *Researches into the Physical
History of Mankind* of 1813 provided support for this theory of
'monogenism' by arguing that all races had diverged from a common
ancestor under the influence of differing climates in the various parts
of the world to which mankind had migrated. But from the start
Prichard had struggled against the problem of explaining how the
very different characters of the various races had been developed in
the few thousand years allowed by the biblical timescale. Critics who
were more conscious of racial differences argued that there must be
several distinct creations corresponding to the progenitors of the
major racial groups, the theory of 'polygenism'.[1] On this interpretation,
Adam and Eve had been the founders of only one branch of
humanity, the others having origins not mentioned in the Bible.

In the middle decades of the century the sense of racial superiority
became so strong in some quarters that an increasing number of
anthropologists began to challenge the view that there could be any
uniformity between the mentality and cultural aspirations of the
different races. New techniques were introduced for identifying racial
types by skull structure and character of hair, as well as colour of skin.
These techniques gave physical anthropologists the opportunity to
attempt a racial analysis of the European population along lines that
were already becoming familiar in the treatment of nonwhite races.
As English historians began to emphasize the genius of the Anglo-
Saxon race in the foundation of the country's power, they inevitably
reinforced prejudices against neighbouring people who were seen as
obstacles to the aspirations of the higher race. This prejudice was
particularly strong against the Irish, who were dismissed as an inferior
Celtic race whose character made it impossible for its members ever
to govern themselves.[2]

Where philology had taught the underlying unity of Celt and
Teuton, anthropologists now began to stress the differences between
the European races. Languages could be transmitted from one race to
another, and physical characteristics were presented as a more
reliable way of classifying races. Yet philology and known history
together provided a model that could be used to integrate the sense of
racial differences into a new form of the cyclic theory of prehistoric
development. The Aryans had originally been seen as a superior

[1] On race theories see Stepan, *The Idea of Race in Science* and Stocking, *Race,
Culture, and Evolution* and *Victorian Anthropology*.
[2] See Curtis, *Anglo-Saxons and Celts*.

racial type invading Europe from the east, while the Saxon invasion of Britain was the last act in the Teutonic conquest of northern Europe. Perhaps all the peoples of Europe could be seen as relics left over from a series of racial invasions, each wave sweeping the earlier populations aside into isolated corners to make room for a superior type. Prehistory and history would thus be united by an interpretation of development which stressed not gradual improvement but the periodic eruption of higher types on to the scene.

The new timescale of the archaeologists created the framework within which the theory of racial migrations could be articulated. While many archaeologists followed de Mortillet in creating a developmental sequence of stone-age cultures, others looked for evidence of abrupt cultural transitions that would denote the appearance of new races. Even de Mortillet admitted that the Neolithic culture had been introduced by invasion rather than by indigenous development. The best hope of confirming the theory of discontinuous progress lay in discovery of the skeletal remains of the ancient toolmakers, which would allow physical anthropologists to challenge archaeology over the reconstruction of prehistory. Enough remains were found to generate a number of rival theories intended to reconstruct the precise sequence of racial invasions and their role in the creation of the modern population. Even the lowly Neanderthals were taken into account as the possible ancestors of some modern European races. Not surprisingly, these reconstructions of racial history tended to reflect the anthropologists' prejudices about the relative status of the modern races. French and German anthropologists blackened each other's racial ancestry as readily as the English denigrated the Irish Celts.

But how had the various races originated? Evolution theory necessarily bore upon this question, but in practice the link between the evolution of species and the origin of human races was difficult to establish. Physical anthropologists often seemed to ignore the question altogether and accept the races as permanently fixed types. But their apparent lack of interest may reflect the fact that some versions of evolutionism permitted one to believe that the appearance of each new species was an abrupt event. Not every biologist followed Darwin's gradualism, and a saltationist form of evolutionism preserved the fixity of species at least in the short term. In theory, evolutionism demanded that all forms of mankind must have a common origin. Yet if the branches had separated suddenly, or had remained distinct for a long time, they might have acquired the status of distinct species. Some anthropologists challenged the normal assumption that all human races can interbreed with one another. Extreme polygenists argued that the various racial types may have originated in different ape species. The concept of fixed racial types was not inconsistent with evolutionism – provided that we recognize the range of non-Darwinian options available in the late nineteenth century. The model of prehistory based on a sequence of racial invasions could itself become part of an evolutionary account of human origins by postulating a centre of progressive development from which new and higher types radiated out to conquer the surrounding territory.

Migration and Conquest

The middle decades of the nineteenth century saw the appearance of a number of works expounding the innate differences between the human races. The authors of these works were all too willing to adopt what Mill had called the 'vulgar' hypothesis of race: they were convinced that the races had distinct mental and moral characters. The nonwhite races had a lower level of intelligence and alien behavioural instincts which left them forever isolated from the march of industrial progress. At best, they might have played an important role at an earlier phase in human history, when they themselves represented the best that nature had as yet produced. Prominent among these early race theorists was Count Arthur de Gobineau, whose *Essay on the Inequality of the Human Races* appeared in 1853. Gobineau was no progressionist; he lamented the decline of the Frankish nobility which in his view had been responsible for creating the civilization of western Europe. He held that race mixture destroyed human progress by diluting the character of the best races. Other writers in the same vein became so convinced of the clarity of racial types that they doubted their ability to interbreed effectively. This paved the way for the emergence of a more triumphant Anglo-Saxonism based on the supposedly permanent superiority of this race.

   This position was advocated by the leading architect of the new race consciousness in the British Isles, Robert Knox. As the anatomist who bought corpses from the bodysnatchers, Burke and Hare, Knox has achieved a certain amount of notoriety, but his *The Races of Men* of 1850 occupies a prominent position in the history of race consciousness. It was Knox who declared that 'With me race, or hereditary descent, is everything; it stamps the man.'[3] Hybrids

---

[3] Knox, *The Races of Men*, p. 6. The second edition cited in the bibliography is identical to the first except for additional material at the end.

between parents of two races were so unnatural, he declared, that a mixed breed could never establish itself, as witnessed by the failure of integration between the Anglo-Saxons and the native Irish. Nor could a race succeed in territory alien to its homeland – unlike most imperialists, Knox doubted that the white race could maintain itself in Australia or North America without constant immigration. It could however, exterminate the native races, while in India and Africa it could exploit the labour of inferior types.

Knox had strong views on the characters of the various races and on the way they interacted. He did not praise the Saxons for their intellectual powers – it was the Sclavonian or South German race that was pre-eminent in this respect. But the Saxons excelled in the practical virtues and in the love of order and liberty. Significantly, the Protestant Reformation had gained ground only in those parts of Europe where the Saxons predominated. The Celts, by contrast, were natural Catholics, since they could only be controlled by power imposed from above. Despite some great achievements, 'the Celtic race does not, and never could be made to comprehend the meaning of the word liberty.' It was characterized by 'furious fanaticism, a love of war and disorder, a hatred for order and patient industry; no accumulative habits, restless, treacherous, uncertain: look at Ireland.'[4] The vast majority of nonwhite races lacked all capacity for civilization and were doomed to extinction. Only the true Negro stood a chance of resisting the Saxon on his own territory. This grudging respect did not, however, prevent Knox from proclaiming the Negro's alien character, which generated instinctive hatred in the Saxon and made the 'mock philanthropy of England' a laughing stock.[5]

Knox had no hesitation in proclaiming that 'might is right' was the only philosophy governing the relationship between races.[6] Race antagonism was the driving force of history and the key to a true understanding of the modern world. Liberals who offered a utopian vision in which the lower races would be educated to play a part in the world were ignoring the true force behind the expansion of Anglo-Saxon power. For all his imperialism, though, Knox was a radical at home. The Saxon was 'the only real democrat on the earth' and the Norman conquest had imposed an alien system of aristocratic government on the British Isles.[7] Despite all efforts at reform, this alien system was still in place, and it could only be shaken by denying

---

[4] Ibid., p. 25.
[5] Ibid., p. 243.
[6] See e.g. ibid., pp. 43–4 and 220–1.
[7] Ibid., pp. 374–5.

control of the land to aristocratic families. Yet a truly democratic Britain would simply restore the Saxon population to its natural state. Knox was no supporter of progress, and believed that the classical civilization of Greece had achieved even more than modern Europe could hope for.

When Knox first started lecturing on race in the 1840s, he saw himself as a voice crying in the wilderness. By the following decade such ideas were becoming commonplace as faith in the Anglo-Saxon's role in history came to the fore. At first Knox had been blackballed by the Ethnological Society, which had been founded earlier in the century by philanthropists interested in other races, but he was admitted in the 1850s as a new generation of race-conscious anthropologists became active in the society. The leading supporter of Knox's approach was James Hunt, who in 1863 led his supporters away to form the rival Anthropological Society of London.[8] The Journal of this society was active through the 1860s in publishing derogatory assessments of other races. Liberal thinkers, including Tylor, Lubbock and many of Darwin's supporters, pointedly remained faithful to the Ethnological Society and its less virulent attitude to the race question. Only in 1871 was the rift healed as the societies amalgamated to form the Anthropological Institute.

One of the factors encouraging Hunt and his followers was the importation of new techniques in physical anthropology from America and the Continent. Knox was an anatomist, but had contented himself mainly with assessing the mental characters of the various races. Now it became possible to identify racial types by what were regarded as unambiguous physical characteristics, allowing a 'scientific' breakdown of the racial components in any nation's population. The science of 'craniology' had been promoted in America by men such as Samuel G. Morton.[9] They measured the cubic capacity of skulls collected from many parts of the world and claimed to detect clear differences between white and nonwhite races. By these measurements (no longer accepted today) nonwhites had smaller brains and hence, by implication, lower levels of intelligence. Equally influential was the 'cranial index' of the Swiss anthropologist Anders Retzius, which related the length and breadth of the skull. Retzius distinguished between the long-headed 'dolichocephalic' races and the round-headed 'brachycephalics'. Whereas assessments

[8] On the Anthropological Society see Stocking, 'What's in a Name?' and *Victorian Anthropology*.

[9] See Stanton, *The Leopard's Spots* and on craniology Gould, *The Mismeasure of Man*.

of the cubic capacity of the skull helped to establish a simple hierarchy of racial intelligence, Retzius's approach allowed the anthropologist to detect a range of different racial types which demanded a much more complex arrangement.

Craniology was taken up with enthusiasm by French anthropologists such as Paul Broca, and Hunt's Anthropological Society of London was modelled on the Paris society, which Broca dominated. British anthropologists were eager to apply the new techniques to the nation's population and contributed their own additional standards of measurement. John Beddoe introduced his 'index of nigrescence' based on the darkness of eyes and hair, and his monumental *Races of Britain* of 1885 claimed to distinguish a wide variety of racial types. The growing emphasis on physical anthropology now undermined some of the ideas promoted by philologists in earlier decades. Philology had pointed to an underlying unity linking Aryan languages such as Celtic and Teutonic, a unity which was widely held to uphold the monogenism advocated by Prichard. Physical anthropologists now insisted that the Celts were racially quite distinct from the Teutons or Saxons, pointing out that a race's language could be changed by interaction with its neighbours and was no indication of a blood relationship. Max Müller's simple assumption that all races speaking an Aryan tongue were related by descent from Aryan ancestors was thus overthrown, creating a vacuum in prehistory that required to be filled with a more complex story of racial migrations.[10]

The resulting separation of Celt and Saxon in the Victorian imagination fuelled the growing contempt for the 'Celtic' race of Ireland. Matthew Arnold was a solitary voice in expressing significant doubts about the cultural capacity of the Saxons and calling for a more sympathetic study of Celtic literature. Not until the last decade of the century did it become fashionable to doubt the role played by the Saxon element in the British character, as the threat posed by the growing power of a united Germany forced a reassessment of the enthusiasm for all things Teutonic which had gripped earlier generations. Folklorists then began to pay more attention to the traditions of the Celtic fringe. Echoing Arnold's view, the philologist Isaac Taylor in 1889 depicted the Teutons as a strong but barbaric race who acquired their more refined Aryan language from the Celts.[11]

[10] See Huxley, 'The Methods and Results of Ethnology' and 'The Aryan Question', reprinted in the 1894 edition of Huxley, *Man's Place in Nature* (*Collected Essays*, VII) and also Taylor, *The Origin of the Aryans*.

[11] Taylor, *The Origin of the Aryans*, pp. 226–46.

The reappraisal of the link between philology and the study of prehistory was brought about by anthropologists who became interested in the new sources of information revealed by archaeology. Knox had avoided any discussion of the racial prehistory of Europe, being convinced that the races had always existed more or less in their present locations. His radical views led him to challenge the biblical chronology, however, and once the antiquity of the human race was confirmed in the 1860s it became obvious that the various races distinguished by the anthropologists had entered Europe at different times. The Saxon invasion of the British Isles in historical times could easily be seen as a late example of the kind of racial migrations that must have taken place throughout prehistory. An article on the Saxon invasion by J. Foster Palmer in 1885 presented this event as the conquest of an indigenous people made up of two Celtic families and a trace of a pre-Celtic race.[12] Palmer admitted that the original inhabitants had been conquered, not exterminated and replaced, but he still maintained that the influx of Saxon blood had been vital to prevent the cultural stagnation of the Britons. The anthropologists were to apply a more vigorous interpretation of the same model to explain how the various racial 'layers' of the British population had been built up.

The original interpretation of European prehistory favoured by archaeologists and philologists in the early nineteenth century also paved the way for the new theory of racial migration. Worsaae and the Scandinavian originators of the three-age system had assumed that bronze and iron were introduced into Europe by more civilized peoples invading from the east. The philologists argued that the Aryan speakers had invaded from the same source, possibly in a series of waves corresponding to the various Aryan languages. The new generation of physical anthropologists severed the blood relationship between the Aryan-speaking races, but preserved the image of higher racial types invading from the east. Only the oldest and most primitive inhabitants of Europe were identified with a darker type of African origin. A new version of the theory of cyclic progress thus emerged, purged of the old hope that a search for the ultimate origin of the races would confirm the unity of the human type. This view of prehistory served as a powerful alternative to the linear progressionism adopted by the archaeologists and cultural anthropologists of the 1860s. Whereas they saw indigenous progress as the source of all technological and cultural innovations, the race theorists held that only the invasion of a new type from some external source could

---

[12] Palmer, 'The Saxon Invasion and its Influence on Our Character as a Race.'

introduce a superior culture into a particular territory. The origin of the higher races was pushed back into a time so remote that it need not concern the European anthropologists. For all the supposed modernity of this new approach, central Asia remained the mysterious source of all human progress.

As a consequence of his analysis of the European population, Retzius suggested that in prehistoric times a dolichocephalic Aryan race represented by the modern Swedes had displaced the indigenous non-Aryan brachycephalics. The Scots anthropologist Daniel Wilson, who coined the term 'prehistoric' in his *Archaeology and Prehistoric Annals of Scotland* (1851), accepted a similar view, although he attributed the primitive state of the earliest inhabitants to degeneration. Studies of Neolithic and bronze-age barrows now began to provide ample information about the racial history of Europe in later prehistoric times. In 1865 the *Crania Britannica* of Joseph Davis and John Thurnham provided detailed descriptions of numerous prehistoric skulls and gave cautious support to Wilson's position.[13]

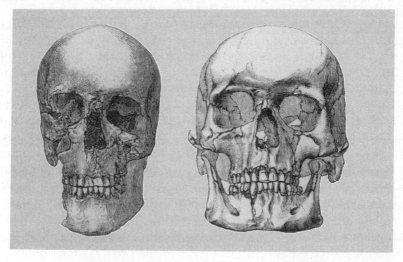

Plate 12   Long- and round-headed skulls.
The skulls are from barrows at Rudstone and Cowlam in the East Riding of Yorkshire. They are depicted separately in Greenwell's book, but were combined as shown here in Isaac Taylor's *The Origin of the Aryans*, p. 71, to illustrate the contrast between the long-headed and round-headed types.
From William Greenwell, *British Barrows*, p. 612 and p. 588

[13] Davis and Thurnham, *Crania Britannica*, p. 55.

Thurnham went on to become a leading proponent of the claim that the earlier long barrows were built by a long-headed race, while the later round barrows contained the remains of a newly introduced short-headed people. This view was endorsed by T. H. Huxley in 1871, by William Greenwell in 1877 and in Beddoe's *Races of Britain*.[14] There was some debate, however, over the exact time of the invasion and over the closest modern representatives of the two races. Huxley argued that the original inhabitants were a dark-skinned race linked to the Iberians, while the later invaders were the much fairer Belgic Gauls described by Caesar and Tacitus. The Iberians, although identified with the Celts of Ireland, were only secondarily Celtic-speaking, while the true Celts were closely related to the Germanic tribes. Beddoe thought the Iberian race could be linked to the Berbers, suggesting an African origin.

Whatever the differences of interpretation, there was growing support for the view that at certain points in European prehistory, the invasion of superior racial types with a higher level of civilization had displaced the earlier inhabitants. Each of these earlier groups could still be found in those areas to which it had retreated, the most primitive of all being found in marginal locations such as the west of Ireland. It was tempting to believe that superior technology was the driving force of racial conquest, with the introduction of bronze being an obvious possibility for explaining the transition from long heads to round. This position was taken up by W. Boyd Dawkins, professor of geology at Owen's College, Manchester, whose *Cave Hunting* of 1874 provided an extensive survey of archaeological discoveries. Dawkins was suspicious of de Mortillet's claim that the various Palaeolithic cultures represented a progressive sequence of technical discoveries, arguing instead that different styles of toolmaking were best seen as contemporary tribal preferences. In particular, he identified the makers of the Magdalenian culture (which included many artefacts of reindeer bone) with the modern Eskimos.

Dawkins's *Early Man* of 1880 developed the racial interpretation of prehistory at greater length. De Mortillet's last three 'stages' of Paleolithic development were now dismissed as contemporaneous cultures based on different local materials. Dawkins objected to the supposed parallel development of culture across the whole of Europe, arguing that there was no evidence of a tendency for people independently to develop the same tools at the same level of culture.[15]

[14] Huxley, 'On Some Fixed Points in British Ethnology', reprinted in *Man's Place in Nature* (1894 edn), pp. 253–70; Greenwell, *British Barrows*; Beddoe, *The Races of Britain*, pp. 11–12.

[15] Dawkins, *Early Man*, pp. 230–1, 241.

The similarity of the reindeer people's artefacts to those of the Eskimos was enough to confirm that the latter were indeed the remains of this Palaeolithic race, driven into the inhospitable lands of the Arctic by later invaders. Asia was the seat of all human progress: 'Probably the centre from which these Palaeolithic tribes swarmed off was the plateau of Central Asia, which in subsequent ages was the aboriginal home of the successive invaders of both Europe and India.'[16] Eventually the Palaeolithic tribes were driven out by the superior civilization of the Neolithic, and 'the origin of domestic animals, as well as of the cereals, proves that the Neolithic peoples migrated into Europe from the South-east, from the mysterious birthplace of successive races, the Eden of mankind, Central Asia.'[17]

Dawkins had no doubt about the nature of the interaction between the Palaeolithic and Neolithic races. Of the Eskimos' ancestors, we can assume 'that at the close of the Pleistocene age, when they came into contact with the Neolithic invaders, there were the same feelings between them as existed . . . between the Eskimos and Red Indians, terror and defenceless hatred being, on the one side, met by ruthless extermination on the other.'[18] A comment to the effect that the Palaeolithic tribes were no lower than the aboriginal Australians suggests that Dawkins's hypothesis of race conflict also drew its inspiration from contemporary white imperialism. To complete his picture of prehistory, he argued that the earliest Neolithic invaders were the non-Aryan Iberians of the long barrows, who were in turn replaced by the first wave of Aryan invaders, the Celts. In time, the Celts were themselves pushed aside by another wave of Aryan invaders, the Germanic tribes. While the Eskimos retreated to the Arctic, the Iberians were forced into marginal areas further south.

Dawkins believed that the Iberians had survived in Britain long after most of the Continent had been conquered by the Celts. Knowledge of bronze had then spread through the Celtic population from a single point of discovery in Asia Minor.[19] This new technology gave the Celts the impetus to undertake the final invasion of the British Isles, since bronze weapons conferred an advantage in war similar to that gained from gunpowder in the middle ages. Iron, too, was discovered in Asia Minor, reaching Britain only just before these islands began to figure in the annals of Rome.

Many authorities disagreed with Dawkins's claim that bronze was

[16] Ibid., p. 173.
[17] Ibid., p. 306.
[18] Ibid., p. 243.
[19] Ibid., pp. 410–12.

brought into Britain by an invading tribe, although this view was supported as late as 1898 by A. C. Haddon.[20] But the notion of successive racial invasions was to dominate Neolithic (although not Palaeolithic) archaeology through the late nineteenth and into the early twentieth century.[21] In general it was assumed that the invaders succeeded because they were more advanced – if not in technology, then at least in organization and general culture. The prehistory of Europe thus consisted of an irregular progress rather than a steady indigenous development. The Germanic tribes, being the last wave of invaders from the east, were thus the highest form of mankind. They may have had to learn the arts of civilization from the classical world, but their moral character and initiative were the foundations upon which the modern achievements of the Anglo-Saxon race would be built.

Only towards the end of the century did a growing suspicion of modern Germany lead to a re-evaluation of the attitudes underlying the assumption of Teutonic supremacy. French and German anthropologists had fallen out as early as the 1860s over the relative standing of their supposed Celtic and Teutonic ancestors. Now some British scholars began to challenge the assumption that the last invaders of Europe were necessarily the most advanced race. We have already noted Isaac Taylor's *Origin of the Aryans* of 1889, which held that the Celts were the true Aryans and dismissed the Teutons as a barbarous tribe of latecomers who had conquered by military skills alone and then absorbed the superior Aryan culture of their victims.[22] Such a claim did not, however, challenge the basic logic of the invasion hypothesis – only the assumption that military strength was a necessary reflection of cultural development. The model of prehistory based on successive invasions was, in fact, to gain new ground in the early years of the twentieth century through its application to the evolution of human types in the Palaeolithic.

Progress through Struggle

Dawkins had suggested a theory that could, in principle, have been applied to the whole evolution of mankind through the Palaeolithic, and even to the origins of the human species itself. His opponents

[20] Haddon, *The Study of Man*, p. 80.
[21] For an account of the eventual collapse of the 'invasion neurosis' see Clark, 'The Invasion Hypothesis in British Archaeology'.
[22] See note 11 above.

among the evolutionary archaeologists and anthropologists used both the 'lower' modern races and extinct ape-like forms such as the Neanderthals to define the phases in what they saw as a continuous progression stretching up to the white race as the highest product of evolution. But perhaps the Neanderthals, like the Eskimos, were just relics of an outdated type waiting to be pushed aside or exterminated by the next wave of conquerors. The story of human progress would thus be divided into a series of distinct chapters, in each of which a new and higher race spread out from some hypothetical centre of creation to dominate the world. Such a theory of human origins was indeed put together in the early decades of the twentieth century, in effect extending the model of Neolithic invasions back into the more distant past. We need to know why this extension of the model did not take place in Victorian times, and why the palaeoanthropologists of the early twentieth century should have been attracted to a model of the past that was so firmly based on Victorian preconceptions about racial origins.

Dawkins said little about the development of mankind in the Palaeolithic, because he did not think there were any human remains available from this era. He even dismissed the Cro Magnon remains as Neolithic burials intruded into Palaeolithic strata. Most authorities, however, accepted the Cro Magnons as genuine examples of Palaeolithic humanity, along with the earlier and more brutish Neanderthals. The Darwinians naturally asked how the two forms were related in the evolutionary ascent from the apes, and, equally naturally, were led to answer in terms of a continuous progression. One explanation of the failure to extend Dawkins's migration theory into the area of human origins is that the anthropologists who were most conscious of racial differences tended to avoid the whole question of origins. They wished to retain the view that races were distinct natural types which had survived more or less intact for many thousands of years. A Darwinian theory of gradual evolution might threaten this 'typological' view of racial purity, and so the anthropologists preferred to evade the question of the ultimate origin of their supposedly distinct types. Some historians of anthropology have suggested that in so doing, the Victorian race theorists turned their backs on the whole evolutionary movement.[23]

In fact, the gulf between the two positions was not as great as we might imagine. Following the triumph of modern Darwinism, we are inclined to believe that any concept of distinct biological types is

<hr>

[23] Stocking, *Race, Culture, and Evolution*, ch. 3 and C. Loring Brace, 'The Roots of the Race Concept in American Physical Anthropology'.

incompatible with evolutionism. But in the nineteenth century there were many concepts of natural development that postulated discontinuous change and hence the relative stability of species once they were created (see chapter 6 below). Darwin and his supporters faced a barrage of objections from biologists who preferred non-Darwinian mechanisms of change. If evolution itself could be seen as an episodic or cyclic process, then the physical anthropologists may have been acting not in ignorance of evolutionism, but with a tacit assumption that non-Darwinian mechanisms would allow them to retain a belief in the stability of races. Their failure to enquire too deeply into the evolutionary origins of races would then reflect a natural reluctance to get involved in a debate which was still by no means settled even among the biologists who directly addressed the question of transmutation.

The possibility of non-Darwinian approaches was recognized from the beginning of the evolutionary debate. In material added to the 1862 edition of his *Races of Men*, Knox hinted that he favoured a discontinuous or saltative form of natural development in which new species (and races) would be produced suddenly when changing conditions triggered off a rearrangement of the forces governing individual growth.[24] We shall see below that similar ideas flourished throughout the late nineteenth century, and were widely used to preserve the supposed fixity of species within an evolutionary context. Nor was it necessary to accept the Darwinian analogy of a branching tree of evolutionary relationships, in which related forms must be linked back to a common point of origin. The French anthropologist Paul Broca argued for a theory in which evolution would have to be seen as a network in which several different lines of development might independently give rise to forms of humanity. Significantly, Broca's attack on the possibility that racial types can interbreed successfully was translated and published by Hunt's Anthropological Society of London.[25] On a slightly different tack, the German anatomist Karl Vogt argued that several different ape species had evolved towards the human form to give the racial types we know today – and again Vogt's work was translated by the Anthropological Society.[26] Knox's, Broca's and Vogt's approaches to evolution would all allow an anthropologist to retain an effective polygenism in which

---

[24] Knox, *The Races of Men*, p. 594.
[25] Broca, *On the Phenomena of Hybridity in the Genus Homo*.
[26] Vogt, *Lectures on Man*. Although never widely accepted, the claim that the various human races have their origins in different ape species survived into the twentieth century, see Klaatsch, *The Evolution and Progress of Mankind*.

the races of mankind were so distantly related that they could still be treated as distinct species.

Even the Darwinian theory of gradual, divergent evolution could be brought into line with the view that the races are stable biological types. If the branches leading to the modern races had begun to diverge at an early stage in the evolutionary ascent from an ape ancestor, sheer antiquity would ensure that the racial divisions had considerable stability. Darwin himself endorsed a suggestion made by Alfred Russel Wallace in 1864 to the effect that racial divisions may have appeared before the human species had acquired its full modern level of intelligence.[27] Wallace saw primitive humans migrating to different parts of the world, where they divided into racial groups by adapting to the local conditions. The advantages to be gained from increasing intelligence ensured that the groups would also continue to evolve in parallel towards the modern human form. There were persistent suggestions that the human species might have appeared much further back in time than archaeology could demonstrate. In his *Man's Place in Nature* of 1863, T. H. Huxley argued that the earliest humans might have appeared as far back as the Eocene period. This view was later endorsed by Samuel Laing, who pointed out that one of its great advantages was that it allowed the racial divisions of mankind to have a high degree of antiquity, guaranteeing their stability.[28]

The Darwinians were thus able to synthesize two distinct approaches to the theory of continuous development. As Darwin and Wallace made plain, their theory required one to assume that the races had diverged from a common ancestor under the influence of different geographical conditions. But Lubbock and the evolutionary archaeologists were tempted by an alternative, linear model of progress in which the 'lower' races were not divergent branches but merely the preserved relics of earlier stages in the ascent from the apes (see chapter 3 above). The two approaches could be reconciled by arguing that adaptive divergence was superimposed on a linear scale of mental development. The blacks of Africa could be seen as having adapted physically to a tropical climate, while at the same time preserving a primitive mental and physical state long surpassed by the races which had continued to evolve in a more stimulating environment. This technique can be seen in the popular writings of the German evolutionist Ernst Haeckel, who divided the human stock

[27] Wallace, 'The Development of Human Races under the Law of Natural Selection', reprinted in *Natural Selection and Tropical Nature*, pp. 167–85.
[28] Laing, *Human Origins*, chs. 10–12.

into two main branches at an early stage in the ascent from the apes. Each branch had diverged into a number of racial types, but the woolly-haired peoples had collectively retained a lower level of evolution than the straight-haired.[29] An 1892 survey of ethnology by A. H. Keane argued that the blacks had been 'left behind' in the tropics while the rest of mankind advanced and diverged into the other modern races in the more stimulating climates of north Africa and Eurasia.[30]

The Darwinians were thus predisposed to accept an early episode of migration followed by continuous evolution in each part of the world. When applied to Palaeolithic Europe, this hypothesis encouraged the belief that higher races had evolved *in situ*, obviating the need to postulate the invasion of higher types from elsewhere. The brutish Neanderthals could be seen as merely the earliest and most primitive form of European man, which had evolved into higher types such as the Cro Magnons in the course of the Palaeolithic. The 'lower' races of modern Africa and Australia would simply have retained a level of development little advanced beyond that of the European Neanderthals. The advantage of this position for the evolutionists was that they could use the Neanderthal specimens to fill in the gap between apes and modern humans, thus providing apparently hard evidence for the most controversial application of evolution theory. As we saw in the interlude 'Missing Links' above, this identification of the Neanderthals was popularized by Haeckel, Gustav Schwalbe and others in the late nineteenth century. It is known as the 'Neanderthal phase of man' theory, a name coined by the American anthropologist Ales Hrdlička who attempted to revive it in the 1920s.[31]

In addition to the anatomists' assumption that the Neanderthals formed a natural step on the path from the apes to modern humans, the archaeologists were also promoting a model of continuous progress. De Mortillet's hierarchical arrangement of the stone-age cultures was designed to stress the continuity of development between the Mousterian and later Palaeolithic toolmakers. As this scheme came to dominate archaeologists' thinking in the late nineteenth century (despite Boyd Dawkins's objections), it inevitably helped to support the idea of a continuous evolutionary progression. Once the discoveries at Spy had confirmed the existence of a Neanderthal race using tools of the Mousterian type, archaeologists

[29] Haeckel, *The History of Creation*, II, pp. 294 and 303–10.
[30] Keane, *Ethnology*, pp. 242, 374–5 and 403.
[31] Hrdlička, 'The Neanderthal Phase of Man'. See also Brace, 'The Fate of the "Classic" Neanderthals'.

were naturally inclined to follow de Mortillet's assumption that subsequent improvements in toolmaking went hand in hand with the gradual evolution of more advanced human types such as the Cro Magnons. The Neanderthals were thus the ancestors of at least some of the modern European races.

Some anthropologists hoped that it would be possible to detect traces of Neanderthal characters in living races. In his 1890 article on 'The Aryan Question', T. H. Huxley noted that the German anthropologist Rudolph Virchow had found Neanderthaloid features in the skulls of modern Frisians.[32] As Isaac Taylor noted in his discussion of the same question, French anthropologists had taken a particular delight in depicting the brutal Neanderthals as the ancestors of the Germanic races.[33] Some English race theorists preferred to see living Neanderthals among the population of western Ireland. Whatever the nature of the direct links to the present, there was widespread acceptance of the contention that the Neanderthals had evolved into at least some of the more primitive races of modern Europe. Neolithic archaeology might demonstrate the subsequent invasion of higher types from Asia, but it was easy to assume that such mass migrations could only have begun after a high degree of social organization had been developed. The advocates of continuous progress thus dominated the study of the Palaeolithic origins of mankind through the late Victorian period. Physical anthropologists and historians might extol the virtues of the Saxon invaders of western Europe, but the first generation of evolutionists were reluctant to complicate their vision of progress with the idea of racial conquests in the distant origins of mankind. The alternative of episodic or discontinuous progress thus lay dormant, waiting for the chance to influence studies of human origins once the basic plausibility of evolution could be taken for granted.

The emergence of a 'progress by invasion' theory of human origins was thus delayed until the early years of the twentieth century. By this time evolutionism itself was no longer controversial, and its supporters no longer felt the need to promote the simplest possible model of human origins. The growing stridency of imperialist rhetoric in the years leading up to the First World War also created a climate of opinion highly receptive to the suggestion that race conflict was the driving force of human evolution. A key figure in the establishment of the new approach was the professor of geology at Oxford, W. J.

[32] Huxley, 'The Aryan Question,' reprinted in Huxley, *Man's Place in Nature* (1894 edn), pp. 271–328, see pp. 326–7.
[33] Taylor, *The Origin of the Aryans*, p. 107.

Sollas, who had begun to take a strong interest in the early phases of human development. Like Boyd Dawkins, Sollas was impressed by the evidence linking the Magdalenian reindeer hunters to the Eskimos, and in his *Ancient Hunters* he set out to reinterpret the whole of prehistory in terms of racial migrations. He believed that each of the Palaeolithic cultures could be identified with a particular group of savages in the modern world. Apart from the Eskimos, the Australian aborigines were little more than living Neanderthals.[34] This identification of modern savages with particular phases in human evolution was, of course, an integral part of the comparative method practised by cultural anthropologists such as Tylor. But Sollas was now convinced that an entirely new interpretation of the link was possible.

In the preface to *Ancient Hunters* Sollas declared: 'I find little evidence of indigenous evolution, but much to suggest the influence of migrating races.'[35] The Eskimos and Australians might each represent a particular stage of Palaeolithic cultural development, but they had each in turn been marginalized by the pressure of later and higher types of mankind expanding across the globe. Indigenous development obviously took place *somewhere*, but the archaeologist might often be unable to locate the precise centre from which each new wave of humanity spread out. From a European perspective, a series of races had occupied the territory in the course of prehistory, but each had been displaced by a higher type invading from elsewhere. There had certainly been a progressive development of culture and of the human form, but it occurred in distinct stages as higher types abruptly displaced the earlier population. 'The surviving races which represent the vanished Palaeolithic hunters have succeeded one another over Europe in the order of their intelligence: each has yielded in turn to a more highly developed and more highly gifted form of man.'[36]

Sollas clearly recognized that his new model of prehistory had broader implications. The principle of 'might is right' was nature's way of ensuring the success of more highly evolved types.

What part is to be assigned to justice in the government of human affairs? So far as the facts are clear they teach in no

[34] Sollas soon gave up this position to join those who claimed that the Neanderthals were a distinct form of humanity, although he continued to argue that the Australians had only a Neanderthal level of culture; see *Ancient Hunters* (3rd edn), pp. 256–7.

[35] Sollas, *Ancient Hunters* (1st edn), p. viii.

[36] Ibid., p. 382; 3rd edn, p. 599.

equivocal terms that there is no right which is not founded on might. Justice belongs to the strong, and has been meted out to each race according to its strength; each has received as much justice as it deserves. What perhaps is most impressive in each of the cases we have discussed is this, that the dispossession by a new-comer of a race already in occupation of the soil has marked an upward step in the intellectual progress of mankind. It is not priority of occupation, but the power to utilise, which establishes a claim to the land. Hence it is a duty which every race owes to itself, and to the human family as well, to cultivate by every possible means its own strength: directly it falls behind in the regard it pays to this duty, whether in art or science, in breeding or in organization for self-defence, it incurs a penalty which Natural Selection, the stern but beneficient tyrant of the organic world, will assuredly exact, and that speedily, to the full.[37]

The imperialist message of this passage is obvious enough, and it would be tempting to dismiss Sollas as the worst kind of 'social Darwinist', obsessed with natural selection as the vehicle of progress. Yet elsewhere in the book he ridiculed the Darwinian mechanism as impotent to explain the generation of higher characters.[38] Like many other critics of Darwinism, Sollas was prepared to accept natural selection as a mechanism for weeding out the types left behind in nature's progress, but confessed himself unable to explain how the higher types were, in fact, evolved. His 'social Darwinism' was more a product of the cyclic model of development that had stood as an alternative to Darwinian gradualism throughout the Victorian era.

In the preface to later editions of his book, Sollas implied that his theory of Palaeolithic migrations had been seen as a great innovation, but had soon gained wide acceptance. The best evidence to support the latter assertion is the sudden revaluation of the status of the Neanderthals which took place in the years leading up to the First World War. By the end of the nineteenth century it had been generally agreed that the Neanderthals were a stage in the continuous evolution of mankind from the apes. This view was supported by the young anthropologist Arthur Keith in his *Ancient Types of Man* of 1911. Yet by the time he wrote his *Antiquity of Man* (published in 1915), Keith had reversed his position to become a leading advocate of the

[37] Ibid., p. 383; 3rd edn, pp. 599–600.
[38] Ibid., p. 405; 3rd edn, p. 666.

claim that the Neanderthals were *not* ancestral to modern humanity. This claim had already been advanced by the French anthropologist Marcellin Boule in his account of a well preserved Neanderthal skeleton unearthed at La-Chapelle-aux-Saints in 1908.[39] There is little evidence that Keith was directly influenced by Boule, however. Their respective support for the new position arose independently and suggests that the time had somehow become right for an application of the theory of progress through migration to the earlier phases of human development.

Boule's analysis of the La-Chapelle-aux-Saints skeleton led him to argue that it had ape-like characteristics marking it off quite distinctly from the modern form of humanity. It was Boule, in fact, who created the popular misconception of the Neanderthals as shambling ape-men (ignoring the large brain-capacity noted by Huxley back in 1863). He may have been misled by the fact that his specimen had been crippled by arthritis. By exaggerating the differences between Neanderthals and modern humans, Boule was able to claim that the transition from one to the other in European prehistory was too abrupt to be explained by gradual evolution. The Mousterian culture was replaced fairly rapidly by the Aurignacian, and since this replacement was assumed to coincide with the transition from Neanderthals to Cro Magnons, it now seemed evident that the latter must have invaded Europe from elsewhere. The Neanderthals of Europe were not ancestral to modern humanity: they were a degenerate offshoot of the human stock who had survived only until their territory was invaded by a higher race.

Keith's *Antiquity of Man* advocated a similar interpretation. If anything, he exaggerated the gulf between the Neanderthals and modern humans even further by claiming that the former had distinct specializations that were not merely relics of an ape ancestry. It is no coincidence that Keith was a leading enthusiast of the notorious Piltdown discovery of 1912, which seemed to provide evidence for a non-Neanderthaloid form of humanity in the early Palaeolithic. We now know, of course, that the Piltdown finds were a hoax or fraud: a human cranium had been deliberately planted alongside an ape jaw.[40] To those who took it seriously at first, though, 'Piltdown man' seemed to provide hard evidence that a form of humanity lacking the distinctive

---

[39] See Boule, 'L'homme fossile de La Chapelle-aux-Saints' and *Fossil Men*. For a more extensive discussion of these developments, see Bowler,. *Theories of Human Evolution*, especially chap. 4.

[40] There is a massive literature on the Piltdown affair; see for instance Weiner, *The Piltdown Forgery* and the most recent survey, Blinderman, *The Piltdown Inquest.*

Neanderthal brow ridges had already evolved before the Neanderthals came to dominate Europe. Some thought that the Piltdown type
may itself have been ancestral to modern humans. Keith did not
accept this, realizing that the ape-like jaw would make it yet another
offshoot from the main line of progress. Yet the discovery gave him a
powerful incentive to argue that the Neanderthals were not truly
human. They were a distinct early species of mankind which had
been replaced quite abruptly when our own ancestors invaded Europe
later in the Palaeolithic. Dubois's even more primitive *Pithecanthropus*
(Java man) was dismissed as another withered twig on the tree of
human evolution, marginalized at the opposite end of the world.

There can be little doubt that the expulsion of the Neanderthals
from human ancestry was a popular move. It became the dominant
view in the 1920s and 1930s, so popular that Hrdlička had to go out
on a limb to revive the 'Neanderthal phase of man' theory in 1927.
The transition was not without its ideological overtones. Michael
Hammond has shown that Boule was motivated by a desire to challenge
the political message that the socialist de Mortillet had associated
with his linear progressionism.[41] Keith – like Sollas – clearly saw the
theory of invasion and extermination as a justification for imperialism.
He had become acutely conscious of the racial differences among
modern humans, and extending the antiquity of the human species
gave him the time he needed to explain the appearance of such
fundamental variations in the non-Neanderthal stock. He favoured
the view that racial interaction would lead to struggle and extinction:
'What happened at the end of the Mousterian period we can only
guess, but those who observe the fate of the aboriginal races of
America and Australia will have no difficulty in accounting for the
disappearance of Homo Neanderthalensis. A more virile form
extinguished him.'[42] In later years Keith went on to develop a whole
theory of human evolution based on racial competition. Natural
selection was the law of evolution, although – again like Sollas – Keith
insisted that selection could not explain the actual production of the
races which competed for mastery.[43]

If we compare the views of Sollas and Keith with those expressed
earlier by Boyd Dawkins, there is only one element missing: the
enthusiasm for central Asia as the 'cradle of humanity' from which

---

[41] Hammond, 'The Expulsion of the Neanderthals from Human Ancestry'.

[42] Keith, *The Antiquity of Man*, p. 136.

[43] Keith's *Darwinism and what it Implies* of 1928 stressed the role of struggle, while
his later *Darwinism and its Critics* insisted that far more than natural selection was
involved.

the higher types migrated out to conquer the rest of the world. Yet this too remained popular with other anthropologists. Dubois's search for 'Java man' in the 1890s had been inspired by Haeckel's promotion of the view that Asia, not Africa, must have been the centre of human evolution. In 1889 A. R. Wallace argued that the development of human intelligence would have advanced more rapidly not in the enervating tropics, but in a more stimulating northern environment, probably in Eurasia.[44] In the 1920s and 1930s, the central Asian theory of human origins was enthusiastically promoted by the American palaeontologist Henry Fairfield Osborn. It was this theory which led Davidson Black to China, where he participated in the discovery of 'Pekin man' (related to Dubois's *Pithecanthropus*) in the late 1920s. Black certainly believed that Asia provided the stimulating environment from which more progressive types migrated out to the rest of the world, pushing their lowly predecessors before them.[45]

It has been argued that the expulsion of the Neanderthals from human ancestry was engineered by anthropologists who wished to downplay the whole idea of evolution.[46] While it is true that the new theory made each fossil race a distinct 'type' of humanity, there is no evidence that Keith and the others wanted to evade the question of how each race originated. Their views on this issue were distinctly non-Darwinian in character, but they believed that some form of natural process generated new races in the most stimulating environments. Their inability to be very precise on the nature of this process illustrates exactly why the previous generation of evolutionists had been unwilling to extend the idea of racial migrations into the area of human origins. At a time when the basic concept of evolution was still controversial, it would have given too much away to their opponents if they had advocated a form of evolution in which the available fossils were not used to plug the gaps in the record of our ascent from the apes. By the early years of the new century, the old controversies had died down and it was possible to explore more complex and (in some respects) more realistic models of how the variety of human fossils might be related.

The palaeoanthropologists of the early twentieth century were thus able to put together a view of human evolution which can be seen as an extension of the cyclic or rhythmic theory of progress advocated throughout the Victorian era. Despite its emphasis on struggle as the

[44] Wallace, *Darwinism*, pp. 459–60. On the central Asian theory of human origins see Bowler, *Theories of Human Evolution*, pp. 174–81.

[45] Black, 'Asia and the Dispersal of Primates', p. 175.

[46] Brace, 'The Fate of the "Classic" Neanderthals'.

means by which higher types displaced their primitive antecedents, this was no product of Darwinian gradualism. Most of its supporters rejected natural selection as the motor of progressive evolution, preferring to invoke some vaguely defined creative force in the central Asian heartland. The fact that both the concept of progress through cycles and the fascination with Asia as the centre of development survived well into the twentieth century reveals the power these Victorian images had to shape the imagination. The echoes of Max Müller's account of Aryan migrations can still be heard in the theories of the 1920s. A fascination with racial conquest had dominated Victorian ideas on late prehistory, but had been excluded from studies of human origins by archaeologists and anthropologists committed to the idea of continuous evolution. But once the faith in continuous progress was undermined by growing militarism in the age of imperial rivalries, the model of progress through conquest emerged from the wings to extend its influence over ideas on human origins. The early twentieth century merely extended the sense of racial destiny that had been growing throughout the Victorian era.

Part III

The Ascent of Life

5

Fossils and Progress

We have seen that the Victorians' ideas on prehistory underwent a dramatic transformation in the 1860s as archaeologists at last began to accept the evidence for human antiquity. Significantly, this event coincided with the emergence of Darwinian evolutionism, thus permitting the creation of a unified progressionist image of animal and human development. Yet the widespread reluctance of many early-nineteenth-century thinkers to accept the great antiquity of the human race must be set against their general willingness to tolerate the emergence of a science of geology in which it was taken for granted that the earth itself was immensely ancient and had undergone vast revolutions before attaining its present state. The geologists had opened up the 'dark abyss of time' but had evaded its full implications by insisting that human history could not be integrated into the later phases of the earth's development.[1] By separating mankind off into a distinctly modern period (by geological standards) the more conservative thinkers were able to retain their belief that the human race possessed a unique spiritual character that lifted it above the rest of creation.

The evidence for a historical process in the formation of the earth's crust was indeed impressive (see the interlude 'Reading the Rocks' below), and to most geologists it seemed to indicate a steady

---

[1] The phrase 'dark abyss of time' was coined by the eighteenth-century naturalist Buffon; see Rossi's book of that title. On nineteenth-century progressionism and the fossil record see Martin Rudwick, *The Meaning of Fossils*, and Bowler, *Fossils and Progress*.

progression towards the present state of affairs. By the 1830s an outline of the fossil record as it is now understood had already begun to emerge, and with it an almost inescapable sense of the progressive development of life from the simplest to the most complex forms. Life had begun in the ancient oceans in the forms of primitive invertebrates and strange armoured fish. Later on, the great reptiles had dominated the planet, both on the land and in the sea. Finally, the first primitive mammals appeared, and after a series of developments began to approach the forms we know today. Only at the very end of the sequence (according to the conventional interpretation) had the modern mammals been joined by human beings.

Nowadays we take it for granted that this sequence records the gradual evolution of life on earth, even if some of the details are missing from the record. This indeed was the position adopted by the Darwinists of the late nineteenth century. But in the period 1830–60 there were many who resisted this interpretation of the fossil record, preferring to see it as evidence that the Almighty had repeatedly exerted His creative power in the course of the earth's history. If the Genesis story of creation could not be accepted as a literal account of the formative process, the basic idea of the miraculous origin of all forms of life – including the human race itself – could be preserved by multiplying the number of creative acts to accommodate the evidence for a succession of extinct populations. In the popular mythology of science, it was Darwin's *Origin of Species* which overthrew this superficially modified creationism and established the case for natural evolution as we accept it today.

Because of its obvious impact on the way we think about ourselves and our relationship to nature, the 'Darwinian revolution' has long formed a focus of attention for historians of science.[2] But the interpretation of this event which has been built into the textbooks offers little scope for integration with our account of how the Victorians approached the past. For their own purposes, scientists – and historians of science – have preferred to see the creation of the 'historical' sciences of geology and evolutionary biology as the triumph of the observational method of science over religious bigotry. In the orthodox picture, the early-nineteenth-century geologists are caricatured as 'catastrophists' who tried to defend as much as possible

---

[2] For orthodox interpretations of the Darwinian revolution, see for instance Eiseley, *Darwin's Century*; Greene, *The Death of Adam*; Himmelfarb, *Darwin and the Darwinian Revolution* and Ruse, *The Darwinian Revolution*. My challenge to the traditional interpretation is outlined more fully in Bowler, *The Non-Darwinian Revolution*.

of the Genesis story. They believed that the earth had been subjected
to periodic upheavals and tidal waves, with Noah's flood being the last
in the series. These catastrophes resulted in the mass extinction of all
forms of life, thus necessitating the miraculous creation of new
species to repopulate the earth. This still largely biblical view of the
earth's past was first challenged in the 1830s by Charles Lyell's
'uniformitarian' geology in which all changes were explained in terms
of observable causes (erosion, earthquakes, etc.) acting over vast
periods of time. Darwin eventually extended Lyell's empiricist
methodology to the organic world, postulating the natural selection of
everyday individual differences to explain the origin of new species.
Once Darwin had published his vast wealth of data in the *Origin of
Species*, the scientific community was soon converted to evolutionism
and Victorian society was forced to confront the theory's materialistic
implications.

Recent developments in the history of science have suggested that
this whole story may be nothing more than the scientists' own version
of Whig history: a reconstruction of the past designed to stress the
role of empirical observation in combatting religious superstition. In
their anxiety to present science as a rationalizing force in western
culture, modern scientists have classified their Victorian predecessors
as heroes or villains according to where they fit into an idealized view
of the path leading towards our modern level of understanding.
Darwinism in particular is hailed as a major scientific and intellectual
force because the *Origin of Species* both verified the basic idea of
evolution and pioneered the theory of natural selection which (after
modernization through a synthesis with Mendelian genetics) is still
accepted by most biologists today. From this whiggish perspective it
seems obvious that if the selection theory is still accepted as valid, it
must have played the central role in converting Darwin's contemporaries to evolutionism.

The alternative view of Victorian geology and evolution theory that
is beginning to emerge from recent research offers a far more
complex picture of what was going on. The old idea of a war between
scientific 'truth' and religious 'superstition' can no longer be
sustained. Equally important for our present purposes, the new
viewpoint allows us to recognize within the evolutionary debates
exactly those themes which we have already discovered in the
Victorians' approach to human history. Even before the establishment
of human antiquity linked archaeology and geology together, the
palaeontologists were debating the alternative versions of development
and progress with which Victorians were already familiar from their
study of history, sociology and philology. There were differences of

emphasis, to be sure, since the concept of a linear scale of development applied to the history of life on earth had materialist implications ensuring that it would at first be espoused only by militant radicals. As the idea of continuous progress was gradually taken up by less radical thinkers, the use of the analogy with the growth of the embryo towards maturity was frequently exploited as a means of implying that evolution has a central, purposeful trend. A progressionist version of biological evolutionism thus became available in time to be synthesized with the cultural anthropologists' linear interpretation of human progress. The history of mankind could then be seen as a direct continuation of the progression apparent throughout the development of life on earth.

The opponents of the early radicals could exploit the alternative cyclic or episodic model of progress already being developed by the liberal Anglican historians and by the philologists. The need to recognize some higher power operating in history was defended by appealing to the discontinuity of the ascent towards mankind revealed by the fossil record. This model was based at first on a simple appeal to miraculous creation, but in later decades more sophisticated ideas of episodic evolution still allowed conservative thinkers to retain their belief that the appearance of mankind represented the start of an entirely new epoch in the history of creation (chapter 6 below). Both sides in the debate assumed that evolution tended towards a goal, but where the radicals saw the efforts of individual animals and humans as the driving force of progress, conservatives invoked the cyclic model to defend their claim that a higher Power sustained the natural and the social hierarchy.

The scientists who figure most prominently in the orthodox story – Lyell and Darwin – seem far more anomalous when viewed against the new background. The 'Darwinian revolution' of the mid-nineteenth century cannot be seen as the inevitable triumph of modern ideas backed up by the accumulation of scientific evidence. Lyell's geology may have stressed the role of natural causes in the earth's history, but we now realize that his methodology was sustained by his faith in a completely cyclic or steady-state world view which denied the element of progress or development altogether. For all his interest in reconstructing the earth's recent past, Lyell believed that the Age of Reptiles could return in the future, when the endless cycle of changes recreated the climatic conditions of that ancient era. Even Darwin could not stomach this total denial of progress, although his own theory of adaptation by natural selection turned evolution into a branching, open-ended process in which there could be no pre-ordained goal towards which life *must* advance. As understood by modern biologists, Darwin's theory threatens the whole foundations of progressionism, and there can be no doubt that Darwin himself realized this, at least to some extent. But in his own time he was successful in promoting the idea of evolution precisely because he adapted his published accounts of natural selection to the prevailing faith in progress. The idea of branching development was important to many biologists, but in popular versions of evolutionism it was subordinated to the widespread assumption that there must be a main line of progress leading towards humankind and, ultimately, to European civilization.

There is thus a very real sense in which Darwinism, as it is understood by modern biologists, did not triumph in the nineteenth century. Studies of late-Victorian evolutionism have increasingly tended to confirm that the most radical implications of Darwin's selection theory were ignored in favour of more 'purposeful' mechanisms of change. The *Origin of Species* played a crucial role, not because it convinced everyone of the power of natural selection, but because it catalysed a transition to evolutionism within a still largely developmental world view. The more radical aspects of Darwin's thought lay hidden until revitalized by the synthesis with genetics in the early twentieth century. The 'Darwinian revolution' that ushered in the theory of evolution was less traumatic than it would have been if these radical ideas had been exploited. Instead of falling into Darwinian materialism, Victorian evolutionists used the idea of progress to retain the traditional belief that the universe is a purposeful system. Teleology was modernized, not abandoned: If the late-Victorian era was dominated by the metaphor of struggle, that metaphor was inspired not so much by Darwinian natural selection as by the increasing willingness to accept that more advanced individuals or societies must displace those who have not participated so actively in the race towards progress. As we have already seen, even the advocates of a cyclic model of development could exploit this image of struggle.

Radical Evolutionism

According to the conventional interpretation of the Darwinian revolution, there was no serious support for evolution in Britain before Darwin published the *Origin of Species*. The geologists and palaeontologists who explored the fossil record during the preceding decades opted instinctively for a series of miraculous creations. It is conceded that evolutionary ideas had been proposed by the French naturalist J. B. Lamarck in works such as his *Philosophie zoologique* of

1809, but Lamarck was supposed to have been completely discredited by his great rival Georges Cuvier and by a lengthy critique of his views in the second volume of Lyell's *Principles of Geology*. For all practical purposes, there was no evolutionism before Darwin, an interpretation which conveniently focuses all our attention on Darwin as the first 'real' evolutionist. The only fact that seemed to jar with this view was Darwin's own recollection of his student days in Edinburgh, when he was surprised to hear the anatomist Robert E. Grant express support for Lamarck.[3] But this episode was generally ignored by historians on the assumption that Grant was an isolated figure who need not be taken seriously.

As mentioned in chapter 4 above, we are now beginning to realize that this conventional interpretation conceals a substantial tradition of radical evolutionism which flourished throughout the early nineteenth century. If Lamarck was completely ignored, why was it necessary for Lyell and many other naturalists to take up a stand against the transmutation theory? Thanks to the work of Adrian Desmond, we can now see that Grant was merely the tip of the iceberg: in fact there was an active movement by political radicals and younger medical men to exploit the materialist implications of evolutionism in their campaign against the political, academic and medical establishments.[4] The conservative Anglicans who controlled Oxford, Cambridge and the medical schools used the idea of divine creation to legitimize a static, hierarchical society. Radicals like Grant opted for evolutionism not only to show that things change, but also to suggest that it is the efforts of hardworking individuals which cause them to change. When the more influential Tory scientists argued against transmutation, they were doing so as part of a deliberate policy to discredit radicals who were seen as a real threat to their authority. In the decades before Darwin published, serious efforts were being made to soften the materialism of this radical evolutionism so that it could become part of a popular vision of natural and social progress.

In his *Philosophie zoologique*, Lamarck had argued that the animal kingdom can be arranged into an essentially linear hierarchy corresponding to the order in which the classes have evolved.[5] At this point, he postulated an inherently progressive evolutionary force and introduced the inheritance of acquired characteristics only to explain

[3] Darwin, *Autobiography*, p. 49.

[4] Adrian Desmond, 'Robert E. Grant: the Social Predicament of a Pre-Darwinian Evolutionist' and *The Politics of Evolution*.

[5] For accounts of Lamarck's work see Burkhardt, *The Spirit of System*; Hodge, 'Lamarck's Science of Living Bodies'; and Jordanova, *Lamarck*.

how the linear pattern had been distorted by the necessity for animals to adapt to an ever-changing environment. In the introduction to his *Histoire naturelle des animaux sans vertèbres* he modified the theory by postulating that the inheritance of acquired characteristics was itself the mechanism of progress as well as of adaptation. As Herbert Spencer and others were to point out later, the Lamarckian mechanism allows individual effort to be portrayed as the driving force of evolution: in the famous example, the giraffes stretch their necks to reach the leaves of trees and the results of their efforts are accumulated over many generations to give the animal we know today. If this mechanism is seen as the driving force of a linear progressive trend, there is an obvious parallel with the philosophical historians' view of social progress. In both cases, the efforts of individuals to cope with the problems of their environment raise the population (animal or human) up the scale of biological or social complexity. It is easy to see why radicals seeking to challenge a static society based on aristocratic privilege should find Lamarckian evolutionism attractive. It was the perfect basis for the claim that progress towards a free society was an inevitable continuation of nature's operations.

Grant was a Scot who studied medicine at Edinburgh and then spent some time in Paris after the defeat of Napoleon. Along with Robert Knox – another radical Scots anatomist whose views on race we have already encountered – he got to know the works of Lamarck and of Geoffroy Saint Hilaire, who continued the defence of transformism against Cuvier in the 1820s.[6] Returning to Edinburgh, he began lecturing on invertebrate anatomy and took an active part in the vigorous intellectual life of the city. An anonymous article defending Lamarck in the *Edinburgh New Philosophical Journal* of 1826 is almost certainly by Grant. It stresses that nature reveals a basically linear pattern linking the lowest forms of animal life to the highest. The meaning of this linear pattern becomes clear when we see that it corresponds to the order in which the forms were introduced in the course of the earth's history. Lamarck, 'one of the most sagacious naturalists of our day', postulates the spontaneous generation of the lowest forms of life and then maintains

> that all other animals, by the operations of external circumstances, are evolved from these in a double series, and in a gradual manner. On that account, the scale of

[6] See Appel, *The Cuvier–Geoffroy Debate*. Geoffroy's transformism did not involve the linear progressionism of Lamarck's theory and was favoured more by Knox than by Grant.

gradation, according to which he arranges the animal kingdom, is, at the same time, the history of their origin; and the discovery of this truly natural method, the most important problem of the natural philosopher.[7]

The newly emerging fossil evidence for progress thus supports Lamarck's theory:

The doctrine of petrifactions, even in its present imperfect condition, furnishes us with accounts that seem in favour of Mr Lamarck's hypothesis. We, in fact, meet with the more perfect classes of animals only in the more recent beds of rocks, and the most perfect, those closely allied to our own species, only in the most recent.[8]

A later article, again probably by Grant, explains the evolution of higher forms as a consequence of the gradual cooling of the earth, which created steadily more demanding environments.[9]

Grant adopted a radical political stance which he actively justified in terms of his evolutionary view of life. As a biologist, he was highly regarded, but his materialism and his political opinions threatened to go beyond what was acceptable in polite society. Many liberals wanted reforms that would give free rein to individual enterprise, a view that was easy enough to justify in terms of the philosophical historians' theory of social progress. But to extend the scale of progress down into the animal kingdom was to raise the obvious spectre of human evolution from the brutes, threatening the traditional view of mankind's spiritual status. Lamarck had made it clear that we had evolved from something like the apes, and Grant himself explained our higher faculties as the end-product of the organic development: 'New organs of sense are unfolded, and the brain becomes the centre of feeling, perception and life, till in man it attains the highest state of perfection, and endows him with consciousness and rationality.'[10] Edinburgh was also the centre from which George Combe promoted the phrenological theory that the brain is the organ of the mind, another extension of the materialist position. Such ideas could be discussed north of the border, but they were anathema to the

---

[7] Grant, 'Observations on the Nature and Importance of Geology', p. 297.
[8] Ibid.
[9] Grant, 'Of the Changes which Life has Experienced on the Globe'. The belief that the earth was gradually cooling down was popular among geologists at this time.
[10] Grant, 'Observations on the Nature and Importance of Geology', p. 296.

Anglican academic establishment of Oxbridge and London. All too often, they were exploited by radicals who were little short of revolutionaries.[11] Those of advanced political views who wished to function within polite society had to tread carefully to avoid being tarred with the materialist brush. It was one thing to advocate social progress by reform; quite another to claim that mankind had evolved from the apes. When Grant took up the Chair of Anatomy and Zoology at the newly founded University of London in 1827, he faced mounting opposition from scientists determined to discredit his radical views. Partly for this reason, and partly because his new job left him no time for research, he soon faded into obscurity.

The challenge faced by less radical thinkers in the following decades was to disengage the idea of organic progression from the materialism represented by Grant and to present it in a more acceptable light. There was an obvious way of doing this, since the linear pattern of development advocated by Lamarck could easily be presented as a divinely pre-ordained sequence leading towards the goal of the human mind. Perhaps both evolution and social progress were merely the unfolding of God's plan in accordance with the laws He had imposed on nature. Robert Knox, who certainly wanted to link mankind with nature, distrusted the idea of simple progression precisely because it implied a divine purpose in evolution.[12] The belief that social development follows a predictable pattern was, of course, implicit in the linear evolutionism of the philosophical historians, but liberal thinkers would have regarded it as counter-productive to stress that the pattern was divinely pre-ordained. In the more controversial area of biological evolution, though, less radical thinkers realized that it was essential to stress the teleological element if the theory was to be uncoupled from the image of materialism it had already acquired. Only by stressing that the direction of evolution had a moral purpose could they explore the possibility that biological and social progress were different phases of the same universal development.

In the decades before the *Origin of Species* appeared the public was gradually introduced to the idea of transmutation in this sanitized form. A key factor in this campaign was the anonymously published *Vestiges of the Natural History of Creation* of 1844. This, not the *Origin*, was the book which introduced the idea of evolution to Victorian England. It outraged the conservative establishment, but sold well enough to ensure that everyone was familiar with its claim that

[11] Desmond, 'Artisan Resistance and Evolution in Britain, 1819–1848'.

[12] Knox, *The Races of Men*, p. 191. As we shall see in chapter 6, Knox did advocate a form of evolution, but invoked sudden transformations or saltations.

transmutation could be regarded as the unfolding of God's plan for universal development.[13] By the 1850s, an increasing number of more liberal thinkers were looking to the idea of natural development as a means of underpinning a progressionist view of society.

As we have already seen in chapter 4, the author of *Vestiges* was the co-founder of the Edinburgh publishing house, Robert Chambers. In the 1830s, Chambers became deeply involved with the radical philosophy associated with phrenology and social reform.[14] He used his *Chambers's Edinburgh Journal* to promote a nonrevolutionary progressionism based on the claim that improvements in society would follow inevitably from the expanding knowledge of how nature works. Already familiar with the philosophical historians' view of social development, Chambers wanted a universal foundation for progressionism and sought it in the science of the earth's past. *Vestiges* was his attempt to justify social reform with the claim that human progress merely continued the trend already built into nature and revealed in the development of life on earth.

Chambers displayed his materialism by arguing for the spontaneous generation of the simplest forms of life by the action of electricity on inanimate matter. Almost a third of the book was devoted to a survey of the fossil evidence for the development of life on earth, with Chambers struggling to convince his readers that, whatever the apparent discontinuities of the advance of life, an overview revealed the underlying trend of gradual progress. The first living things were primitive invertebrates, followed by fish whose cartilaginous skeletons revealed their status as immature vertebrates. More advanced fish, reptiles and finally mammals then appeared in steady progression. The mammals advanced gradually towards their modern forms and culminated in the appearance of mankind. The size of the brain had increased throughout the history of life, allowing Chambers to present the human mind as the inevitable product of the progressive trend in the animal kingdom. Phrenology, with its explanation of mental powers in terms of brain structure, was the ideal foundation for such an attempt to bridge the gap between the animals and human phases of progress. Once again, Chambers revealed his materialism – much to the disgust of his conservative critics.

And yet *Vestiges* went out of its way to portray the advance of life towards mankind as the unfolding of a divine plan. Chambers's aim was to use the unity and regularity of the progression as a means of showing that the whole sequence of development was the result of

[13] For an account of the *Vestiges* debate see Millhauser, *Just before Darwin*.
[14] On Chambers's intellectual development see Secord, 'Behind the Veil'.

divine contrivance. God did not create individual species; He created the law of progress and then left it to unfold in accordance with the programme He had built into it. To emphasize the purposeful character of the progression, Chambers used the growth of the embryo towards maturity as his model for the history of life on earth. Indeed, he argued that evolution worked through the gradual lengthening of the process of individual growth, carrying life onwards and upwards to ever higher levels of maturity:

> the simplest and most primitive type, under a law to which that of like production is subordinate, gave birth to the next type above it . . . this again produced the next higher, and so on to the very highest, the stages of advance being in all cases very small – namely, from one species to another; so that the phenomenon has always been of a simple and modest character.[15]

The human race itself was the last stage in this steady development of the animal kingdom – although curiously Chambers seems to have been reluctant to specify the apes as our most probable ancestors.

It would be a mistake to dismiss Chambers's theory as merely an immature version of Darwin's.[16] Apart from the fact that he saw new species being 'born' instantaneously from old, Chambers had no interest in the process of adaptation to the environment that was central to both Lamarckism and Darwinism. As he wrote in later editions of *Vestiges*, the great weakness of Lamarckism lay in its 'giving this adaptive principle too much to do'.[17] For Chambers, the central theme of evolution was progress, not adaptation, and he exploited the analogy with the growth of the embryo to bring out the idea that progress was essentially the ascent by means of a linear pattern towards a predetermined goal. In effect, the lower animals merely stepped off the escalator of development before reaching the top. *Vestiges* offered not a theory of branching, divergent evolution, but a linear progressionism. In later editions, when Chambers responded to criticism by trying to make his theory more sophisticated, he invoked parallel lines of evolution all advancing through a basically similar pattern of development. This emphasis on the directed nature

---

[15] Chambers, *Vestiges of the Natural History of Creation* (1st edn), p. 222.

[16] The title of Millhauser's *Just before Darwin* illustrates how Chambers has often been portrayed as a forerunner of Darwin. For an account that stresses the non-Darwinian character of Chambers's theory see Hodge, 'The Universal Gestation of Nature'.

[17] Chambers, *Vestiges of the Natural History of Creation*, (1860 edn), p. 161.

of evolution was ideal for the purpose of stressing that the whole process was no more than the unfolding of a divinely pre-ordained plan.

Because it attributed progress to a divine plan, rather than to the cumulative efforts of animals to deal with their environment, Chambers's theory provided only an indirect link between the organic and the social phases of progress. He could not really argue that human progress worked by exactly the same mechanism as animal evolution, and in this respect the theory was a compromise between the idealist vision of progress as a divinely imposed pattern of development and a truly naturalistic evolutionism. Perhaps such a compromise was necessary in the sensitive years of the 1840s. Even with its concessions to divine providence, *Vestiges* was roundly condemned by conservative thinkers as a vehicle for promoting seditious materialism. Most of the biologists who had closed ranks to resist Grant's Lamarckism reiterated their claims that the fossil record exhibited a discontinuous, not a gradual advance (see chapter 6 below). Yet the book's popularity ensured that its message could not be ignored. The possibility that progressive evolution might be used to underpin a radical, but nonrevolutionary, call for reform had been firmly introduced into the public debate.

By the 1850s some of the more advanced thinkers even within the Anglican establishment had begun to suspect that a philosophy of 'creation by law' was preferable to reliance on the outdated notion of a vast sequence of miracles. The Oxford mathematician and philosopher Baden Powell wrote his *Essays on the Inductive Philosophy* of 1855 partly to argue that the regularity of law was a better indication of design by God than arbitrary miracles.[18] In the post-Darwinian era, Chambers's position would increasingly be taken up by moderate conservatives as a more sophisticated alternative to the fully naturalistic evolutionism of Darwin and Spencer. By the time Darwin published the *Origin*, Spencer had already begun to advocate a unified evolutionary philosophy in which individual effort was the driving force of both the organic progression and the historical development of society. Chambers's compromise was abandoned by the radicals as they found themselves at last free to advance a theory of natural progress without being branded as revolutionaries. *Vestiges'* legacy to liberal thought was its emphasis on the linearity of the progressive trend in nature, which dovetailed neatly with the philosophical historians' thesis that society advances naturally towards the mature state of industrial capitalism. To a surprisingly large

[18] See Corsi, *Science and Religion*.

extent, post-Darwinian evolutionism retained the model of a sequence of developmental stages that Chambers had introduced into the popular consciousness.

What, then, was the role of the *Origin of Species*? Darwin's theory played a valuable part because the idea of evolution could only become an integral part of the social debates if it could also be made scientifically respectable. Many biologists distrusted *Vestiges* because of its cavalier approach to the scientific evidence. Even those who were on the lookout for a new initiative to replace creationism were suspicious of the 'law of development' precisely because it still left the ultimate explanation of change in the hands of the Almighty. This can be seen in the attitude of the young T. H. Huxley, who attacked *Vestiges* bitterly in an 1853 review because it offered no scientifically testable mechanism of change.[19] Huxley's subsequent enthusiasm for Darwinism was prompted by his belief that natural selection filled the explanatory gap left by Chambers's appeal to a divinely pre-ordained pattern of development.

In the years immediately before Darwin published, Herbert Spencer tried to break the deadlock by boldly opting for Lamarckism as the mechanism of both biological and social evolution. This was, perhaps, less adventurous than it had been in Grant's time, but there is little evidence that working biologists were willing to give Lamarckism another chance. The theory was to become popular in the later nineteenth century, but in the 1850s something else was needed to convince biologists that evolution could be turned into a respectable scientific programme. Darwin's theory provided the new intiative that was needed and thus broke the conceptual logjam created by the blacklisting of Lamarckism and the too-obvious compromise of 'creation by law'. Natural selection had no previous convictions for materialism, was supported by a wealth of new evidence, and was presented in a form that deliberately emphasized its progressionist implications. Although vulnerable to a number of objections, it convinced scientists that a new approach to the whole question of organic origins was worthwhile and precipitated their conversion to evolutionism – thus allowing the topic to emerge as a central feature of progressionist thought.

Darwinism Triumphant?

Darwin's *Origin of Species* converted the scientific community to evolutionism and went on to become a major influence on Victorian

[19] Huxley, 'Vestiges of the Natural History of Creation'.

thought. Historians of culture naturally take the book seriously, but our understanding of its impact has been drastically skewed by hindsight owing to the fact that Darwin's theory of natural selection was belatedly resurrected to become the foundation stone of the modern synthetic theory of evolution. This fact has all too often blinded us to the relative lack of success enjoyed by the selection theory in Darwin's own time. Indeed, Darwin's whole model of evolution as an ever-branching tree proved very difficult for the Victorians to accommodate into their progressionist world view. In the eyes of most late-nineteenth-century thinkers, natural selection lacked the driving force that would explain why life constantly advanced towards higher levels of development. Everyone admitted that the fittest deserved to survive – but where did the supply of fitter individuals or races come from? Darwin himself did his best to ensure that the theory would be seen as a contribution to progressionism, and 'Darwinism' was thus absorbed into the popular culture of the time. In the process, natural selection was supplemented by various concepts of directed evolution and those aspects of Darwin's thought most highly regarded by modern biologists were ignored.

There is thus a sense in which the emergence of Darwinism as we now understand it should not be treated as the main theme in the development of Victorian evolutionism. Darwin proposed a theory that was too radical for most of his contemporaries because it denied that there was a guiding force leading organic development towards a higher goal. He realized that this would be unacceptable and sought for metaphors that would encourage his readers to believe that a moral purpose lay behind the apparently blind activities of nature. The extent of his success can be judged from the fact that the *Origin* catalysed the transition to evolutionism despite the steady flow of arguments intended to demonstrate the ineffectiveness of natural selection. Darwin provided the scientific respectability that had been lacking in Chambers's *Vestiges*, but was unable or unwilling to sever the link between evolutionism and the developmental way of thinking that Chambers had already imprinted on the public consciousness.

The anomalous character of Darwin's theory can be judged from its origins, which include many factors quite alien to the main thrust of Victorian progressionism. The most obvious of these atypical factors is the uniformitarian geology of Charles Lyell. Lyell's *Principles of Geology* (1830–3) was another book which, like the *Origin*, exerted great influence despite the rejection of its most fundamental thesis. Modern geologists hail Lyell as one of their heroes, but their adulation rests on an interpretation of his work which picks out only those aspects which seem to anticipate modern ideas.[20] They see him as a champion of the scientific method whose appeal to observable causes in geology discredited the catastrophists' attempt to retain a role for Noah's flood in shaping the earth's surface. No one doubts that the *Principles* did force geologists to think more carefully about the possibility of gradual change, but historians now realize that Lyell linked his apparently 'scientific' methodology to a world view that rejected not only the central tenets of Victorian historicism but also certain crucial aspects of modern geology.

Although Lyell's gradualism represented a challenge to the biblical orthodoxy which he, at least, attributed to the catastrophists, he had no intention of using the idea of social evolution as his model for the earth's history. He set out, in fact, to replace the catastrophists' developmental view of the earth's past with a purely steady-state model in which all change is cyclic or nondirectional. He argued that since scientific geology should only work with observable causes, we must accept that we do not have access to any rocks formed under conditions differing significantly from those we observe today. We should abandon all hope of trying to discover the remains of a 'primitive' period when the earth was affected by causes no longer in operation. Lyell tried to show that however far back in time we look, we see only the evidence of changes similar to those now in progress. As far as scientific geology is concerned, the earth has always been more or less the same, because the constructive forces of elevation which create mountains and continents are exactly balanced by the destructive forces of erosion. This perfect adjustment allows the earth to maintain itself indefinitely as a suitable habitat for living things, thus demonstrating the perfect workmanship of its Creator. For all we know, it will continue in this state for an indefinite time in the future.

Lyell certainly believed that it was possible to reconstruct what had happened in the more recent periods of the earth's past from the fossil record, but he insisted that we should not expect the record to reveal an irreversible process of historical development. He tried to discredit the evidence that was being used to argue for a progressive development of life on the earth. According to Lyell, the record is so imperfect that we cannot use it to support rigid conclusions about what kinds of life did *not* exist during the earlier geological periods. The fact that the fossilized remains of higher animals have not been found in these early rocks does not prove that such animals did not exist when these rocks were laid down; only that we have not yet

[20] For a recent account of how historians have begun to challenge the orthodox account of Lyell see Gould, *Time's Arrow, Time's Cycle.*

Plate 13   The Temple of Serapis at Puzzuoli.
The marks on the columns indicate that the temple has been
partially submerged beneath the sea and then re-elevated since
Roman times. Lyell argued that over a greater timespan, natural
earth movements could have more substantial effects, including
the elevation of mountain ranges. The illustration also suggests a
parallel with the rise and fall of empires in human history.
From Charles Lyell, *Principles of Geology*, vol. 1, frontispiece

found any of their fossils. He was, in fact, able to show that the record did not support a simple, linear scheme of progress, since a very small number of mammal fossils had been found along with the dinosaurs in the heart of the so-called 'Age of Reptiles'. Perhaps future discoveries would reveal mammals at the very beginning of the known record, thus disproving progress altogether.[21] According to Lyell, the Age of Reptiles was merely a period when minor fluctuations in the earth's climate had created an environment more favourable to reptiles than to mammals, so that the ratio between the two classes was the inverse of that observed today. Throughout the great cycles of continental elevation and depression, there had been fluctuations in the character of the earth's inhabitants, but no directional change. In theory, the Age of Reptiles may be recreated in some future cycle – a possibility caricatured by Henry de la Beche in a cartoon depicting a 'Professor Ichthyosaurus' lecturing on a fossil human skull![22]

There was considerable support for Lyell's effort to explain the past in natural terms, but hardly anyone accepted his steady-state view of the earth's history. Even Darwin – in some respects Lyell's greatest disciple – accepted that the fossil record confirmed the sequential appearance of new types in the course of time. Darwin's great achievement was to extend Lyell's appeal for explanations based on observable causes into the one area that Lyell himself had excluded from the system: changes in the organic world. For all his Whig sympathies, Lyell wished to protect the traditional concept of the soul as a distinct spiritual entity. He refused to admit that man might have evolved from the brutes and rejected the whole idea of transmutation. He included a detailed refutation of Lamarck's claims in the second volume of the *Principles*, thus sealing the fate of that theory for the time being. But Darwin, who became a convert to Lyell's gradualism while on a voyage around the world aboard HMS *Beagle*, saw that the new geology opened up the possibility of a similarly naturalistic explanation of organic change. If Lamarckism had been branded as scientifically inadequate and morally suspect, it would be necessary to search for another, more acceptable, mechanism.

By the time he set out on the *Beagle*'s voyage of exploration in 1831, Darwin had already gained a substantial, if unofficial, training as a naturalist during his abortive studies at Edinburgh and while gaining a BA at Cambridge. Although traditional accounts of his career stress

[21] For accounts of Lyell's evidence see Rudwick, *The Meaning of Fossils*, ch. 4 and Bowler, *Fossils and Progress*, ch. 4.
[22] See Rudwick, 'Caricature as a Source for the History of Science' and Gould, *Time's Arrow, Time's Cycle*.

Lyell's geology and the biogeographical studies of the *Beagle* voyage as the ·key factors in his conversion to evolutionism, extensive modern research has confirmed that many of his interests were established at an early age.[23] Even Grant may have played a role in stimulating certain lines of thought, although it is clear that Darwin soon realized the social vulnerability of Grant's Lamarckism and began to distance himself from it. At Cambridge, he accepted the uncritical creationism of his teachers, including the catastrophist professor of geology, Adam Sedgwick. When the results of the *Beagle* voyage forced Darwin once again to confront the possibility of natural transmutation, he was acutely conscious of the need to dissociate the idea from the materialist label that earlier radicals had attached to it. The selection theory was to be developed in private while Darwin explored the best avenues for presenting it in an acceptable light.

Observations in South America convinced Darwin that Lyell was right: geological change was gradual rather than catastrophic. He soon began to think about the implications of this position for the origin of new species, especially when he realized that simple creationism was incapable of providing a satisfactory explanation of how species were distributed around the globe. He was *not* led to the topic through a study of the ascent of life in the fossil record – indeed, his own fossil discoveries convinced him that the record was too imperfect to allow the detailed reconstruction of evolutionary links. At best, the record reveals general trends, but not precise genealogies. Geography, not geology, was the crucial factor, because the concept of divine creation could not explain why species were located only in certain parts of the globe. The particular experience that had most effect on Darwin's mind was, of course, his stay on the Galapagos islands. If each of these tiny islands, hundreds of miles out in the Pacific, had its own species of finch or mockingbird, could one really believe that the Almighty had made a personal visit to perform the act of creation? The only rational explanation was that the birds had been accidentally transported to the islands from the American mainland and had gradually adapted to the conditions they encountered. New species had evolved from samples of the old through the necessity of each population adapting to its own local environment.

Darwin became convinced of this conclusion shortly after his return from the *Beagle* voyage and spent the late 1830s searching for a mechanism of adaptation based on observable causes. Unlike the

---

[23] For an extensive collection of modern Darwin scholarship, see Kohn, ed., *The Darwinian Heritage*. De Beer's *Charles Darwin* is a good traditional biography, but there is no account of his life which takes proper account of the latest research.

majority of mid-nineteenth-century evolutionists, he began to study the breeding of domesticated animals in the hope that this would provide him with a clue. He was soon alerted to the possibility that nature might select out individual variants in a manner paralleling the breeders' technique for producing new varieties of dogs or pigeons. The breeders taught Darwin that every population contains a fund of apparently random variability, from which an acute eye can select those individuals better endowed with the preferred characteristics. After reading Thomas Malthus's *Essay on the Principle of Population* – a classic of *laissez-faire* political economy – Darwin saw that the constant tendency of the population to expand beyond the available food supply would generate a 'struggle for existence' in which those individuals best adapted to the local conditions would survive and reproduce better than their less well adapted brethren. Assuming that favourable variations could be accumulated over many generations, here was a mechanism of 'natural selection' that would explain how a population exposed to a new environment might eventually change sufficiently to become a new species.

The central theme of Darwin's new mechanism was that evolution is not directed towards any predetermined goal. The variation within a population is essentially random and is incapable of 'pushing' the species in any particular direction. Selection acts purely by adapting the population to its way of life within the local environment, and if the environment changes, the direction of evolution will change. Species that cannot adapt quickly enough will be driven to extinction. The evidence from geography made it essential for Darwin to see evolution as a branching process, rather than as the ascent of a ladder of complexity. When samples from a single original population are transported to a series of new environments (as on the Galapagos islands), each sample will adapt to its own local conditions as best it can. Each will evolve in its own direction and the result will be a group of 'daughter' species evolved from the common parent. There can be no 'main line' of development, because each branch is merely 'doing its own thing' and cannot be judged by standards derived from other branches. Darwin realized that the divergent character of evolution would make the concept of progress difficult to define. There may be a tendency for animals and plants to become more complex in the course of time, but it will be difficult to compare the level of development reached by two very different types. Nor does evolution always yield progress, since some life styles lead to degeneration, as in the case of parasites. In this kind of theory there can be no goal towards which evolution is striving, and progress will become at best an irregular by-product of the endless pressure to adapt.

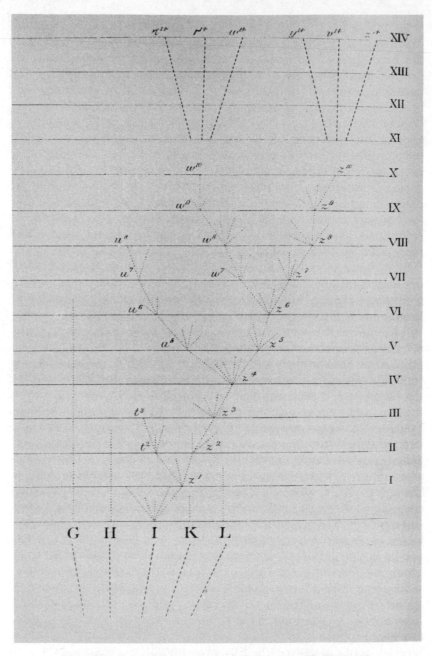

Plate 14   Part of Darwin's evolutionary tree. In Darwin's
theory, the lines of evolutionary development divide and move
apart from one another solely as the result of geographical
factors and environmental pressures. There is no implication
here that one branch can be regarded as superior to the others.
From Darwin, *On the Origin of Species by Means of Natural Selection*,
facing p. 117

Darwin's approach to evolution encouraged the naturalist to look for generalizations relating the known living and fossil species, but offered little hope of reconstructing the detailed path along which each had evolved. It might be impossible for us ever to discover the exact sequence of events by which American species had migrated to the various Galapagos islands, for instance; but the general pattern of divergence was clear. To a considerable extent, this technique paralleled that already developed by the philologists in their effort to work out the historical relationships between languages. Similar languages were seen as descendants of a single parent tongue, the divergence being brought about by migrations that would be difficult to reconstruct in detail. (In this respect, the isolated written remains from dead languages are like the naturalists' fossils, since in both cases the record is too imperfect to allow any more than the most general links to be discerned.) The diagram given in the *Origin of Species* to illustrate the branching character of biological evolution is similar to that used by philologists to depict the evolution of languages, and Darwin was well aware of the parallels between the two fields.[24]

In effect, Darwin's approach synthesized the two great traditions of nineteenth-century historical thought. His starting point was the liberals' emphasis on individual activity and natural development. Thanks to the influence of Lyell and of his geographical studies, he was able to uncouple this tradition from the naive progressionism represented by the assumption that industrialization is the goal towards which all social development must tend – an assumption still paralleled in Chambers's vision of life's ascent towards the goal of mankind. In his search for an alternative model of development, Darwin was led to propose an equivalent of the philologists' branching evolutionary tree, but he had no interest in their assumption that each family is descended from a mysterious archetypical founder. For Darwin, all levels of evolution, including the origin of the major groups, must occur through the summing-up of minute individual variations. The result was a theory of open-ended development that fell between the two stools of Victorian historicism and could not hope to be incorporated into the popular thought of the time without a good deal of reinterpretation.

There can be little doubt that Darwin realized from the start how radical the implications of his theory would be and how difficult it would be for his contemporaries to accept the incorporation of mankind into such a system. As he gradually refined the scientific

[24] Darwin, *Origin of Species*, pp. 422–3.

basis of his theory in the course of the 1840s and 1850s, he debated with himself and with a few close colleagues (including Lyell and the botanist J. D. Hooker) on how best to present the idea to the public. Natural selection offered a genuinely scientific hypothesis that would attract the more adventurous biologists in a way that Chambers's vague law of development could not. Yet it was unencumbered as yet with the kind of materialistic associations now firmly linked to Lamarckism. Darwin realized that, whatever his own views on the implications of the theory, it would have to be presented as a contribution to progressionism.

In 1858, the appearance of a similar theory by A. R. Wallace at last prompted Darwin to write the popular account of his theory that became the *Origin of Species*.[25] To minimize public anxiety, he concentrated on the scientific arguments, ignored (except for a single sentence) the controversial issue of human origins, and included a series of comments that would allow a sympathetic reader to believe that natural selection was, at least indirectly, a mechanism of progress. We can see this most clearly in the conclusion:

> Thus, from the war of nature, from famine and death, the most exalted object which we are capable of conceiving, namely, the production of the higher animals, directly follows. There is grandeur in this view of life, with its several powers, having been originally breathed into a few forms or into one; and that, whilst this planet has gone cycling on according to the fixed law of gravity, from so simple a beginning endless forms most beautiful and most wonderful have been, and are being, evolved.[26]

If he could not offer a simple ladder of progress, Darwin certainly intended his readers to see evolution as the progressive unfolding of a potential that God had originally 'breathed' into life.

Conservative thinkers were unwilling to accept Darwin's assurances and dismissed natural selection as a mechanism that left evolution at the mercy of chance.[27] As we saw in chapter 3 above, they were particularly upset by the obvious implication that mankind would have

---

[25] Much has been written on the independent discovery of natural selection by Darwin and Wallace, but in fact there were significant differences between their ideas; see Malcolm Kottler, 'Charles Darwin and Alfred Russel Wallace', in Kohn, *The Darwinian Heritage*, pp. 367–432.

[26] Darwin, *Origin of Species*, p. 490.

[27] For a survey of the religious controversy surrounding evolutionism see Moore, *The Post-Darwinian Controversies*.

to be treated as the product of such a meaningless system. Yet the very fact that a progressionist account of human origins was widely accepted in the later nineteenth century suggests that the initial debate over the *Origin* was something of a flash in the pan. For all their efforts, the conservatives could not stop the rising tide of evolutionism. A new generation of biologists, led by T. H. Huxley, recognized that Darwin's initiative at last opened up the question of organic origins to their researches, and they were no longer willing to concede the theologians' right to block their efforts. Scientists welcomed evolution as a weapon in the fight to establish their profession as the new arbiter of truth in an increasingly industrialized world. Within a decade or so, 'Darwinism' had become an integral feature of the new scientific establishment.

For all their efforts, conservative thinkers were unable to prevent the basic idea of evolution from gaining wide acceptance. A survey of the British periodical press by A. Ellegård shows that within a decade of the *Origin*'s appearance, there had been a fairly general conversion to evolutionism.[28] The same survey reveals, however, that natural selection remained highly controversial, with many writers preferring some more purposeful mechanism of development. Liberal thinkers went along with the progressionist philosophy of Herbert Spencer, while conservatives explored various means of 'modernizing' traditional values so that they could be preserved within an evolutionary framework (see chapter 6). In a sense, Darwin's public-relations exercise had been too successful. It had allowed evolutionism to escape its old materialist label and become acceptable in polite society. But at the same time, it had ensured that the theory would be incorporated into the framework of progressionism, thus concealing the more radical aspects of Darwin's message that are of interest to twentieth-century biologists. Darwin became the figurehead of evolutionism while his own theory of natural selection was left on the sidelines.

There was a widespread assumption that natural selection was only a destructive force: it removed the unfit but did not explain the origin of the fittest. Random variation must be supplemented by some more purposeful agent that would ensure the progress of life towards higher states. For Herbert Spencer, this supplementary agent was Lamarckism, the inherited effects of the organisms' efforts to better themselves. Spencer's *Principles of Biology* coined the term 'survival of the fittest' to denote Darwin's mechanism, but repeated Spencer's earlier insistence that the inheritance of acquired characteristics was a major

[28] Ellegård, *Darwin and the General Reader*.

force in evolution. As we saw in chapter 1 above, Spencer's social evolutionism was based on the assumption that more complex societies evolve out of the efforts of individuals to improve their lot. Lamarckism was the perfect counterpart to this philosophy of progress through effort, and Spencer continued to defend it throughout his career. In the later decades of the century, Lamarckism would become a major force in both biological and social evolutionism.[29]

It would be wrong to pretend that Lamarckism gained an immediate hold on scientists' imaginations. As Samuel Butler found to his cost when he tried to invoke Lamarck's name against Darwin's in his *Evolution, Old and New* of 1879, the British scientific community rallied around their hero and dismissed the challenger as a crank.[30] Butler's personal attack on Darwin did more harm than good to the cause of Lamarckism, however, and should not blind us to the growing popularity of the theory. In America and in many European countries, 'neo-Lamarckian' movements became very active, while even in Britain there was more support as the century drew to a close. The popularity of Spencer's philosophy more or less guaranteed the prevalence of Lamarckian ways of thought, even if many of his readers found it difficult to distinguish between the Lamarckian and Darwinian approaches. It was all too easy to think that the individual's struggle to better itself was part of the Darwinian theory, forgetting that for Darwin the individual was at the mercy of its biological inheritance and would die however hard it struggled if it was born with an unfit character.

In principle, Spencer recognized the divergent character of evolution. But we have already seen that his theory of social development allowed one to believe that *laissez-faire* capitalism was the 'highest' form of society. Similarly, in biology, his readers would have been led to assume that there was something special about the line of evolution leading towards the human race. This line had been the first to reach the threshold at which social and mental evolution began to reinforce one another, and hence could be identified (at least by hindsight) as the 'main line' of development. Other post-Darwinian evolutionists were even more explicit in their recognition of certain key steps in evolution defining a hierarchy of progress with mankind at the top. The great German biologist Ernst Haeckel wrote popular surveys of evolution that were translated into many different languages. His *The History of Creation* (1876) and *The Evolution of Man*

[29] For an account of the anti-Darwinian evolutionism of the late nineteenth century see Bowler, *The Eclipse of Darwinism*.

[30] See Willey, *Darwin and Butler* and Bowler, *Eclipse of Darwinism*, pp. 72–5.

(1879) helped to shape the public image of 'Darwinism' even in Britain. It was Haeckel, not Darwin, who created the popular assumption that evolutionism is principally concerned with the detailed reconstruction of the history of life on earth. He also created the equally popular myth that the growth of the human embryo offers a speeded-up model of how evolution advanced towards its goal – the recapitulation theory or 'biogenetic law'. Like Spencer, Haeckel offered a Lamarckian explanation of how new characteristics are formed and saw selection as only a secondary mechanism. His illustrations of the ascent of life include the one reproduced here which explicitly gives the tree of evolution a 'trunk' with mankind at the top (see plate 15).

Even T. H. Huxley seems to have taken his inspiration more from Haeckel than from Darwin.[31] Although he defended Darwin vigorously in the *Origin* debate and went on to become the leader of the 'Darwinian' faction in the scientific community, Huxley had little interest in natural selection and preferred to believe that evolution was somehow predisposed to advance along restricted channels. He seems to have been excited by Darwin's book mainly because it offered an opportunity to argue that professional scientists could now tackle a subject once reserved for theologians. He made no effort to exploit even the basic idea of evolution in his palaeontological work during the early 1860s, and only began to do so after reading Haeckel's progressionist interpretation. At this stage in his career, Huxley seems to have been anxious to stress the idea of progress as a means of convincing the working classes that reform was inevitable.[32] Haeckel's approach was exactly what was needed in this context, and Huxley now began to stress the importance of fossils such as *Archaeopteryx* as 'missing links' that would fill in the main steps of progressive evolution.

Although Huxley was never an advocate of the view that individual growth recapitulates evolutionary history, Haeckel's 'biogenetic law' was taken up with enthusiasm by younger naturalists such as E. Ray Lankester. After supervising the translation of Haeckel's *History of Creation*, Lankester published a number of articles in which comparative anatomy and embryology were used to reconstruct the course of evolution. In a technical article of 1877 and in his 'Zoology'

---

[31] See Desmond, *Archetypes and Ancestors*, ch. 5 and Mario di Gregorio, *T. H. Huxley's Place in Natural Science*.

[32] Huxley's enthusiasm for progressionism was short-lived – in his 1893 address 'Evolution and Ethics' (reprinted in *Collected Essays*, IX) he attacked Spencer's position on the grounds that natural evolution is not progressive, thus adopting a more Darwinian perspective. See the epilogue to this volume.

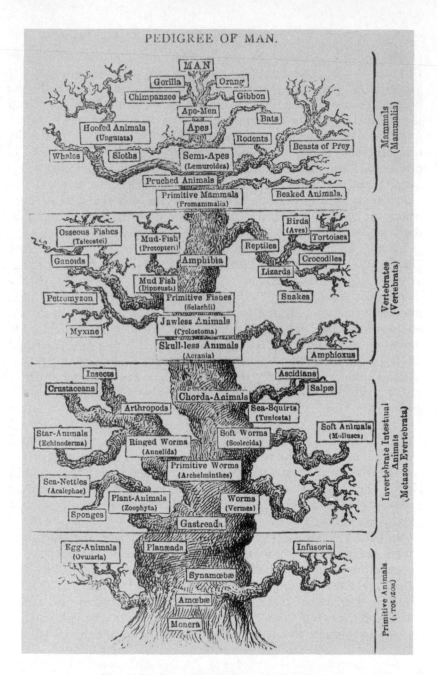

Plate 15   Ernst Haeckel's evolutionary tree.
Although apparently naturalistic, Haeckel's tree has a main
'trunk' running up to mankind at the top. Unlike Darwin's tree
of life, it thus represents evolution as an inherently progressive
and goal-directed process.
From Ernst Haeckel, *The History of Creation*, vol. 2, facing p. 188

article for the ninth edition of the *Encyclopaedia Britannica*, he argued that there were several distinct stages in the ascent of life, at each of which a number of lines branched out away from the main line of development.[33] Lankester realized that living things could degenerate if they adopted a less active lifestyle (as in the case of parasites) and even warned against the perils this tendency might create for the human race.[34] But his main emphasis was on the progressive trend in evolution which resulted from the normal efforts of organisms to cope with their environment. Lankester has been depicted as a 'Darwinian', and his efforts to reconstruct the history of life on earth were certainly typical of late-nineteenth-century evolutionism. But his concept of a main line of evolution and his emphasis on struggle against the environment as the driving force of progress suggest that even in scientific biology, the non-Darwinian ideas of Spencer and Haeckel were the real driving force.

The last great defender of the recapitulation theory, the embryologist E. W. MacBride, linked a similar thesis directly to the Lamarckian mechanism of adaptation through use and effort. He urged that there is a main line of evolution leading towards the vertebrates, while 'the Invertebrates collectively represent those branches of the Vertebrate stock which, at various times, have deserted their high vocation and fallen into lowlier habits of life.'[35] After 1900 MacBride became increasingly isolated as he attempted to defend Lamarckism against the rise of Mendelian genetics, but his overall view of evolution can be seen as one of the last and most explicit expressions of the Victorians' faith in effort as the driving force of progressive evolution towards mankind. The fact that he was prepared to argue explicitly for Lamarckism suggests that the superficial enthusiasm for 'Darwinism' among the first generation of evolutionists had now evaporated, allowing the non-Darwinian implications of their position to be recognized more explicitly.

Thus 'Darwinism' triumphed only because the open-ended, undirected character of evolution in Darwin's original theory was ignored or misrepresented. The majority of late-Victorian evolutionists did not believe in random variation and advocated selection only as a means of eliminating those who got left behind in the race for progress. Implicitly at first, and later quite explicitly, biologists

[33] Lankester, 'Notes on the Embryology and Classification of the Animal Kingdom' and 'Zoology'.

[34] Lankester, *Degeneration*; for further discussion of this topic, see the epilogue to this volume.

[35] MacBride, *A Textbook of Embryology*, p. 662; see Bowler, 'E. W. MacBride's Lamarckian Eugenics'.

promoted a largely non-Darwinian view of evolution that drew heavily on Spencer's Lamarckism and on Haeckel's assumption that there is a main line of progressive development leading towards mankind. Darwinism was thus absorbed into the liberal progressionist view of things, providing the perfect natural foundation for the theory of social progress towards industrialization and the Whig interpretation of history. The Victorian form of 'social Darwinism' drew on a Spencerian image of progress through struggle which ignored those aspects of Darwin's thinking that were to be taken up by modern biologists. The purpose of struggle was to promote the organism's efforts to better itself, and only secondarily to eliminate hereditary defects. The Darwinian revolution thus ended not with the destruction of traditional morality, but with the establishment of a modernized version of the liberals' faith in hard work as the key to personal and social improvement.

Interlude:

Reading the Rocks

The evolutionary debates of the mid-Victorian era took place within an intellectual framework which accepted that the earth had a history far more extensive than that of mankind. The planet and its inhabitants had undergone a vast sequence of changes long before the first primitive humans appeared. It is a popular misconception that the 'catastrophist' geologists of the early nineteenth century still wanted to defend a literal interpretation of the Genesis story of the creation and the deluge. By the 1820s the majority of educated people had accepted that the earth's crust has a structure whose complexity could only be explained in terms of a long sequence of physical changes in which rocks had been laid down, folded into mountains, partially eroded, and in many cases overlaid by yet more deposits. Fossils were at this time being studied in detail for the clues they offered to the inhabitants of the earth during the periods in which the rocks were laid down.

To be sure, most early geologists thought that the earth's development had been punctuated by violent catastrophes – but at the most, only the last of these events could be associated with the biblical deluge. Under the influence of Lyell even this claim was abandoned, and the scale of the hypothetical catastrophes was gradually reduced. The fossil record was at first supposed to be consistent with a series of divine creations, not with continuous evolution, but no one could doubt that life had undergone a process of development leading towards the modern species of animals and plants. Geology was thus a *historical* science: it used the monuments preserved in the earth's crust to reconstruct a sequence of events through time. Not surprisingly, then, it shared the preconceptions that influenced other areas of historical study. Fossils aroused great interest because they revealed a bizarre array of extinct creatures that could satisfy the most Gothic of imaginations. But they were also an indication that the earth's history fulfilled a moral purpose. The sequence was almost universally interpreted as the record of a progressive development of life from the simplest forms up to mankind. But the actual structure of the progressive sequence could be interpreted in different ways according to the geologists' views on the nature of historical development. The history of life on earth was a prelude to the great drama of human history, and even the advent of Darwinism would be unable to shake this faith.

The years around 1800 had witnessed a highly acrimonious debate between the supporters of rival geological theories. But in the early decades of the new century, geologists turned to the study of the fossil record with renewed hope of reaching a consensus on the interpretation of the earth's past. The Geological Society of London was founded in 1807 to coordinate the new wave of research. Although ostensibly intended to promote a purely empirical study of the rocks, the society did, in fact, preside over the erection of a thoroughly developmental interpretation of the earth's past.[1] British geologists liked to pretend that the new techniques for dating rocks by their fossil contents had been worked out by William Smith, the 'father of English geology', but much of the original inspiration came from France. Here Georges Cuvier and Alexandre Brongniart had worked out the sequence of deposition in the Paris basin, while Cuvier pioneered the careful reconstruction of extinct vertebrates from their fossil remains. British geologists and palaeontologists took up these new techniques with enthusiasm, and were soon playing a major role in establishing the earlier phases of the development of life on earth.

Interest in the large bones found in some very recent geological deposits had begun to grow in the late eighteenth century. It was soon apparent that these were not the bones of giant humans. Some, at least, had belonged to elephant-like creatures; the mammoth from Siberia and the mastodon from America. When Georges Cuvier began to apply his skills as a comparative anatomist to the reconstruction of these creatures from their skeletal remains, one question soon became critical. Were the ancient elephants merely variants of living species, or were they distinct forms that must be counted as extinct in

---

[1] On the development of geology and palaeontology in the nineteenth century see Gillispie, *Genesis and Geology*; Rudwick, *The Meaning of Fossils*; Bowler, *Fossils and Progress*; and Buffetaut, *A Short History of Vertebrate Palaeontology*.

the modern world? As early as 1799 Cuvier had decided in favour of extinction; the mammoth was quite distinct from the living elephants and such a large creature could hardly have remained undiscovered in an age of world-wide exploration. The mastodon turned out to be even more clearly distinct from living elephants, and soon Cuvier was caught up in a wave of frantic activity as he described the ever-growing array of fossils that was now being unearthed. His collected papers, published in 1812 under the title *Recherches sur les ossemens fossiles*, are taken as the foundation stone of modern vertebrate palaeontology.

At first Cuvier may have believed that he was dealing with a single ancient population which had been replaced by the earth's modern inhabitants. But his work in stratigraphy with Brongniart made him aware of the fact that geological deposits are not all of the same age. It soon became clear that some of the extinct vertebrates were much older than others. Even within the most recent or Tertiary series of rocks, there was a sequence of deposits, each with its distinct population of fossil vertebrates and invertebrates. The mammoth came from deposits so recent that its bones were not even mineralized, and Cuvier's reconstruction of the creature was triumphantly vindicated when a frozen carcass, flesh, hair and all, was discovered in the Siberian tundra. In the older Tertiary deposits, the extinct creatures seemed much less familiar, allowing Cuvier to see a pattern of development through time. The most recently extinct creatures were similar (but not identical) to living species, while those of the older strata were increasingly unlike anything now alive. The *Palaeotherium* ('ancient beast') of the oldest Tertiary rocks, for instance, seemed to combine features now found only among a number of distinct groups. It was a kind of amalgam of tapir, rhinoceros and pig. Beneath the Tertiary lay the even more ancient Secondary and Transition series of rocks, and here the remains of mammals seemed completely lacking. There were, however, strange reptiles such as the aquatic carnivore *Mosasaurus*. In effect, Cuvier had begun to establish evidence for the progressive development of life on earth, although his views on biological classification led him to distrust the common assumption that mammals are 'higher' than reptiles.

One point Cuvier did insist upon: the fossil populations seemed to change abruptly from one stratum to the next. There was no sign of the gradual transmutation predicted by Lamarck's theory – a theory to which Cuvier was deeply hostile in principle and which he opposed with all his influence. The 'Discourse préliminaire' to the *Recherches sur les ossemens fossiles* (translated into English as the *Essay on the*

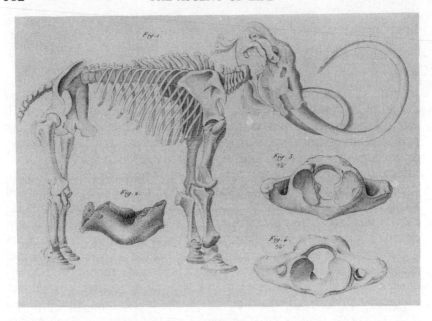

Plate 16   Skeleton of the mammoth.
Such reconstructions of extinct species helped to generate a
sense of wonder at the exotic character of the earth's earlier
inhabitants.
From Georges Cuvier, *Recherches sur les ossemens fossiles*, vol. 1, plate 11

Theory of the Earth) argued for the abrupt disappearance and
replacement of the fossil populations in geological 'revolutions'. At
one time, the term 'revolution' might have been used to signify a cycle
of change analogous to the revolution of the planets around the sun,
but Cuvier was a child of his time and his 'revolutions' carried all the
overtones of violent change that would have been familiar to anyone
who had experienced the Reign of Terror and the rise of Napoleon.
He insisted that many features of the earth's surface indicated violent
changes that could not have been brought about by causes now in
operation. Yet his support for 'catastrophism' should not mislead us
into dismissing him as a biblical fundamentalist. He made no effort to
identify the last catastrophe with Noah's flood and strove to establish
palaeontology as an independent source of information about the
past. Nor did he call in miracles to explain the sudden appearance of
new forms in the record – he thought they had merely migrated in
from areas not affected by the catastrophe.
    It was Cuvier's British followers who at first tried to retain a link
between the new geology and traditional accounts of the creation and

deluge. The colourful reader in geology at Oxford, William Buckland, discovered a cave at Kirkdale in Yorkshire in which the bones of hyaenas and their prey were buried in a layer of mud. In his *Reliquiae Diluvianae* of 1823 he interpreted this as evidence for a geologically recent flood which could be identified with that recorded in Genesis. But Buckland was anything but a simpleminded diluvialist, since he realized that the most recent catastrophe was the last in a vast sequence of events not recorded by the Bible. Indeed, he played a major role in expanding our knowledge of the earth's distant past.[2] Thanks in part to the activity of Lyell, Buckland and his fellow catastrophists gradually scaled down the violence of their hypothetical events, but they never abandoned their basic position. In particular, they resisted Lyell's steady-state interpretation of the past and continued to see the earth's history as a development from a primitive to the modern state. In the 1830s, the vast majority of geologists were convinced that the earth was gradually cooling down, having begun as a globe of molten rock. This explained why past earthquakes were more violent than those of today and tied catastrophism firmly to the idea of development through time.

The strength of this directional synthesis was enhanced by the growing fossil evidence for the progressive development of life on earth. British geologists played a major role in extending Cuvier's techniques to the study of the older rocks of the Secondary and Transition series. They helped to establish the sequence of the oldest fossil-bearing rocks, creating the geological periods we know today.[3] More important for our present purpose, they greatly extended our knowledge of the extinct creatures which inhabited these distant epochs of the past. Strange aquatic reptiles, *Plesiosaurus* and *Ichthyosaurus*, were added to those already recorded by Cuvier from the Secondary rocks. In 1824 Buckland described a giant terrestrial reptile from the Jurassic slate of Stonesfield, Oxfordshire, a fearsome carnivore which he named *Megalosaurus*. In the following year a Sussex doctor, Gideon Mantell, found the fossilized teeth of a large herbivorous reptile in a pile of stones left for road-mending. He named it *Iguanodon*. The term 'dinosaur' was coined by the anatomist Richard Owen in 1841 to denote these spectacular extinct reptiles. But long before this, Mantell had drawn attention to the new evidence suggesting that the era of the Secondary rocks constituted

---

[2] See Rupke, *The Great Chain of History*.

[3] For recent studies of the complex developments in Victorian stratigraphy see Rudwick, *The Great Devonian Controversy*; and Secord, *Controversy in Victorian Geology*.

an 'Age of Reptiles'.[4] The yet older Transition rocks seemed to lack any sign of terrestrial life. Strange armoured fish were described from the Old Red Sandstone of Scotland by the stonemason-turned-geologist Hugh Miller.[5] These seemed to be the oldest vertebrates, since beneath them lay the Silurian and Cambrian periods inhabited only by invertebrates such as Trilobites.

By the 1840s, then, the evidence for a progressive development of life in the course of the earth's history had begun to seem incontrovertible. Life had appeared first in the form of primitive invertebrates, and then the vertebrate classes had been added in the order fish, reptiles and mammals. The mammals showed a steady advance towards the modern forms, and mankind appeared as the very last step in the grand advance of life. Even among the invertebrates, there were distinct epochs of development, each with its own characteristic types. It was on the basis of this evidence that in 1841 John Phillips introduced the modern terms 'Cainozoic' 'Mesozoic', and 'Palaeozoic' to denote the three great epochs of the history of life. As indicated by figure 2, the earth's past had now been interpreted as a great sequence of development, with each geological period assigned to its place in the overall progress of life.

At first the evidence seemed to support Cuvier's claim that each fossil population was distinct from all the rest. As the century progressed, however, new discoveries helped to reveal detailed patterns within the overall development of life. There were never enough intermediate fossils to satisfy the critics of evolutionism, but in the decades following the publication of the *Origin of Species* Darwin's followers could point to several discoveries which seemed to fit in with their predictions. Most spectacular was *Archaeopteryx* from the Jurassic limestone of Solnhofen, Bavaria, the first specimen of which was purchased for the Natural History Museum in London in 1872. Although Richard Owen dismissed this specimen as merely an unspecialized bird, T. H. Huxley saw that it represented a 'missing link' between reptiles and birds. Here was a creature with teeth rather than a beak, but with the clear impression of feathers in the surrounding rock. Also in the 1870s, the American palaeontologist O. C. Marsh discovered a series of fossils linking the modern horse back to a primitive four-toed ancestor which he named *Eohippus* ('dawn horse'). Huxley proclaimed Marsh's sequence of horse fossils to be 'demonstrative evidence of evolution'.[6]

    [4] Mantell, 'The Geological Age of Reptiles'. Owen coined the term 'dinosaur' in his 'Report on British Fossil Reptiles'.
    [5] Miller, *The Old Red Sandstone.*
    [6] Huxley, *American Addresses*, pp. 85–90.

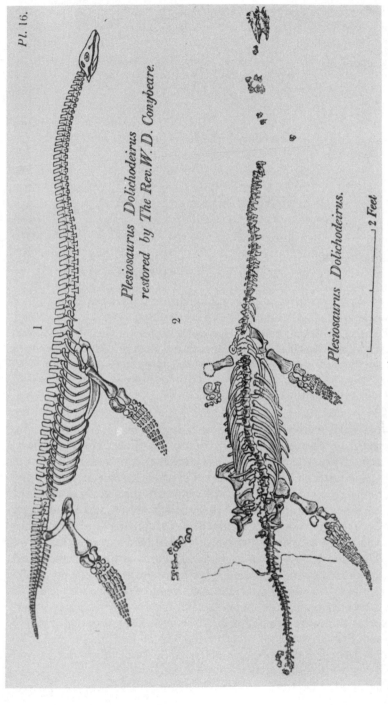

Plate 17 *Plesiosaurus.*

The first specimen of this aquatic reptile was described in 1821. The almost complete skeleton shown here was discovered a few years later at Lyme Regis in Dorset and reconstructed by W. D. Conybeare.

From William Buckland, *Bridgewater Treatise: Geology and Mineralogy Considered with Reference to Natural Theology*, vol. 2, plate 16

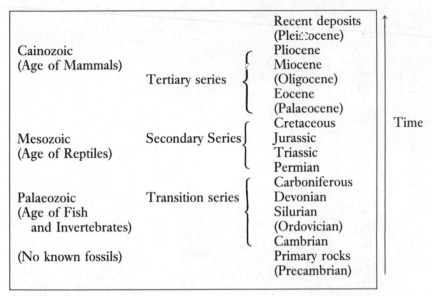

		Recent deposits (Pleistocene)	
Cainozoic (Age of Mammals)	Tertiary series	Pliocene Miocene (Oligocene) Eocene (Palaeocene)	Time
Mesozoic (Age of Reptiles)	Secondary Series	Cretaceous Jurassic Triassic Permian	
Palaeozoic (Age of Fish and Invertebrates)	Transition series	Carboniferous Devonian Silurian (Ordovician) Cambrian	
(No known fossils)		Primary rocks (Precambrian)	

Figure 2   Sequence of geological formations as established in the mid-nineteenth century, with later names added in brackets. The terms Pliocene, Miocene and Eocene were introduced by Charles Lyell. Catastrophists such as Adam Sedgwick and Roderick Murchison worked out the sequence of older rocks and introduced the terms Devonian (which also covers the Old Red Sandstone of Scotland), Silurian and Cambrian.

The fossil discoveries had an immense impact on Victorian thought quite apart from their role in the evolution debates. Many ordinary people were impressed by this evidence for the former state of life on the earth, and especially by the more spectacular creatures such as the dinosaurs. Great museums were built to house the fossil collections. In London, the Natural History Museum was designed by Owen in the 1860s, although not built until 1881. Its romanesque splendour still attracts a host of visitors, who are greeted by a statue of Owen at the head of the great staircase, with his great rivals, Darwin and Huxley, confined to a room beneath his feet. Owen also played a role in the creation of another Victorian monument to the distant past, the life-sized reconstructions of *Megalosaurus*, *Iguanodon* and many other extinct forms that were erected at Sydenham in the grounds to which the Crystal Palace was moved after the Great Exhibition of 1851. They are still there today, rather inaccurate by modern standards, but impressive nonetheless (see plate 18 below).

Novelists and poets were also struck by the evidence for the bizarre and transitory nature of the earth's early inhabitants. When Dickens tried to evoke the archaic character of a London fog in the opening passage of *Bleak House*, a dinosaur helped to complete the image.

> London. Michaelmas term lately over, and the Lord Chancellor sitting in Lincoln's Inn Hall. Implacable November weather. As much mud in the streets, as if the waters had but newly retired from the face of the earth, and it would not be wonderful to meet a Megalosaurus, forty feet long or so, waddling like an elephantine lizard up Holborn Hill.

More seriously, the fossils are brought in to illustrate the impermanence of life in one of the most pessimistic sections of Tennyson's *In Memoriam*.

> 'So careful of the type?' but no.
>   From scarped cliff and quarried stone
>   She cries, 'A thousand types are gone:
> I care for nothing, all shall go.'
>
> 'Thou makest thine appeal to me:
>   I bring to life, I bring to death:
>   The spirit does but mean the breath:
> I know no more.' And he, shall he,
>
> Man, her last work, who seem'd so fair,
>   Such splendid purpose in his eyes,
>   Who roll'd the psalm to wintry skies,
> Who built him fanes of fruitless prayer,
>
> Who trusted God was love indeed
>   And love Creation's final law –
>   Tho' Nature, red in tooth and claw
> With ravine, shriek'd against his creed –
>
> Who loved, who suffer'd countless ills,
>   Who battled for the True, the Just,
>   Be blown about the desert dust,
> Or seal'd within the iron hills?
>
> No more? A monster then, a dream,
>   A discord. Dragons of the prime,
>   That tare each other in their slime,
> Were mellow music match'd with him.[7]

[7] Tennyson, *In Memoriam*, §LVI.

Tennyson's vision of nature's cruelty has often been seen as an anticipation of the attitude displayed by Darwin's theory, and certainly this passage very effectively evokes the fears that must have disturbed many Victorians when contemplating the vast sequence of bizarre forms that the geologists had unearthed. As Tennyson himself eventually realized, the idea of progress was now essential to give meaning to what would otherwise become a senseless chaos.

6

Progress by Leaps

The majority of early Victorian naturalists still accepted that some form of supernatural intervention was needed to explain the origin of the new species appearing at various stages in the earth's history. But as the number and diversity of the available fossils increased, it became obvious that even divine creation must follow some sort of pattern – these 'miracles' were not totally arbitrary violations of natural law. The ascent through the vertebrate classes from fish to reptiles and mammals was the first regularity to become apparent, making it clear that creation followed a roughly progressive sequence. The evidence for this progressive trend did not at first disturb the advocates of supernatural origins, because the advance was so obviously discontinuous or episodic that it seemed to confirm the need for major creative innovations at several points in the earth's history. The fact that the record could be broken up into distinct eras and periods confirmed that progress worked in cycles. As the century progressed, other trends were recognized within the main episodes of the history of life, allowing the establishment of a sophisticated theory in which creative innovation was followed by developments that were not, in themselves, progressive.

There are obvious parallels between this approach to the history of life on earth and the models of human history proposed by liberal Anglicans such as Thomas Arnold and by the philologists investigating the development of human languages. These parallels are no coincidence, and arise from the fact that within each field of historical study, the model of development was being designed for a similar purpose. To assume that the pattern of development was always a simple progression towards the next highest class was to give the game away to the evolutionists, as Chambers showed in his *Vestiges of Creation*. Mankind would then become merely the last and highest of the animal species. In the 1850s, more conservative naturalists – like the historians and philologists – had to balance the need to concede at least some developmental trends against their desire to retain major creative steps in history. As long as the trend *within* each class was not a simple progression, one could concede the regularity of development at this level while still insisting that there was no overall progressive trend linking mankind directly to the brutes. The internal trend might parallel the phases of individual growth and decline, allowing the next highest class to be seen as a renewal or rebirth at a higher level. Or the various members of the class could be seen as the unfolding of potentials latent within some original archetype. In either case, the step towards the next class represented something more than a continuation of the internal trend, and required a distinct injection of creative energy. History was a process of development, but it was a development that worked through phases or cycles, thus disproving the radicals' claim that individual effort was the driving force of a single, continuous, progressive trend.

This approach could even survive the transition to evolutionism. In the post-Darwinian era, there were many naturalists who supported transmutation, but rejected both the Darwinian and the Spencerian explanation in favour of a cyclic model of development. For them, evolution was the unfolding of God's plan, just as Chambers had proposed. But they preferred to believe that the plan was far more complex than a simple progression. It included regular adaptive trends (far *too* regular for them to be the product of random variation) alternating with 'leaps' in which some higher power seemed to take direct control. This element of discontinuity allowed the appearance of mankind to be presented not as the final outcome of a gradual progression, but as the last and most important of the major steps in the ascent of life. There might be parallels between the various stages of human and animal history, but the introduction of mind had lifted creation on to an entirely new plane.

In the final years of the nineteenth century, it became less fashionable for biologists openly to invoke the Creator's guiding hand to explain the pattern of evolution. The divine plan was replaced by theories based on variation-trends somehow built into the very constitution of living matter. Yet even at this late stage, when the basic concept of natural evolution seemed to have been accepted at last, the cyclic model of development continued to flourish. The claim that each group of living things ultimately undergoes a degeneration to senility and extinction remained popular among palaeontologists through into the early twentieth century, representing one of the last and most bizarre manifestations of the analogy between individual growth and the development of life on earth. For the supporters of this theory of 'orthogenesis', evolution still followed a cyclic rather than a linear pattern of progress. Their theory could even be applied directly to the origins of the human species, thereby substantiating a distinctly non-Darwinian approach to this key step in the development of life on earth.

Catastrophes and Progress

Recent studies of radical evolutionism (outlined in chapter 5 above) have thrown new light on the attitudes of conservative naturalists in the decades before the *Origin of Species* appeared. Not long ago, historians (myself included) were rather puzzled to find that evolutionism was under open attack during the 1830s and 1840s. If Lyell had so effectively discredited Lamarck in the second volume of his *Principles of Geology*, what was the need for further refutation? Now that we know about the underground current of radical Lamarckism, we can see that the opponents of transmutation were responding to a genuine threat. The scientific establishment was determined to resist materialism, and a new generation of naturalists now came to the fore precisely because they could use their skills to create a more sophisticated view of the history of life. They retained scientific credibility by going beyond simple creationism, yet resisted the transmutationists by showing that the fossils did not support a linear progress towards mankind. Richard Owen was the most influential of these younger naturalists, a man from a negligible social background who rose to a pre-eminent position in British science because he exploited his anatomical skills to defend the conservative Anglican establishment. Owen has frequently been dismissed as a nonentity by historians because his rejection of Darwinism is seen as the action of a totally negative thinker. Yet we can now see that his theoretical position underwent a continuous development towards a non-Darwinian view of evolution. Far from being a backward-looking thinker, Owen was a leading exponent of a nonlinear form of progressionism which formed the main bulwark against the liberal developmentalism that culminated in Spencer's philosophy of social evolution. Nor was Owen a scientific lightweight; his theoretical position generated insights that were of permanent value to biology.

The catastrophist geologists of the 1820s and 1830s often appealed to the theory of the cooling earth to explain why the Creator had not formed higher animals during the early periods of the planet's development.[1] Only as the conditions improved towards the modern state had God been able to introduce the higher elements in His plan of Creation, culminating in mankind. Catastrophism was thus built upon an inherently developmental model of the earth's physical history. The notion of cooling also gave a perfect explanation of why earlier geological events were more violent than those of today, thus validating the appeal to catastrophes as natural 'punctuation marks' in the earth's history. Lyell's uniformitarianism challenged not only the appeal to catastrophes, but also the developmentalism of the cooling earth theory.

Palaeontologists accepted that new populations appeared in the fossil record after a catastrophe had wiped out the earth's previous inhabitants. But where did the new species come from? Cuvier's theory of migrations was never taken seriously as an explanation of the appearance of new species at various points in the fossil record. His British followers simply assumed that the apparently abrupt appearance of new forms in the strata indicated that they had been miraculously created to replace those wiped out by the catastrophes which separated the periods of rock formation one from another. All species were new creations, but at certain points in the earth's history, the introduction of higher classes provided clear evidence of major steps forward in the divine plan. As more fossils were discovered, however, it seemed possible that at least some of the gaps might be filled in. Radicals such as Grant began to argue that the record would ultimately confirm the existence of a continuous progressive trend as predicted by Lamarck's theory. Simple creationism was no longer acceptable in the face of growing fossil evidence suggesting some form of regularity in the history of life. The conservatives thus needed to identify those crucial upward steps that could be defended as clear instances of the Creator's intervention, while conceding that there might be regular patterns of development in between.

One of Richard Owen's first major contributions to this anti-transmutationist form of progressionism came in the 'Report on British Fossil Reptiles' which he delivered to the British Association for the Advancement of Science in 1840 and 1841. In the second part of this report, Owen coined the term 'dinosaur' to denote the great terrestrial reptiles such as *Megalosaurus* and *Iguanodon*. Here, he claimed, the fossil record revealed a group of reptiles quite different from any alive today. This was a valid point, but Owen's definition of

---

[1] On early-nineteenth-century progressionism, see Bowler, *Fossils and Progress*, ch. 2.

the dinosaurs was clearly part of his campaign against Grant and the transmutationists.[2] He went out of his way to stress that the dinosaurs were more advanced than the modern reptiles (a view which may anticipate the claim by some modern palaeontologists that the dinosaurs were warm-blooded). Yet they appeared *before* the lower reptiles in the fossil record, showing that the history of the class revealed the very opposite of a continuous progression towards the mammals.

> The evidence acquired by the researches which are detailed in the body of this Report, permit of no other conclusion than that the different species of Reptiles were suddenly introduced upon the earth's surface, although it demonstrates a certain systematic regularity in the order of their appearance. Upon the whole, they make a progressive approach to the organization of the existing species, yet not

Plate 18　Life-sized reconstruction of the carnivorous dinosaur *Megalosaurus* designed by Richard Owen and erected at Crystal Palace along with many other representations of extinct species. It was later discovered that *Megalosaurus* in fact walked only on its hind legs.

---

[2] Owen, 'Report on British Fossil Reptiles'. See Desmond, 'Designing the Dinosaurs' and *Archetypes and Ancestors*, ch. 4.

by an uninterrupted succession of approximating steps. Neither is the progression one of ascent, for the Reptiles have not begun by the perrenibranchiate type of organization, by which, at the present day, they most closely approach the fishes; nor have they terminated at the opposite extreme, viz., at the Dinosaurian order, where we know that the Reptilian type of structure made the nearest approach to the mammals.[3]

Note that Owen concedes some regularities in the sequence of development, but insists that these are not of the kind that would support a continuous progression. Indeed, since the dinosaurs came first, he had actually shown that there was a decline in the overall level of reptilian development. Within the next couple of decades, amphibians would be discovered below the dinosaurs, thus destroying Owen's generalization. But in the 1840s he could quite legitimately claim that his new order of fossil reptiles completely undermined the evidence for gradual progress.

Another exponent of discontinuity in the ascent of life was the Swiss naturalist Louis Agassiz, who went on to become one of the founding fathers of American biology. Agassiz – like Owen – was deeply influenced by German nature-philosophy, with its vision of the material world as the expression of an underlying unity originating in the mind of God. As an expert on fossil fish, he became convinced that there was a parallel between the geological history of that class and the development of a modern fish embryo towards maturity. The fish of the Old Red Sandstone resembled the embryos of modern fish. More significantly, the whole history of vertebrate life on earth paralleled the growth of the human embryo towards maturity. Agassiz knew that there were many specialized branches leading away from the 'main line' of development, but he was convinced that the human embryo passed through stages corresponding to the ages of fish, reptiles and mammals in the fossil record.

This advance was no mere response to the cooling of the earth, however. For Agassiz, the similarity between the pattern of development exhibited by the human embryo and that exhibited by the history of life on earth confirmed the existence of a rational God who wished to give us a symbol of mankind's position at the head of creation: 'The history of the earth proclaims its Creator. It tells us that the object

---

[3] Owen, 'Report on British Fossil Reptiles', p. 202. The 'perrenibranchiate reptiles' are those amphibians which retain their gills and are thus closest to the fish. (The amphibians were not treated as a distinct class in the early nineteenth century.)

and term of creation is man. He is announced in nature from the first appearance of organized beings; and each important modification in the whole series of these beings is a step toward the definitive term of the development of organic life.'[4] Unlike Chambers, however, Agassiz was convinced that the advance of life occurred through a series of discontinuous steps. The history of each class was not a gradual progression toward the next, so the actual appearance of new classes had to be seen as the direct product of the Creator's will. Nor was this position incompatible with his concern for the embryological analogy: we are so used to thinking of the growth of the human individual as a continuous process that we forget the discontinuous nature of many species' development. Metamorphosis advances the tadpole or the caterpillar to an entirely new phase of growth, and for Agassiz the appearance of a new class was the equivalent of the transition from the tadpole to the frog.

The stonemason-turned-geologist-and-journalist, Hugh Miller, came into contact with Agassiz's philosophy when the latter was called in to describe the fossil fish of the Old Red Sandstone of northern Scotland. Miller was deeply influenced by Agassiz's vision of progress, and his native religious sentiments led him to place even greater emphasis on the discontinuity of the advance. Miller's book, *The Old Red Sandstone* of 1841, was a popular exposition of the new discoveries and their implications. Where the transmutationist expected the fish to progress in the course of their history as a class, the fossil record showed that there was no such advance. If the first fish had cartilaginous rather than bony skeletons, their nervous system was as fully developed as that of their modern counterparts.

> Now it is a geological fact, that it is fish of the higher orders that appear first on the stage, and that they are found to occupy exactly the same level during the vast period represented by five succeeding formations. There is no progression. If fish rose into reptiles, it must have been by sudden transformation, – it must have been as if a man who had stood still for half a lifetime should bestir himself all at once, and take seven leagues at a stride. There is no getting rid of miracle in the case – there is no alternative

[4] Agassiz, 'On the Succession and Development of Organized Beings', p. 399. On the parallel between individual growth and the development of life on earth, see Gould, *Ontogeny and Phylogeny*, esp. ch. 3. On Agassiz's life and work see Lurie, *Louis Agassiz*.

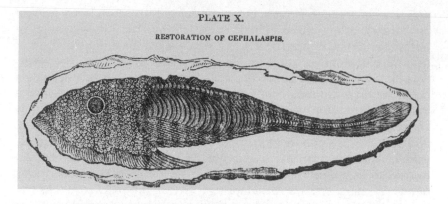

PLATE X.

RESTORATION OF CEPHALASPIS.

Plate 19   *Cephalaspis.*
This armoured fish from the upper Old Red Sandstone
(Devonian) of Scotland illustrated the bizarre character of the
first vertebrates. Nevertheless, Miller insisted that it was a fully
developed fish, showing that the vertebrate type had not evolved
graduall*y* from an invertebrate ancestor. Modern evolutionists
still have no fossils to illustrate the sequence by which the first
vertebrates evolved.
From Hugh Miller, *The Old Red Sandstone*, plate 10

between creation and metamorphosis. The infidel substitutes
progression for Deity; Geology robs him of his god.[5]

After the publication of the *Vestiges of Creation*, Miller repeated his
arguments in another book, *Footprints of the Creator*. He conceded that
belief in a Creator who allowed His plan to unfold by natural law
rather than by miracle was not a step towards atheism. But he insisted
that the true Christian must retain the idea of divine intervention in
order to sustain the unique spiritual character of mankind. In fact the
fossil record showed that all progress worked through the sudden
appearance of a new level of creation followed by a subsequent
decline or degeneration.

> The general advance in creation has been incalculably
> great. The lower divisions of the vertebrata precede
> the higher; – the fish preceded the reptile, the reptile
> preceded the bird, and the bird preceded the mammiferous
> quadrupeds. And yet, is there one of these great divisions
> in which, in at least some prominent feature, the present,

[5] Miller, *The Old Red Sandstone*, pp. 44–5.

through this mysterious element of degradation, is not inferior to the past?[6]

Miller drew a comparison with the fall of man, in which God's fairest creation became morally lost and degraded. Thus human history and the history of life on earth were linked together – but via a cyclic model of development which made it quite clear that the origin of mankind represented the last and greatest step forward in the plan of creation.

The claim that the development of life occurred through a series of distinct waves or phases continued to be used as an argument against transmutation even after the *Origin of Species* appeared. In 1860, John Phillips's *Life on Earth* surveyed the fossil record and concluded against transmutation or any form of continuous development. Phillips had introduced the modern terms Palaeozoic, Mesozoic and Cainozoic to denote the three great eras in the history of life, and he saw each era as a separate phase in the history of life. In each era, certain characteristic groups had multiplied to a great level of diversity and then declined to extinction in preparation for the next wave. In each era, 'the characteristic and prevalent fauna begins at a minimum, rises to a maximum, and dies away to a final minimum, to be followed by another system having similar phases.' Phillips also gave a diagram showing the wave-like character of living development.[7]

These efforts to show that the history of life follows a cyclic pattern of development suggest an obvious parallel with the model of history proposed by Thomas Arnold and the liberal Anglicans. In the cyclic scheme, progress occurs only through the sudden appearance of higher types of organization, whether in organic species or in human societies. Subsequent developments within each stage might follow a regular pattern, but that pattern did not lead on towards the next upward step. Any early progress was followed by an inevitable decline and eventually by replacement with a new and higher type which in turn underwent its own cycle of rise and fall. Progress was the result of creative intervention, and the laws of natural development led only to stagnation or decay. As with the cyclic model of human development, the theory of discontinuous progress in the history of life on earth was designed to highlight the need for something more than animal or human effort at the start of each new phase. As evolutionism became more popular, the need to emphasize a

---

[6] Miller, *Footprints of the Creator*, p. 179.
[7] Phillips, *Life on Earth*, pp. 64 and 66.

discontinuity marking the appearance of mankind became all the more pressing. The phases in the history of life and the history of mankind might follow the cyclic pattern, but the fact that all the cycles were to some extent distinct episodes made it impossible to argue that human progress was merely a continuation of animal evolution.

Although Miller and Phillips seem to have accepted the need for miraculous creation at numerous points in the history of life, other naturalists were willing to explore the possibility that nonmiraculous forces might be at work even here. As long as the history of life was divided into distinct episodes, it might still be possible to think in terms of some form of natural development without falling into the trap of outright materialism. The most powerful force encouraging moves in this direction was the 'transcendental anatomy' that became popular both in Germany and in France during the early decades of the nineteenth century. The transcendental anatomist sought the underlying unity of type linking all the diverse species within a group, and was thus predisposed to see natural relationships between species. At first, this was greeted by British naturalists as yet another form of materialism – but the concept of an underlying unity of type had obvious possibilities as the source of a new argument for God's presence in nature. In the end, even naturalists of quite conservative opinions were able to use this approach as a way of arguing that the cycles of living development followed patterns that were recognizable and might even be due to a natural unfolding of the potentials built into life by its Creator. Some of their suggestions were to become integral parts of modern evolutionism.

Cuvier had always opposed Lamarck's theory of continuous progression, but in the 1820s he was forced to confront a new and quite different challenge. This stemmed from the transcendental anatomy of Geoffroy Saint Hilaire, who set out to unify the whole animal kingdom by showing that all the distinct specific forms could be seen as manifestations of a basic underlying pattern.[8] Because he was able to see the morphological links between related forms, Geoffroy was willing to argue that one species might actually be transformed into another by a sudden change in the direction of the growth process. When the reptiles of the Mesozoic were exposed to new environmental conditions, the growth of future generations was distorted or diverted into a new channel, leading to the production of the modern reptiles and birds. This was a theory of transmutation quite different to Lamarck's, since it relied not on continuous progress, but on the sudden transformation of one variant of the basic

[8] See Appel, *The Cuvier–Geoffroy Debate.*

vertebrate pattern into another. For Geoffroy and his followers, evolution took place by saltations or sudden mutations and gave rise to a divergent pattern of development rather than a linear progression.

Radical naturalists supported Geoffroy because his theory implied the possibility that mankind might be just another variant of the basic vertebrate pattern. In Britain, this position was developed by Robert Knox, who included in his *Races of Men* of 1850 a powerful statement of the view that the races have absolutely distinct mental and physical characteristics (see chapter 4 above). Knox praised Geoffroy's search for the unity of natural forms and emphasized that he argued for the appearance of new variants upon the basic type by natural generation.[9] Noting that a similar view had been adopted in the *Vestiges of Creation*, Knox went on to reject the claim that the successive new types appeared in accordance with a law of progress. His implication was that new species (and, of course, new races of men) were merely new variants produced by the action of changed conditions upon the growth process. This was made explicit in the material added to the second edition of 1862, where he argued that 'the young of every species is a generic animal, having a form so modifiable by altered circumstances as to assume under these alterations a distinct specific adult form.'[10]

In the post-Darwinian era, the theory of evolution by saltations would become important to many conservative naturalists (see below), but when first proposed by Geoffroy and Knox it was far too radical. Yet the basic relationships assumed by transcendental anatomy were of interest to those who wanted to resist radical materialism, because the idea of an underlying unity of organic type could be exploited as evidence of a divine plan linking the apparent diversity of nature into a single whole. In Germany, transcendentalism had developed in a less radical way that used the unity of organic form to argue that the whole of nature was an expression of the divine Mind. Richard Owen now realized that such an approach offered a means of updating the traditional idea of divine creation without giving ground to the materialists. He was determined to oppose the theory of linear progression, and – as Knox himself pointed out – Geoffroy's 'unity of type' implied a divergent rather than a linear scheme of relationships. Ignoring the possibility of sudden transmutation, at least for the time being, Owen now proposed a new form of natural theology in which God's handiwork would be seen not in the adaptation of each species to its environment, but in the overall unity that lay behind the adaptive

[9] Knox, *The Races of Men*, p. 176.
[10] Ibid, p. 594.

variations of the vertebrate type. At the same time, he began to see divergence as a clue to understanding the nonprogressive trends that were now being discovered in the fossil record.

In 1848 Owen proposed his concept of the vertebrate 'archetype', an idealized representation of the most basic or primitive vertebrate form. All real vertebrate species were but specialized modifications of this basic type. Despite its idealist foundations, the archetype theory allowed Owen to promote the important concept of 'homology', a term he introduced to denote cases in which the same skeletal structure is used for different purposes by different species. Thus the human hand, for instance, contains exactly the same pattern of bones as the wing of the bat and the paddle of the whale. In his *On the Nature of Limbs* of 1849, Owen argued that such underlying similarities can only be seen as evidence that the diversity of nature has been built upon a rational plan established by its Creator. In the conclusion of this work he came close to evolutionism himself by hinting that the variants upon the archetype might unfold in the course of geological time by 'secondary', i.e. nonmiraculous, causes.

> The archetypical idea was manifested in the flesh, under divers such modifications, upon this planet, long prior to the existence of those animal species that actually exemplify it. To what natural laws or secondary causes the orderly succession and progression of such organic phenomena may have been committed we are as yet ignorant. But if, without derogation of the Divine power, we may conceive the existence of such ministers, and personify them by the term 'Nature', we learn from the past history of our globe that she has advanced with slow and stately steps, guided by the archetypical light, amidst the wreck of worlds, from the first embodiment of the Vertebrate idea under its Ichthyic vestment, until it became arrayed in the glorious garb of the human form.[11]

Lest this seems to give the whole game away to the progressionists, Owen's admission should be viewed in the light of his already established position that the appearance of each new class must represent a sudden manifestation of creative power, lifting life on to a

---

[11] Owen, *On the Nature of Limbs*, p. 89. For a recent assessment of Owen's attitude towards evolution, see Richards, 'A Question of Property Rights'. On the idealist version of the argument from design, see Bowler, 'Darwinism and the Argument from Design'.

new plane. He was now prepared to accept that the developments taking place *within* each class followed a regular pattern indicating creation by law rather than by miracle – but only because he had already established that there was no simple overall progression that would allow mankind to be seen as merely the end-product of a continuous line of ascent. Even in this highly qualified form, however, Owen's veiled support for transmutation aroused hostility among some conservatives, and he said no more on the origin of species until after Darwin's book was published.

Despite evading the issue of transmutation in the 1850s, Owen continued to think about the pattern of living development. Along with the physiologist W. B. Carpenter, he now saw that it would be possible to create a new kind of parallel between individual growth and the development of life on earth.[12] The German embryologist Karl Ernst von Baer had challenged the simple image of growth as an ascent through a linear hierarchy of animal forms. Chambers's idea that the lower animals were merely immature or underdeveloped manifestations of the human form was wrong. Each living organism grows by acquiring the specialized characteristics of its own species, and the 'higher' animals do not pass through stages identical to the adult forms of 'lower' ones. Owen and Carpenter realized that much of the fossil evidence for development within each class showed a parallel with the trend towards specialization postulated in von Baer's embryology. This trend corresponded neither to progression nor to degeneration; instead, the class began with very generalized types, from which radiated many lines of specialization, each adapting to a particular way of life. The earliest mammals, for instance, were all unspecialized, but the fossil record showed a series of lines diverging towards the highly specialized modern species. Owen suggested a similar pattern of divergence within each of the classes which had succeeded one another as the dominant forms of vertebrate life. The lines of specialization in the lower classes advanced not towards the next highest class, but towards more specialized modifications at their own level. The appearance of new classes was *not* an inevitable outcome of developments taking place within the preceding classes. Owen was thus still in a position to accept gradual change, even transmutation, within each class, while denying that the main upward steps in the history of life were a product of the same trend.

Owen remained convinced that divergent evolution represented the unpacking of potentials built into the class by its Creator. The

---

[12] See Ospovat, 'The Influence of Karl Ernst von Baer's Embryology', and Bowler, *Fossils and Progress*, ch. 5.

vertebrate archetype was an idealized model of the most unspecialized vertebrate form – a means of understanding the underlying unity of the Creator's plan. In this respect, Owen's theory of divergence exactly parallels the model of historical development used by Max Müller and the philologists to highlight the mystical archetypical foundation of each language group. But Darwin was able to incorporate Owen's evidence for divergence into his own, more materialistic theory, because specialization for the species' way of life was exactly the kind of trend that natural selection would be expected to produce.[13] The critical problem remained the origin of the classes themselves. As Owen pointed out, specialization did not represent an ascent towards the next highest class, so progress was not a mere continuation of the normal historical trend. Later evolutionists even came to see specialization as a trap into which most species were led as a prelude to extinction – a specialized form is highly efficient within a stable environment, but is incapable of adjusting to major disturbances of its surroundings. As the Lamarckian palaeontologist E. D. Cope pointed out, only those species which avoid this trap and retain a more generalized structure have any hope of advancing to form the nucleus of an entirely new class.

The origin of classes thus remained a crucial point of dispute between the exponents of continuous and of cyclic development. Darwin had no time for mystical archetypes and was convinced that the evolution of each new class must take place by the same process as that responsible for evolution within classes. In certain circumstances, natural selection acting upon the remaining unspecialized species of one class must drive them towards a higher level of organization so that they become the pioneers of the next class. When a successful new group appears, it will obviously cause a decline in the membership of rival groups, but that decline will be a result of normal competition, not of a mysterious parallel with individual birth and death. Progressive evolution might be unusual, but it must occasionally be possible under the normal laws of organic change. There could be no exceptions to the rule of adaptive evolution, no interruptions of 'higher' powers responsible for advancing life to a new level, and no mysterious cycles of life and death.

For Spencer and Haeckel, of course, the occasional progressive episodes leading to the production of a new vertebrate class could be fitted together to define the main line of evolution towards mankind, thus concealing the fact that such steps were really quite anomalous. But for Owen and his conservative backers, a distinction between the

---

[13] See Ospovat, *The Development of Darwin's Theory.*

normal and the progressive phases of evolution was necessary to allow the appearance of mankind to be seen as the last of the great surges forward that confirmed the involvement of the Creator in the evolutionary process. The sequences of progressive steps might represent the main line of development, but the steps must be discontinuous in a way that would preserve the idea of creative surges in history. Darwin might convert the world to evolutionism, but there were many naturalists anxious to preserve a cyclic model of progress that would leave room for occasional steps or breaks in the advance of life.

Growth and Decline

Owen's reluctance to speak out on transmutation during the 1850s ensured that it was Darwin's *Origin of Species* which precipitated the scientific community's conversion to evolutionism. Once incorporated into the Spencerian philosophy, Darwin's theory of continuous, natural development was an ideal foundation upon which the liberals could build their ideology of progress through individual effort. But there remained a strong conservative opposition, which was now forced to admit that the concept of evolution as the unfolding of God's plan formed the only plausible alternative to Darwinian 'materialism'. Owen was at last free to speak out, becoming the leader of a group of naturalists who resisted Darwinism by trying to show that evolution exhibited regularities which could not be explained by a simple process of adaptation. This group was never as well organized as the Darwinians, partly because Owen himself had an abrasive personality which prevented him from properly exploiting his academic eminence. Nevertheless, the group published widely and ensured that the scientific weaknesses of simple progressionism were not ignored. Certain aspects of the cyclic model of development thus survived into late-Victorian biology. When we recollect that in the study of human history and prehistory, the empire-builders of the late nineteenth century continued to argue for distinct racial or cultural episodes in the rise of mankind, we should not be surprised to find biologists still upholding the claim that evolution is a discontinuous or cyclic process. Like the great empires of the past, each of the vertebrate classes had had its period of glory before being displaced by the next highest manifestation of the Creator's power.

The earliest efforts to construct a non-Darwinian form of evolutionism were made by naturalists who quite explicitly wanted to retain the belief that God's power can be seen directly in the pattern of living development. This was 'theistic evolutionism', in which the allegedly haphazard mechanism of change postulated by Darwin was to be disproved by showing that evolution displayed regularities that could only represent the unfolding of a divine plan.[14] Individual efforts to cope with an ever-changing environment were not enough to explain why evolution should follow an artificially regular pattern both within each class and, more importantly, in the production of new and higher classes. These naturalists conceded that creation took place by 'law', but they saw the laws of nature as forces imposed by the Creator's will, capable of driving evolution in a preconceived direction whatever the demands of the environment. In effect, Chambers's vision of a divinely planned law of development had been uncoupled from simple progressionism so that it could become the foundation for conservative resistance to Darwinism. Owen and his followers were still determined to show that mankind was not the end-product of a continuous progressive trend, and for this they needed a more complex model of how the advance of life had taken place.

Owen wrote a bitterly critical review of Darwin's *Origin* which has misled some historians into treating him as an anti-evolutionist. But in fact the growing acceptance of evolutionism in the 1860s allowed Owen to come out of the closet and openly proclaim his support for transmutation as the mechanism by which the divine plan unfolded. In the third volume of his *Anatomy of the Vertebrates* (1868) he advanced his theory of 'derivation': 'Derivation holds that every species changes in time, by virtue of inherent tendencies thereto. "Natural Selection" holds that no such change can take place without the influence of altered external circumstances. "Derivation" sees among the effects of the innate tendency to change irrespective of altered circumstances, a manifestation of creative power in the variety and beauty of the results.'[15] Evolution is not an open-ended response to the environment because variation is directed along channels defined by predispositions built into living things by their Creator. The best line of evidence against Darwin was the regularity of the resulting developments, as displayed in the fossil record and in the beauty of modern species.

Perhaps the greatest exponent of theistic evolutionism was Owen's disciple, the anatomist St George Jackson Mivart, whose *Genesis of Species* of 1871 launched a barrage of arguments against natural selection, many of which are still used by modern creationists.[16]

[14] On theistic evolutionism, see Bowler, *The Eclipse of Darwinism*, ch. 3.
[15] Owen, *Anatomy of the Vertebrates*, III, p. 808.
[16] On Mivart's critique of Darwinism see Gruber, *A Conscience in Conflict*, and Vorzimmer, *Charles Darwin: the Years of Controversy*.

Mivart was a Catholic, deeply concerned about the materialistic implications of Darwinism. His attack on the theory was so comprehensive that it was seen as an attempt to discredit Darwin personally, and he was ostracized from the group. (Some theistic evolutionists retained links with the Darwinians – not as surprising as it sounds, given that Huxley also preferred directed evolution.) Apart from attacking the plausibility of the selection mechanism, Mivart pointed to numerous patterns in the development of life which seemed incompatible with any theory based purely on adaptation to the environment. Quoting Owen on derivation, Mivart supported the view that the environment might at best serve as a trigger to elicit changes whose real cause was an inbuilt tendency for species to develop in a pre-ordained direction.

At first sight it might be thought that Owen and Mivart were conceding too much. Even if the regularity of evolutionary trends precluded an explanation in terms of natural selection, surely the very fact of continuous development threatened that bastion of orthodoxy, the spiritual status of mankind. In fact, both naturalists were determined to show that the human race was not merely the end-product of a continuous progressive trend. In the early 1860s, Owen debated with Huxley on the relationship between humans and apes, with Owen insisting that the human brain contained structures that were totally lacking in the brains of apes. Eventually Huxley's *Man's Place in Nature* demolished Owen's arguments, but the basic issue was not so easily settled. Mivart's *Man and Apes* of 1873 attacked Huxley's position from a new direction, arguing that the relationships between humans and the various ape species were far too complex for them to be arranged into an evolutionary hierarchy. The relationships form a network, not a ladder, suggesting that if mankind *had* evolved from the apes, it was by a process far more complex than a simple progression.

Mivart's views on human origins illustrate one of the directions in which the theistic evolutionists were moving in their effort to concede the possibility of natural development without giving the whole game away to liberal progressionism. He now insisted that there was no single genealogical tree linking all the vertebrate classes. Instead, evolution should be visualized as an interlocking grove of trees, with several different trees often producing similar forms which the Darwinians mistakenly assumed to be linked by common descent from a single ancestor.[17] Development was often parallel rather than divergent, with independent lines being driven in the same direction

[17] On this aspect of Mivart's work, see Desmond, *Archetypes and Ancestors*, ch. 6.

by the mysterious inbuilt forces that direct variation. Thus the human race might not be closely related to the apes, since these animals could have acquired independently the characters by which they resemble us. Mivart and Owen also suggested that evolution was saltative rather than continuous. Just as Geoffroy had argued several decades earlier, they now supposed that evolution worked in sudden spurts, when a stimulus from the environment finally became strong enough to trigger off the next phase in the developmental pattern built into the species. Mivart compared evolution to a polyhedron rolling along from face to face – a series of linked but discrete events rather than a continuous motion.[18] Again, this argument had the implication that humans did not arise from apes by a continuous progression.

The claim that evolution is sometimes parallel rather than divergent led Owen and Mivart to a distinctly anti-Darwinian view of life's history, which turned out to be surprisingly fruitful as a guide to the fossil record. As Adrian Desmond has shown, their theory led them to visualize each vertebrate class not as the collective descendants of a single 'pioneer' species, but as a grade of organization that might be reached independently by a number of evolutionary lines.[19] Once a new grade was reached, the line might throw off a number of branches diverging towards various specializations, as Owen had shown in the 1850s, but the link through into the next class would have to advance in a direction that was not governed by this adaptive radiation. The reptile grade, for instance, had been passed through independently by the dinosaurs, on the way to becoming birds, and by the 'mammal-like reptiles' of the early Mesozoic which had, of course, gone to become the ancestors of the mammals. Inspired by this view, Owen correctly appreciated the significance of the mammal-like reptiles then being discovered in the rocks of South Africa – fossils which were ignored by Huxley because he dismissed the idea of a reptilian 'grade' as idealist moonshine. Mivart also developed the view, taken seriously by many later palaeontologists, that the marsupials and the placental mammals are derived from discrete lines that have separately reached the mammalian grade of organization.[20]

Owen and Mivart had thus preserved the idea that progressive evolution leading to the origin of new classes was the product of a

[18] Mivart, *Genesis of Species*, pp. 109–10. Note that Mivart explictly connected the forces that control variation with those governing individual growth; see his 'On the Development of the Individual and of the Species'.

[19] Desmond, *Archetypes and Ancestors*, ch. 6, esp. pp. 193–201.

[20] Mivart, 'On the Possible Dual Origin of the Mammalia'.

different form of directed evolution to that responsible for the adaptive radiation within each class. On this model, a single progressive line could ascend through a series of grades, each representing a recognizably distinct phase in the hierarchy of organic development. Although the concept of a sudden burst of creative energy at the beginning of each class had now been abandoned in favour of continuous development, the cyclic model of history had been preserved by treating the origin of classes as a unique phenomenon that could not be explained in terms of adaptive evolution. The mysterious forces that governed progressive evolution had laid down a pre-ordained pattern that would be followed by many different lines, each in turn passing through the phases of development defined by the grades or classes. The critical episodes marking the transition to a new grade were each the start of something entirely new in the history of life – a position that would still give comfort to anyone wishing to treat the origin of mankind as a unique event rather than just another response to the environment.

It may be significant that in his 'Natural Theology of the Future' of 1871, Charles Kingsley praised Mivart's *Genesis of Species* as exactly the kind of evolution theory required by his view of nature as a manifestation of the divine power.[21] Kingsley's best known accounts of evolution, in his *Water Babies*, seem to convey a strong Darwinian or Spencerian message by emphasizing the importance of effort and the failure of those who do not measure up to what is required of them. But we know from his approach to human history (see chapter 2 above) that Kingsley saw effort as important only in so far as it contributed to the realization of the nation's destiny. It is thus not surprising that he preferred a view of evolution in which the Creator's purpose was more clearly apparent. In 1863 he welcomed the advent of evolutionism because it got rid of the idea of an interfering God and forced everyone 'to choose between the absolute empire of accident, and a living, immanent, ever-working God.'[22] The Spencerians were anxious to show that their version of progress was not the 'absolute empire of accident', but many conservatives saw the natural selection of random variation as implying exactly that principle, and Kingsley may well have preferred the theistic evolutionists' vision of the history of life as the unfolding of a divine plan through a series of distinct progressive episodes.

[21] Kingsley, 'The Natural Theology of the Future', reprinted in Kingsley, *Scientific Lectures and Essays*, pp. 313–36, see p. 313n.
[22] Kingsley to F. D. Maurice, quoted in *Charles Kingsley: His Letters and Memories of his Life*, II, p. 171.

An inevitable consequence of the cyclic model's emphasis on the distinction between progressive and divergent evolution was a recognition of the inevitability of each group eventually losing its place at the head of creation in favour of something more advanced. Some evolutionists became positively fascinated by the image of the rise and fall of classes in the history of life. Perhaps the strangest manifestation of this fascination was the theory of 'racial senility' proposed by the American palaeontologist Alpheus Hyatt. As a student of Agassiz at Harvard, Hyatt found Darwinism implausible; but he welcomed the idea of evolution and tried to reconcile it with Agassiz's idealist view of creation. In 1866 he used his studies of fossil Ammonites to argue that the evolution of the whole order followed a pattern identical to that seen in the life cycle of an individual organism.[23] The earliest members were simple, youthful forms, which gradually evolved into flamboyant mature forms when the Ammonites dominated the ancient seas.

But Hyatt did not stop here: he realized that the individual organism declines from maturity towards old age and death, and he was convinced that he could see a similar decline into racial senility and extinction in his fossil invertebrates. The last Ammonites recapitulated the whole rise and fall of the class in the course of their growth, preserved in the inner segments of their coiled shells. In later papers Hyatt argued that each class is born with a certain amount of evolutionary energy, which it uses to conquer its environment as it advances towards maturity. Hyatt was a prominent member of the American school of neo-Lamarckism, which stressed the purposeful character of evolution for much the same reasons as Samuel Butler. But unlike Butler, the Americans insisted that Lamarckian evolution must exhibit regular trends advancing towards a purposeful goal. Hyatt extended this theory by supposing that a group's evolutionary energy eventually becomes exhausted; the group can no longer cope with environmental challenges and it degenerates back to simple forms which are the inevitable prelude to extinction. Hyatt suggested that all groups undergo the same pattern of birth, growth, decline and extinction, after which they are replaced by new types formed through some mysterious injection of a new supply of creative energy.

The Darwinists found it difficult to explain the apparently degenerative trends that Hyatt found in some invertebrates, and in

---

[23] Hyatt, 'On the Parallelism between the Different Stages of Life in the Individual and those in the Entire Group of the Moluscous Order Tetrabranchiata'. On Hyatt's theory see Bowler, *Eclipse of Darwinism*, ch. 6, and Gould, *Ontogeny and Phylogeny*, ch. 4.

the later decades of the century many vertebrate palaeontologists also took up the idea of racial senility in a somewhat different form. The theory of 'orthogenesis' was based on the assumption that each line of evolutionary development acquires a kind of momentum which carries it inexorably forward whatever the adaptive consequences of the resulting changes.[24] In many cases, the results appeared to be disastrous: structures such as horns continued to grow in size to a point where they became so large that the animals could no longer function and the line became extinct. Like Hyatt, the supporters of orthogenesis saw the evolution of each class as an inevitable cycle of progress and decline, a pattern through which all members of the class advanced in parallel, driven by forces built into their very constitution. Progress occurred only through the occasional episodes when a new class was formed, but within each class the lines of development led towards increased specialization, overdevelopment of once-useful structures, and extinction. Even the rise and fall of the dinosaurs was attributed to this inevitable cycle of growth and decay.

At the turn of the century, one of the leading exponents of orthogenesis was Arthur Smith Woodward, Keeper of Geology at the Natural History Museum in London. In his studies of the pattern of evolution in many vertebrate groups, Woodward was convinced that he could see the operations of a force directing variation, an 'inherent property in living things, which is as definite as that of crystallization in inorganic substances.'[25] He applied the same theory to explain the origin of the human brain, pointing out that in this case there could be no harmful effect from overdevelopment.

> Now the study of many kinds of fossils has shown that when, in successive generations, one part of the body begins to increase in size or complication much more rapidly than other parts, this increase rarely stops until it becomes excessive. As a rule, it passes the limit of utility, becomes a hindrance, and even contributes to the extermination of the race of animals in which it occurs. In the case of the brain, however, a tendency to overgrowth might become an advantage, and it seems reasonable to imagine that such an overgrowth in the early apelike animals eventually led to the complete domination of the brain, which is the special hallmark of man.[26]

[24] On the theory of orthogenesis, see Bowler, *Eclipse of Darwinism*, ch. 7.
[25] Woodward, 'President's Address', p. 468.
[26] Woodward, *Guide to the Fossil Remains of Man*, p. 3. On orthogenesis and theories of human origins, see Bowler, *Theories of Human Evolution*, ch. 8.

Thus, the human mind – which Woodward agreed had ushered in a new era in evolution – was a product of the last and greatest of those mysterious variation-trends which from time to time had raised evolution on to a higher plane.

Nowadays Woodward is remembered only for his involvement in the Piltdown affair of 1912, when an ape jaw and a human cranium were at first attributed to a 'dawn man', *Eoanthropus*.[27] There can be little doubt that he and other palaeoanthropologists were taken in by these deliberately planted 'fossils' because they wanted to find an early form of humanity in which the brain was developing faster than any other part of the body. The discovery fitted in nicely with Woodward's theory of a trend towards brain expansion, because it seemed to reveal an early form of humanity in which the cranium was more highly developed than the rest of the anatomy. (Nationalism may also have been a factor; unlike the French and Germans, British scientists had found no really ancient specimens of humanity on their home territory.)

Both the Piltdown discovery and the theory of directed evolution helped to promote the growing belief that human prehistory could be interpreted as a series of racial conquests (see chapter 4 above). We know that Woodward shared the view of Sollas and Keith that new and higher forms of mankind had appeared from time to time, and had spread out to conquer their inferior predecessors.[28] We also know that Sollas and Keith shared Woodward's suspicion of natural selection as an explanation of progressive evolution. All three preferred to see the purposeful component of evolution as the product of some mysterious force, possibly linked to individual growth. The theory of parallel evolution by orthogenesis formed the perfect basis for such an interpretation, since it implied that many different lines of primate evolution were independently striving towards the human form. The Neanderthals were one such line, eventually displaced by higher types (which might or might not have evolved from 'Piltdown man'). Nature had experimented with the production of various forms of humanity, allowing racial conflict to determine which, in the end, would inherit the earth. Far from being a form of social Darwinism, this emphasis on racial conflict arose directly from the alternative concept of directed evolution. The theory of orthogenesis thus upheld a cyclic view of progress in two

[27] The classic account of the Piltdown affair is Weiner, *The Piltdown Forgery*; for a recent survey see Blinderman, *The Piltdown Inquest*.

[28] This is especially clear in his last work, written much later: Woodward, *The Earliest Englishman*.

quite different ways: it allowed each stage of prehuman evolution to be seen as the rise and fall of a distinct group or family, and it supported the 'waves of conquest' interpretation of human prehistory that became so popular in the early years of the twentieth century.

Thus we have come full circle in our study of the cyclic model of development. The palaeontologists' theory of parallel, orthogenetic evolution was used to support the ideology of racial conquest that was the end-product of the same model when applied to human history and prehistory. Far from seeing the triumph of Darwinian or Spencerian progressionism, the late nineteenth century experienced a resurgence in all fields of historical study of the rival, more conservative view of development. By uncoupling progress from the individual's response to its environment, and making it instead a product of mysterious and episodic forces built into living matter, the cyclic model of evolution sought to undermine the liberal position. The history of life exhibited phases of development over which living things themselves had no control – just as human history saw the rise and fall of the empires founded by each race as it took its turn as the driving force of the Creator's plan. Species, races and civilizations rose and fell at the command of the divine will. The prevalence of orthogenetic theories in late-Victorian evolutionism parallels the contemporary emergence of imperialism, both trends confirming the survival of a model of history whose origins lay in an idealist and hence more conservative value-system. Darwinian or Spencerian progressionism was a passing phase, although the image of racial conflict used in later decades has misled some historians into thinking that 'social Darwinism' was still all the rage. In fact, as we have seen throughout this study, the cyclic model of progress was equally capable of generating indifference to those who were pushed aside in the advance towards higher things.

Epilogue:
Progress and Degeneration

The three sections of this book have shown how the Victorians' knowledge of the past increased in scope as the study of history was extended into human prehistory (philology, archaeology and anthropology) and into the development of life on earth (palaeontology and biological evolutionism). We have also seen how, at each level of penetration into the past, the same basic models of development came up for debate. To a large extent this was an inevitable consequence of the desire to create a complete philosophy of history. A particular theory of human progress soon came to depend for its conceptual foundations upon a compatible interpretation of the origin of mankind, and hence of the history of life on earth. The parallels were also a consequence of the theories' ideological perspectives: each model of progress had definite implications for the Victorians' views on human nature and hence for their attitudes towards change in society. It was thus all the more necessary to ensure consistency of interpretation across the whole spectrum of historical development.

Those historians who saw the growth of free-enterprise commercialism as the driving force of progress paved the way for a social evolutionism in which the attainment of middle-class values was the last step in the ascent of a linear hierarchy of developmental stages. In principle, the whole human race must tend to advance through the same pattern of development, although some nations and races have become stuck at earlier stages in the process. As archaeologists extended the linear model of social development back down into the stone age, anthropologists appealed to modern 'primitives' for information on how the Europeans' own ancestors had lived in the distant past. At every level of the hierarchy, social evolutionists saw the individual's effort to conquer his environment through the exploitation of better technology as the driving force of social change. Once extended into the realm of biological evolution, this model of continuous change could be uncoupled from the traditional faith in the constancy of human nature. A primitive culture became the sign of a primitive mentality, with the 'lower' races being dismissed as relics of earlier stages in man's progress up from the apes. Spencer's philosophy allowed one to assume that the ascent of life was driven throughout by the same force: Lamarckian evolution and social progress both depended on the accumulated effects of individual effort. Just as exposure to a less stimulating environment had caused some human races to be left behind in the march of progress, so the lower animals were preserved as relics of earlier stages in the ascent of life.

Although sometimes branded as irreligious, the theory of continuous social evolution retained a sense of cosmic teleology by supposing that all efforts were ultimately directed towards the same, morally significant goal. For more conservative thinkers, however, this was not enough. They preferred to see human history as a more obvious expression of the divine plan. It was not enough to claim that human effort was the driving force of progress; God's purpose must transcend our own efforts, at least in the establishment of new levels of social development. Individual effort was meaningful only to the extent that it allowed full expression of the purpose underlying the current phase of history. The cyclic or episodic model of progress was used to retain the belief that history was something more than an accumulation of selfish actions. Each new phase of development moved the human spirit on to a new plane, and could not be accounted for in purely naturalistic terms. From the liberal Anglican view of history to the race consciousness of later historians and anthropologists, we find the same concept of progress advancing by sudden impulses followed by stagnation and decline. The belief that each race has contributed in turn to the ascent of man, only to give way before higher types, provided another excuse for branding non-European races as relics of the past. The same image of the birth and decay of successively higher types was used by palaeontologists opposed to gradual evolution. It continued to flourish in the post-Darwinian era and was exploited in theories of human origins even in the early twentieth century.

The philologists adopted a slightly different model, in which the branching evolution within each stage of development could be seen as the unpacking of potentials created within the original archetype.

Their effort to unify the various 'Aryan' races represented one of the last vestiges of the old biblical view of human origins. It foundered on the growing evidence for the vast antiquity of stone-age mankind and on the increasingly blatant racism of the age of imperialism. Even so, the theory of archetypes played a substantial role in the exploration of the fossil record and, at least indirectly, in the development of Darwin's views on the history of life.

It was at the intersection of the history of life and the history of mankind that the most explosive consequences of the theory of continuous progress became apparent. If gradual progress by everyday natural causes could be extended to cover the evolution of the first primitive humans from ape ancestors, then the liberal virtues of effort and initiative would become the driving forces of nature itself. At the same time, one of the most fundamental bastions of religious orthodoxy – the unique spiritual character of mankind – would be undermined. Those who argued for distinct cycles of development in the fossil record thus had two purposes in mind. They wanted to preserve a clearer indication of God's power operating in nature, and to show that the appearance of mankind was something more than a mere extension of what had gone before. As the idea of progress was extended to include the history of life on earth, both sides of the debate had to accept some form of link between animal and human evolution. But where the Spencerians sought complete integration, their more conservative opponents preferred to see parallels between the phases of human and animal development that would allow each to be treated as a distinct stage in the expression of God's purpose.

Both sides of the debate accepted that struggle, in one form or another, was essential for progress. Liberals saw individual competition as the means by which everyone (and ultimately every organism) was encouraged to do their best. Without the stimulus of competition, individuals would stagnate and progress would come to a halt. Imperialists saw the periodic replacement of one nation or race by another as essential to move progress on to higher levels, and thus took it for granted that the newcomers would have to conquer and dispossess their predecessors. Both sides seized upon Darwinian metaphors to justify their harsh attitudes towards those nations or individuals that were not pulling their weight. Yet neither was prepared to accept the natural selection of purely random variation as the source of progress. Evolution had to arise from something more purposeful; either the initiative of the individual, or underlying natural forces directing variation towards its goal. Natural selection was welcomed only as a secondary or negative mechanism, and the 'modern' aspects of Darwin's thinking were ignored. The *Origin of*

Species triggered off a general conversion to evolutionism because both sides in the debate over progress had become blocked in their efforts to create a unified view of human and animal development. Darwin himself allowed his theory to be seen as a new variety of progressionism, thus facilitating its incorporation into the Spencerian philosophy.

The underlying trend of Darwin's thinking nevertheless ran counter to the prevailing faith in progress. Natural selection left the organism at the mercy of both the environment and its own biological inheritance. Precisely because variation was not directed towards a goal, evolution could be seen as a branching, open-ended process in which even the appearance of a human level of intelligence was unpredictable. The majority of Victorians were quite unable to accept that there was no 'main line' of evolution leading towards themselves, and late-nineteenth-century 'Darwinism' was firmly progressionist in character. Only a few individuals – Robert Knox is one example – rejected progress altogether as a vestige of old-fashioned cosmic teleology. Even Charles Lyell, with his cyclic or steady-state theory of the earth's physical history, saw the appearance of mankind as a distinct upward step. As the Victorians faced up to the problems of living in a changing world, in general they preferred to believe that change must be moving in a purposeful direction.

A few thinkers were willing to accept the possibility that western civilization had already passed its zenith and was moving into its own period of decline. Ruskin saw modern art as degenerating from the mediaeval ideal, and the widespread nostalgia for the past suggests that others shared his distaste for the values of industrialism. But only in the *fin-de-siècle* atmosphere of the 1890s did concern for the possibility of degeneration become widespread. The notoriety surrounding artists such as Aubrey Beardsley and writers such as Oscar Wilde generated a feeling that something might be going wrong with modern values. The German sociologist Max Nordau gave expression to this fear in his survey, *Degeneration*, translated in 1895. Even here, though, modern historical studies suggest that concern over the possibility of short-term degeneration only occasionally extended into wholesale doubts about the future progress of the human race.[1]

As early as 1879, the biologist E. Ray Lankester had pointed out that degeneration was a frequent characteristic of evolution. Any species which began adapting to a less stimulating way of life would lose its active powers and fall back to resemble earlier stages in the

---

[1] See Chamberlin and Gilman, eds, *Degeneration: the Dark Side of Progress*.

ascent of life. Lankester also saw the potential applicability of his thesis to mankind. He warned that 'primitives' such as the Australian aborigines might be the degenerate remnants of once-civilized peoples, not merely relics of our stone-age past. The decline of Rome was used as an example of what could happen to a culture that became too used to luxury. Lankester warned that the same danger could threaten modern civilization, but expressed the hope that science itself would provide a stimulus capable of generating further progress.[2] The fact that Lankester thought it necessary to warn biologists about the effects of degeneration shows how effectively Darwin's theory had been incorporated into progressionism. Lankester's own theory did not challenge the view that the individual's response to its environment is the chief cause of progress – it merely noted that any branch of evolution that was diverted into a less stimulating environment would experience the opposite effect.

In his early career T. H. Huxley had opposed the progressionist interpretation of the fossil record, but in the 1870s his enthusiasm for Haeckel's evolutionism led him to withdraw his opposition. By 1890 Huxley had become dissatisfied with Spencer's social philosophy, and in his Romanes Lecture 'Evolution and Ethics' he revived his anti-progressionist view of life's development as a means of undermining the case for *laissez-faire*.[3] He now insisted that Darwin's theory offered no guarantee of progress, and argued that if most natural evolution was unprogressive, then there was nothing to be gained by allowing nature to take its course in human society. Huxley adopted a philosophy of 'cosmic pessimism' in which human moral values were seen as standing in violation of all natural trends. As a consequence of this, he was prepared to accept that nature would eventually strike back, undermining all human efforts at improvement. Here the essentially nonprogressive character of Darwin's theory had at last begun to assert itself.

This more pessimistic view of evolution was popularized in the science-fiction stories of H. G. Wells, especially *The Time Machine* of 1895. Wells expressed great admiration for Huxley, under whom he had studied briefly at the Normal School of Science. He also wrote a popular article on biological degeneration, which almost certainly

---

[2] Lankester, *Degeneration*, pp. 59–61. This book originated in an address to the British Association in 1879. For a more detailed discussion of the biological side of degenerationism, see Bowler, 'Holding Your Head Up High'.

[3] This essay is reprinted in *Evolution and Ethics*, Huxley's Collected Essays, IX, pp. 46–116. On Huxley's philosophy, see Paradis, *T. H. Huxley: Man's Place in Nature*, esp. pp. 141–63.

owes something to Lankester's earlier discussion.[4] Wells's time traveller is carried to a future in which the human race has degenerated through achieving too perfect a control over the environment. The development of science and technology may have offered a stimulus at first, but eventually they created the two quite different, but equally stultifying environments in which the frail Eloi and the grisly Morlocks had evolved. At the end of the book, Wells offers the even more chilling thought that eventually the sun must die and the whole earth freeze over. The inevitability of this descent into universal night was made apparent by that other great Victorian science, thermodynamics, and Wells graphically portrays the anti-progressionist implications of the physicists' alternative model of a cosmos governed completely by natural law.

To some extent, a concern over the possibility of degeneration was a natural outgrowth of the liberal belief that effort and initiative are the driving forces of evolution. But the alternative theory of cyclic evolution also held open the prospect that the human phase of development might have passed its peak and be heading towards inevitable decline. In 1897, the palaeontologist Alpheus Hyatt extended his theory of racial senility into an argument against the emancipation of women. He claimed that anything tending to bring about an identity between the two sexes would favour the onset of evolutionary senility in mankind.[5] According to Hyatt's own theory, nothing could prevent the eventual degeneration of mankind in the long run. Even so, he expressed the hope that in this case, prompt action could reverse the trend and allow further progress to occur. We have already noted (in chapter 6) how Smith Woodward modified the theory of orthogenesis in the case of human evolution so he could argue that overdevelopment of the brain did not lead to degeneration. Max Nordau's *Degeneration* argued that the human race must eventually run out of evolutionary energy, but insisted that this point had not yet been reached. The problems of modern culture were only temporary, 'because humanity has not yet reached the term of its evolution; because the over-exertion of two or three generations cannot yet have exhausted all its vital powers. Humanity is not senile. It is still young, and a moment of over-exertion is not fatal for youth; it

---

[4] Wells's article 'Zoological Retrogression' is reprinted in Philmus and Hughes, *H. G. Wells: Early Writings in Science and Science Fiction*, pp. 158–68. On *The Time Machine* see Mackenzie and Mackenzie, *The Time Traveller*, ch. 8 and Morton, *The Vital Science*, ch. 4.

[5] Hyatt, 'The Influence of Woman in the Evolution of the Human Race'.

can still recover itself.'[6] Progress may have faltered, but it was not yet at an end.

Wells's account of future degeneration was thus received more as a warning than as a prediction. If modern civilization must inevitably decline, the crisis point had not yet been reached. The exponents of imperialism entered the new century still fairly confident that the white race would continue to dominate the world. Even here, though, there was a growing feeling that active steps would have to be taken if the perils of racial degeneration were to be avoided. The eugenics movement, founded by Darwin's cousin, Francis Galton, warned that the quality of the white race would be diminished if the unfit masses huddled in the slums were allowed to go on breeding at an unchecked rate.[7] For Galton it became almost a religious duty to protect the biological character of the race. At first, his calls for action had been ignored: the Victorians were not ready for a truly hereditarian view of human nature in which a person's character and ability were totally determined by biological inheritance. But in the early years of the new century, Galton at last began to attract significant support. His disciple, Karl Pearson, linked the movement firmly to imperialism by pointing out the dangers to the empire if the nation could not keep up with its rivals. This was especially easy in the aftermath of the Boer War, which had exposed the weaknesses of the army and even of the race itself (many recruits had been rejected as unfit). The future lay not with *laissez-faire* but with active management of the population as well as the economy.

The early eugenics movement was typical of an age which still thought progress was possible, even if it accepted that major efforts were required to counter the threat of degeneration. But the new biology that was called in to support the hereditarian social policies had far-reaching implications for the evolutionism which had sustained the late-Victorians' faith in progress. Eugenics made sense only if one believed that the organism's character is completely determined by its heredity. No amount of effort in response to environmental challenge could produce significant improvement in the organism, or in the characteristics it transmitted to future generations. As Pearson recognized, such a hereditarian theory undermined Lamarckism and all the other non-Darwinian mechanisms that had flourished in the era of progressionism. The natural selection of random variations at last could be seen as the only plausible mechanism of evolution. Although Pearson himself would

---

[6] Nordau, *Degeneration*, p. 540.
[7] On the eugenics movement see Searle, *Eugenics and Politics in Britain*.

never admit it, the new science of Mendelian genetics was, in fact, the clearest expression of this new faith in the power of heredity.[8] In the new biology, the process of individual growth was irrelevant for evolution, thus making clear the illegitimacy of using growth as a model for the ascent of life towards mankind. Eventually the Mendelians too would realize that natural selection was the only available mechanism of evolution, paving the way for the emergence of the modern Darwinian theory.

Opponents of Darwinism – including the modern creationists – have always blamed the theory for undermining the moral fibre of western society. Yet it is difficult to believe that the belated recognition of the full potential of Darwin's theory in the early twentieth century played any more than a minor role in the crisis of confidence that eventually destroyed the Victorian concept of progress. Even at the purely intellectual level, there are many other factors of at least equal significance. Anthropologists now began to turn their backs on the simpleminded evolutionism which had assumed that all modern 'primitives' are merely relics of earlier stages in the development of western society. Under the influence of W. H. R. Rivers, other cultures were studied for the light they threw on the human capacity for social invention, thus implying a cultural relativism that made it harder to depict western values as the goal of an inevitable historical development. Later on, the 'functionalism' of A. R. Radcliffe-Brown would also adopt a strongly nonhistorical perspective on cultural divergence.[9]

Perhaps even more significant were a series of challenges to the very foundations of the assumption that we can perceive a purposeful trend in nature and in human affairs. In the years immediately before the outbreak of the Great War, Sigmund Freud's theory of the unconscious mind began to attract attention in the English-speaking world. Freud himself saw his theory as one of the three greatest blows administered to mankind's self-esteem, following those of Copernicus and Darwin.[10] The new psychology would have been unthinkable without the assumption that mankind had evolved from the animals –

[8] On the controversies surrounding the new theories of heredity see Bowler, *Evolution: The History of an Idea*, chs. 9 and 11, and Bowler, *The Mendelian Revolution*.

[9] See Slobodin, *W. H. R. Rivers* and Langham, *The Building of British Social Anthropology*. On later developments in anthropology, see Stocking, ed., *Functionalism Historicized*.

[10] See Freud's *Introductory Lectures on Psychoanalysis* of 1916–17 in *The Standard Edition of the Complete Psychological Works of Sigmund Freud*, XVI, p. 284. Freud's ideas became known in the English-speaking world after he was invited to lecture in America in 1909.

indeed, Freud's model of the mind as an accumulation of layers established in the course of progressive evolution was a direct product of the developmental philosophy.[11] In this case, however, the extension of progressionism was self-destructive. If the mind were still driven by unconscious and irrational impulses, what hope could there be of controlling, or even of understanding, the development of society? The growing popularity of Freud's approach made it difficult to sustain the claim that western man was somehow elevated further above the level of his animal ancestors.

The American writer Henry Adams identified other factors that had precipitated an intellectual crisis at the start of the new century: Karl Pearsons's positivist philosophy and the revolutionary discoveries of the physicists. Nature was not the neat, orderly system that had been used to uphold the Victorians' faith in evolutionary progress. 'Chaos was the law of Nature; Order the dream of Man.'[12] Evolutionists such as Haeckel had tried to impose a purposeful direction upon nature's activities, but that order had turned out to be purely imaginary. Now even the physicists had discovered that nature was not as rigidly lawbound as they had once assumed. The 'metaphysical bomb called radium' had led Arthur Balfour and others to recognize that 'the human race without exception had lived and died in a world of illusion until the last years of the century.'[13] Thus biology, anthropology, psychology and even physics were all conspiring to undermine the cosmic teleology which had underpinned the Victorians' faith in progress. T. H. Huxley's pioneering efforts to suggest that nature itself was without purpose had now been vindicated, while at the same time his faith in the moral character of mankind had been undermined. The technological superiority that had allowed ·the western nations to dominate the world was no sign either of a more advanced mentality or of a superior level of culture.

By themselves, these revolutionary insights might have had little impact outside intellectual circles. Throughout the Edwardian period, ordinary people were still encouraged to believe that the empire stood for the expansion of civilized values as well as the accumulation of profits. But the very fact that the rivalries between the European nations were becoming ever more intense can, in retrospect, be seen as a growing realization that power was not linked to moral superiority. The carnage of the First World War brought

[11] On the role of evolutionism in Freud's thought, see Sulloway, *Freud: Biologist of the Mind*, ch. 7.
[12] Adams, *The Education of Henry Adams*, p. 451.
[13] Ibid., pp. 452 and 457.

home to everyone the moral bankruptcy of the western nations. The technological skills that had once been used to dominate the world were now exploited to destroy commercial rivals. The threat of degeneration had been realized in an unexpected but horrifying way. If faith in the conceptual foundations of Victorian progressionism had been shaken in the Edwardian era, it was totally destroyed in the war. Paradoxically, the imperialists' emphasis on national competition was itself a product of an important version of the progressionist thesis. It was no coincidence that the theory of Neanderthal extinction was introduced in the years immediately before the outbreak of war. Now the amoral implications of what was misleadingly called 'social Darwinism' had become apparent to all. Oswald Spengler's *Untergang des Abendlandes* (*The Decline of the West*) appeared in 1918, heralding a new and more pessimistic view of history in which the cycle of development for European civilization was now seen to be moving inexorably on to a downward path.

Bibliography

Ackerman, Robert. *J. G. Frazer: His Life and Work*. Cambridge: Cambridge University Press, 1987.

Adams, Henry. *The Education of Henry Adams: An Autobiography*. Boston: Houghton Mifflin, 1918.

Agassiz, Louis. 'On the Succession and Development of Organized Beings at the Surface of the Terrestrial Globe'. *Edinburgh New Philosophical Journal* 33 (1842): 388–99.

Annan, Noel. *Leslie Stephen: The Godless Victorian*. New edn. London: Weidenfeld and Nicolson, 1984.

Appel, Toby. *The Cuvier–Geoffroy Debate: French Biology in the Decades Before Darwin*. New York and Oxford: Oxford University Press, 1987.

Argyll, G. D. Campbell, Duke of. *Primeval Man: An Examination of Some Recent Speculations*. London: Alexander Strahan, 1869.

Arnold, Matthew. *Complete Prose Works*. Ann Arbor: University of Michigan Press, 1960–77, 11 vols.

Arnold, Thomas. *The Life and Correspondence of Thomas Arnold, D.D.* 3rd edn. London: B. Fellowes, 1844, 2 vols.

—— *History of Rome*. New edn. London: T. Fellowes, 1871, 3 vols.

—— *Introductory Lectures on Modern History*. 7th edn. London: Longman, Green, 1885.

Ashton, Rosemary. *The German Idea: Four English Writers and the Reception of German Thought, 1800–1860*. Cambridge: Cambridge University Press, 1980.

Bannister, Robert C. *Social Darwinism: Science and Myth in Anglo-American Social Thought*. Philadelphia: Temple University Press, 1979.

Beddoe, John. *The Races of Britain: A Contribution to the Anthropology of Western Europe.* Reprinted London: Hutchinson, 1971.

Black, Davidson. 'Asia and the Dispersal of Primates'. *Bulletin of the Geological Society of China* 4 (1933): 133–83.

Blinderman, Charles. *The Piltdown Inquest.* Buffalo, NY: Prometheus Books, 1986.

Boule, Marcellin. 'L'homme fossile de La Chapelle-aux-Saints'. *Annales de paléontologie* 6 (1909): 109–72; 7 (1910): 18–56, 85–192; 8 (1911): 1–71.

—— *Fossil Men: Elements of Human Palaeontology.* Edinburgh: Oliver and Boyd, 1923.

Bowler, Peter J. 'The Changing Meaning of "Evolution"'. *Journal of the History of Ideas* 36 (1975): 95–114.

—— *Fossils and Progress: Paleontology and the Idea of Progressive Evolution in the Nineteenth Century.* New York: Science History Publications, 1976.

—— 'Darwinism and the Argument from Design: Suggestions for a Re-evaluation'. *Journal of the History of Biology* 10 (1977): 29–43.

—— *The Eclipse of Darwinism: Anti-Darwinian Evolution Theories in the Decades around 1900.* Baltimore: Johns Hopkins University Press, 1983.

—— *Evolution: The History of an Idea.* Berkeley: University of California Press, 1984.

—— 'E. W. MacBride's Lamarckian Eugenics'. *Annals of Science* 41 (1984): 245–60.

—— *Theories of Human Evolution: A Century of Debate, 1844–1944.* Baltimore: Johns Hopkins University Press; Oxford: Basil Blackwell, 1986.

—— 'The Invention of the Past'. In Lesley M. Smith (ed.), *The Making of Britain: The Age of Revolution*, 159–71. London: Macmillan, 1987.

—— *The Non-Darwinian Revolution: Reinterpreting a Historical Myth.* Baltimore: Johns Hopkins University Press, 1988.

—— *The Mendelian Revolution: The Emergence of Hereditarian Concepts in Modern Science and Society.* London: Athlone Press, 1989.

—— 'Holding Your Head Up High: Degeneration and Orthogenesis in Theories of Human Evolution'. In James R. Moore (ed.), *History, Humanity and Evolution: Essays in Honour of John C. Greene.* Cambridge: Cambridge University Press, forthcoming.

Brace, C. Loring. 'The Fate of the "Classic" Neanderthals: a Consideration of Hominid Catastrophism'. *Current Anthropology* 5 (1964): 3–43.

—— 'The Roots of the Race Concept in American Physical

Anthropology'. In Frank Spencer (ed.), *A History of American Physical Anthropology*, 11–29. New York: Academic Press, 1982.

Broca, Paul. *On the Phenomena of Hybridity in the Genus Homo.* Ed. C. Carter Blake. London: Longman, Green, Longman and Roberts, for the Anthropological Society, 1864.

Brown, David. *Walter Scott and the Historical Imagination.* London: Routledge and Kegan Paul, 1979.

Buckland, William. *Reliquiae Diluvianae: or Observations on the Organic Remains Contained in Caves . . . Attesting the Action of a Universal Deluge.* 2nd edn. London: John Murray, 1824.

—— *Bridgewater Treatise: Geology and Mineralogy Considered with Reference to Natural Theology.* 2nd edn. London, 1837, 2 vols.

Buckle, Henry Thomas. *History of Civilization in England.* London: Longman, Green, 1903, 3 vols.

Buckley, Jerome Hamilton. *The Triumph of Time: A Study of the Victorian Concepts of Time, History, Progress, and Decadence.* Cambridge, Mass.: Harvard University Press, 1966.

Buffetaut, Eric. *A Short History of Vertebrate Palaeontology.* London: Croom Helm, 1987.

Bulwer-Lytton, Edward. *The Last Days of Pompeii.* Leipzig: Tauchnitz, 1879.

Bunsen, Christian Carl Josias. *Christianity and Mankind: Their Beginnings and Prospects.* London: Longman, Brown, Green and Longman, 1854, 7 vols.

Burkhardt, Richard W. Jr. *The Spirit of System: Lamarck and Evolutionary Biology.* Cambridge, Mass.: Harvard University Press, 1977.

Burrow, J. W. *Evolution and Society: A Study in Victorian Social Theory.* Cambridge: Cambridge University Press, 1966.

—— 'The Uses of Philology in Victorian England'. In Robert Robson (ed.), *Ideas and Institutions of Victorian Britain: Essays in Honour of George Kitson Clark*, 180–204. London: G. Bell, 1967.

—— *A Liberal Descent: Victorian Historians and the English Past.* Cambridge: Cambridge University Press, 1981.

Bury, J. B. *The Idea of Progress: An Inquiry into its Growth and Origins.* 1932; reprinted New York: Dover, 1955.

Butler, Samuel. *Evolution, Old and New.* London: Harwicke and Bogue, 1879.

Butterfield, Herbert. *The Whig Interpretation of History.* London: G. Bell, 1931.

Bynum, William F. 'Charles Lyell's *Antiquity of Man* and its Critics'. *Journal of the History of Biology* 17 (1984): 153–87.

Calder, William M., III, and Trail, David A. (eds). *Myth, Scandal and*

History: The Heinrich Schliemann Controversy. Detroit: Wayne State University Press, 1986.

Carlyle, Thomas. *Past and Present*. London: Chapman and Hall, n.d.

Chamberlin, J. Edward, and Gilman, Sander L. (eds). *Degeneration: The Dark Side of Progress*. New York: Columbia University Press, 1985.

[Chambers, Robert.] *Vestiges of the Natural History of Creation*. London: John Churchill, 1844; 5th edn, 1846; 11th edn, 1860.

Chandler, Alice, *A Dream of Order: The Medieval Ideal in Nineteenth-Century English Literature*. London: Routledge and Kegan Paul, 1971.

Clark, Graham. 'The Invasion Hypothesis in British Archaeology'. *Antiquity* 40 (1966): 172–92.

Clive, John. *Thomas Babbington Macaulay: The Shaping of a Historian*. London: Secker and Warburg, 1973.

Combe, George. *Of the Constitution of Man*. Edinburgh, 1828.

Condorcet, M. J. A. N. *Sketch for a Historical Picture of the Progress of the Human Mind*. Trans. J. Barraclough. London: Weidenfeld and Nicolson, 1965.

Cooter, Roger. *The Cultural Meaning of Popular Science: Phrenology and the Organization of Consent in Nineteenth-Century Britain*. Cambridge: Cambridge University Press, 1985.

Corsi, Pietro. *Science and Religion: Baden Powell and the Anglican Debate, 1800–1860*. Cambridge: Cambridge University Press, 1988.

Cottrell, Leonard. *The Bull of Minos: The Discoveries of Schliemann and Evans*. New edn. London: Bell and Hymann, 1984.

Cramb, J. A. *The Origins and Destiny of Imperial Britain*. London: John Murray, 1915.

Culler, A. Dwight. *The Victorian Mirror of History*. New Haven: Yale University Press, 1985.

Curtis, L. P., Jr. *Anglo-Saxons and Celts: A Study of Anti-Irish Prejudice in Victorian England*. Bridgewater, Conn.: Conference on British Studies, 1968.

Cuvier, Georges. *An Essay on the Theory of the Earth*. Edinburgh, 1813.

—— *Recherches sur les ossemens fossiles*. 3rd edn. Paris: Dufour et D'Ocagne, 1825, 5 vols.

Dale, Peter Alan. *The Victorian Critic and the Idea of History: Carlyle, Arnold, Pater*. Cambridge, Mass.: Harvard University Press, 1977.

Daniel, Glyn. *A Hundred and Fifty Years of Archaeology*. London: Duckworth, 1975.

—— (ed.). *Towards a History of Archaeology*. London: Thames and Hudson, 1981.

Darwin, Charles Robert. *On the Origin of Species by Means of Natural Selection: or The Preservation of Favoured Races in the Struggle for Life*. London, 1859; reprinted Cambridge, Mass.: Harvard University Press, 1964.

—— *The Descent of Man and Selection in Relation to Sex*. London: John Murray, 1871, 2 vols. 2nd edn, revised, 1885.

—— *The Autobiography of Charles Darwin*. Ed. Nora Barlow. New York: Harcourt, Brace, 1958.

Davis, Joseph Barnard, and Thurnham, John. *Crania Britannica: Delineations and Descriptions of the Skulls of the Aboriginal and Early Inhabitants of the British Isles*. London: For the Subscribers, 1865.

Dawkins, W. Boyd. *Cave Hunting: Researches on the Evidence of Caves Respecting the Early Inhabitants of Europe*. London: Macmillan, 1874.

—— *Early Man in Britain and His Place in the Tertiary Period*. London: Macmillan, 1880.

de Beer, Sir Gavin. *Charles Darwin*. London: Nelson, 1963.

de Mortillet, Gabriel. *Le Préhistorique: antiquité de l'homme*. Paris: Reinwald, 1883.

—— 'Promenades préhistoriques à l'exposition universelle'. *Matériaux pour l'histoire positive et philosophique de l'homme* 3 (1867): 181–368.

de Quatrefages, A. *The Human Species*. 2nd edn. London: Kegan Paul, 1879.

Desmond, Adrian. 'Designing the Dinosaurs: Richard Owen's Response to Robert Edmund Grant'. *Isis* 70 (1979): 224–34.

—— *Archetypes and Ancestors: Palaeontology in Victorian London 1850–1875*. London: Blond and Briggs, 1982.

—— 'Robert E. Grant: The Social Predicament of a Pre-Darwinian Evolutionist'. *British Journal for the History of Science* 17 (1984): 189–223.

—— 'Richard Owen's Reaction to Transmutation in the 1830s'. *British Journal for the History of Science* 18 (1985): 25–50.

—— 'Artisan Resistance and Evolution in Britain, 1819–1848'. *Osiris* 2nd series 3 (1987): 77–110.

—— *The Politics of Evolution: Morphology, Medicine, and Reform in Radical London*. Chicago: University of Chicago Press, forthcoming.

Dickens, Charles. *Bleak House*. London: Hazell, Watson & Viney, n.d.

di Gregorio, Mario. *T. H. Huxley's Place in Natural Science*. New Haven: Yale University Press, 1984.

Dilke, Sir Charles Wentworth. *Greater Britain: A Record of Travel in English-Speaking Countries during 1866 and 1867*. 5th edn. London: Macmillan, 1870.

Draper, J. W. *History of the Conflict between Religion and Science.* New York: Appleton, 1874.

Drummond, Henry. *The Ascent of Man.* New York: James Pott, 1894.

Dubois, Eugene. 'Remarks on the Brain-Cast of *Pithecanthropus erectus*'. In A. Sedgwick (ed.), *Proceedings of the Fourth International Congress of Zoology*, 78–95. Cambridge: Cambridge University Press, 1898.

Dunn, Waldo Hilary. *James Anthony Froude: A Biography.* Oxford: Clarendon Press, 1961–3, 2 vols.

Durant, John (ed.). *Darwinism and Divinity: Essays on Evolution and Religious Belief.* Oxford: Basil Blackwell, 1985.

Eiseley, Loren. *Darwin's Century: Evolution and the Men who Discovered it.* New York: Doubleday, 1958.

Ellegård, Alvar. *Darwin and the General Reader: The Reception of Darwin's Theory of Evolution in the British Periodical Press, 1859–1872.* Goteburg: Acta Universitatis Gothenburgensis, 1957.

Evans, John. *The Ancient Stone Implements, Weapons, and Ornaments of Great Britain.* London: Longman, Green, Reader and Dyer, 1872; 2nd edn. London: Longman, Green, 1897.

Farrar, Frederic W. *Families of Speech: Four Lectures Delivered before the Royal Institution of Great Britain.* London: Longman, Green. 1870.

Feaver, William. *The Art of John Martin.* Oxford: Clarendon Press, 1975.

Ferguson, Adam. *An Essay on the History of Civil Society.* Dublin: Boulter Grierson, 1787.

Flammarion, C. *Le monde avant la création de l'homme.* Paris: Marpon and Flammarion, 1886.

Fleishman, Avrom. *The English Historical Novel: Walter Scott to Virginia Woolf.* Baltimore: Johns Hopkins University Press, 1971.

Forbes, Duncan. *The Liberal Anglican Idea of History.* Cambridge: Cambridge University Press, 1952.

Frazer, J. G. *Psyche's Task: A Discourse Concerning the Influence of Superstition on the Growth of Institutions.* London: Macmillan, 1913.

—— *The Golden Bough: A Study in Magic and Religion.* Abridged edn. London: Macmillan, 1924.

Freeman, Edward A. *The History of the Norman Conquest of England: Its Causes and its Results.* Oxford: Clarendon Press, 1870–6, 5 vols.

—— *Comparative Politics: Six Lectures read before the Royal Institution in January and February 1873.* 2nd edn. London: Macmillan, 1896.

—— *The Chief Periods of European History: Six Lectures read in the University of Oxford in Trinity Term 1885.* London: Macmillan, 1896.

Freud, Sigmund. *The Standard Edition of the Complete Psychological Works of Sigmund Freud.* London: Hogarth Press, 1959–74, 24 vols.

Froude, James Anthony. *The Nemesis of Faith*. London: John Chapman, 1849.

—— *History of England from the Fall of Wolsey to the Death of Elizabeth*. London: John W. Parker/Longman, Green, 1856–70, 12 vols.

—— *Short Studies on Great Subjects*. New edn. London: Longman, Green, 1881, 3 vols.

—— *The English in Ireland in the Eighteenth Century*. London: Longman, Green, 1881, 3 vols.

—— *Oceana: or England and her Colonies*. London: Longman, Green, 1896.

—— *English Seamen in the Sixteenth Century: Lectures delivered at Oxford, Easter Terms, 1893–94*. London: Longman, Green, 1895.

Gillespie, Neal C. 'The Duke of Argyll, Evolutionary Anthropology, and the Art of Scientific Controversy'. *Isis* 68 (1977): 40–54.

Gillispie, Charles C. *Genesis and Geology: A Study in the Relations of Scientific Thought, Natural Theology, and Social Opinion in Great Britain, 1790–1850*. Cambridge, Mass.: Harvard University Press, 1951.

Gould, Stephen Jay. *Ontogeny and Phylogeny*. Cambridge, Mass.: Harvard University Press, 1977.

—— *The Mismeasure of Man*. New York: Norton, 1981.

—— *Time's Arrow, Time's Cycle*. Cambridge, Mass.: Harvard University Press, 1987.

[Grant, Robert E.] 'Observations on the Nature and Importance of Geology'. *Edinburgh New Philosophical Journal* 1 (1826): 293–302.

—— 'Of the Changes which Life has Experienced on the Globe'. *Edinburgh New Philosophical Journal* 3 (1827): 298–301.

Grayson, Donald K. *The Establishment of Human Antiquity*. New York: Academic Press, 1983.

Green, John Richard. *The History of England*. London: Macmillan, 1881.

—— *The Conquest of England*. 2nd edn. London: Macmillan, 1884.

Greene, John C. *The Death of Adam: Evolution and its Impact on Western Thought*. Ames: Iowa State University Press, 1959.

Greenwell, William. *British Barrows: A Record of the Examination of Sepulchral Mounds in Various Parts of England*. Oxford: Clarendon Press, 1877.

Grote, George. *A History of Greece from the Earliest Period to the Close of the Generation Contemporary with Alexander the Great*. New edn. London: John Murray, 1888, 10 vols.

Gruber, Jacob W. *A Conscience in Conflict: The Life of St George Jackson Mivart*. New York: Columbia University Press, 1960.

—— 'Brixham Cave and the Antiquity of Man'. In Milford E. Spiro (ed.), *Context and Meaning in Cultural Anthropology*, 373–402. New York: Free Press; London: Collier–Macmillan, 1964.

Haddon, A. C. *The Study of Man.* London: John Murray, 1898.

Haeckel, Ernst. *The History of Creation: or The Development of the Earth and its Inhabitants by the Action of Natural Causes. A Popular Exposition of the Doctrine of Evolution in General and of that of Darwin, Lamarck, and Goethe in Particular.* New York: Appleton, 1876, 2 vols.

—— *The Evolution of Man: A Popular Exposition of the Principal Points of Human Ontogeny and Phylogeny.* New York: Appleton, 1879, 2 vols.

—— *The Last Link: Our Present Knowledge of the Descent of Man.* London: A. & C. Black, 1898.

Halévy, Elie. *The Growth of Philosophic Radicalism.* Boston: Beacon Press, 1955.

Hamburger, Joseph. *Macaulay and the Whig Tradition.* Chicago: University of Chicago Press, 1976.

Hammond, Michael. 'Anthropology as a Weapon of Social Combat in Late-Nineteenth-Century France'. *Journal of the History of the Behavioral Sciences* 16 (1980): 118–32.

—— 'The Expulsion of the Neanderthals from Human Ancestry: Marcellin Boule and the Social Context of Scientific Research'. *Social Studies of Science* 12 (1982): 1–36.

Harris, Marvin. *The Rise of Anthropological Theory: A History of Theories of Culture.* London: Routledge and Kegan Paul, 1968.

Hatch, Melvin. *Theories of Man and Culture.* New York: Columbia University Press, 1973.

Henty, G. A. *By England's Aid: or The Freeing of the Netherlands (1585–1604).* London: Blackie, n.d.

Himmelfarb, Gertrude. *Darwin and the Darwinian Revolution.* New York: Norton, 1959.

Hodge, M. J. S. 'Lamarck's Science of Living Bodies'. *British Journal for the History of Science* 5 (1971): 323–52.

—— 'The Universal Gestation of Nature: Chambers' *Vestiges* and *Explanations*'. *Journal of the History of Biology* 5 (1972): 127–52.

Hofstadter, Richard. *Social Darwinism in American Thought.* Revised edn. Boston: Beacon Press, 1959.

Houghton, Walter E. *The Victorian Frame of Mind, 1830–1870.* New Haven: Yale University Press; London: Oxford University Press, 1957.

Hrdlička, Ales. 'The Neanderthal Phase of Man'. *Journal of the Royal Anthropological Institute* 56 (1927): 249–74.

Hume, David. *The History of England from the Invasion of Julius Caesar to the Revolution of 1688.* New edn. Basle: J. J. Tourneson, 1789, 12 vols.

Huxley, T. H. 'Vestiges of the Natural History of Creation'. *British and Foreign Medico-Chirurgical Review* 13 (1853): 332–43.

—— *Man's Place in Nature.* London: Williams and Norgate, 1863.

—— *American Addresses: With a Lecture on the Study of Biology.* New York: Appleton, 1888.

—— *Collected Essays.* London: Macmillan, 1893–4, 9 vols. (VII, *Man's Place in Nature*; IX, *Evolution and Ethics.*)

Hyatt, Alpheus. 'On the Parallelism between the Different Stages of Life in the Individual and those in the Entire Group of the Moluscous Order Tetrabranchiata'. *Memoirs of the Boston Society of Natural History* 1 (1861): 193–209.

—— 'The Influence of Woman in the Evolution of the Human Race'. *Natural Science* 11 (1897): 89–93.

Jenkyns, Richard. *The Victorians and Ancient Greece.* Oxford: Basil Blackwell, 1980.

Jensen, J. Vernon. 'Return to the Wilberforce–Huxley Debate'. *British Journal for the History of Science* 21 (1988): 161–80.

Jones, Greta. *Social Darwinism and English Thought.* London: Harvester, 1980.

Jordanova, L. *Lamarck.* Oxford: Oxford University Press, 1984.

Keane, A. H. *Ethnology.* Cambridge: Cambridge University Press, 1896.

Keith, Arthur. *Ancient Types of Man.* London and New York: Harper, 1911.

—— *The Antiquity of Man.* London: Williams and Norgate, 1915.

—— *Darwinism and What it Implies.* London: Watts, 1928.

—— *Darwinism and its Critics.* London: Watts, 1935.

Kemble, John Mitchell. *The Saxons in England: A History of the English Commonwealth till the Period of the Norman Conquest.* London: Longman, Brown, Green and Longman, 1849, 2 vols.

King, William. 'The Reputed Fossil Man of the Neanderthal'. *Quarterly Journal of Science* 1 (1864): 88–97.

Kingsley, Charles. *Charles Kingsley: His Letters and Memories of his Life.* 4th edn. London: Henry S. King, 1877, 2 vols.

—— *Scientific Lectures and Essays.* London: Macmillan, 1890.

—— *Hypatia: or New Foes with an Old Face.* London: Macmillan, 1895.

—— *The Roman and the Teuton: A Series of Lectures Delivered before the University of Cambridge.* New edn. London: Macmillan, 1897.

—— *Westward Ho!* London: Macmillan, 1917.

—— *Hereward the Wake: 'Last of the English'.* London: Macmillan, 1919.

Kipling, Rudyard. *Puck of Pook's Hill.* London: Macmillan, 1906.

—— *Rewards and Fairies.* London: Macmillan, 1910.

Klaatsch, Hermann. *The Evolution and Progress of Mankind.* Trans. Joseph McCabe. London: T. Fisher Unwin, 1923.

Knoll, Elizabeth. 'The Science of Language and the Evolution of Mind: Max Müller's Quarrel with Darwinism'. *Journal of the History of the Behavioral Sciences* 22 (1986): 3–22.

Knox, Robert. *The Races of Men: A Philosophical Enquiry into the Influence of Race on the Destiny of Nations.* 2nd edn. London: Henry Renshaw, 1862.

Kohn, David (ed.). *The Darwinian Heritage.* Princeton: Princeton University Press, 1985.

Kottler, Malcolm J. 'Alfred Russel Wallace, the Origin of Man, and Spiritualism'. *Isis* 65 (1974): 145–92.

Kuper, Adam. 'The Development of Lewis Henry Morgan's Evolutionism'. *Journal of the History of the Behavioral Sciences* 21 (1985): 3–21.

Laing, Samuel. *Human Origins.* London: Chapman and Hall, 1892.

Lamarck, J. B. *Zoological Philosophy.* Trans. Hugh Elliot. London: Macmillan, 1914.

Langham, Ian. *The Building of British Social Anthropology: W. H. R. Rivers and his Disciples in the Development of Kinship Studies, 1898–1931.* Dordrecht: D. Reidel, 1981.

Lankester, E. Ray. 'Notes on the Embryology and Classification of the Animal Kingdom'. *Quarterly Journal of Microscopical Science* 17 (1877): 399–454.

—— *Degeneration: A Chapter in Darwinism.* London: Macmillan, 1880.

—— 'Zoology'. *Encyclopaedia Britannica.* 9th edn (1888) 24: 799–820.

Layard, Austen Henry. *Nineveh and its Remains.* London: John Murray, 1849, 2 vols.

—— *Discoveries in Nineveh and Babylon.* London: John Murray, 1853.

Lecky, W. E. H. *History of the Rise and Influence of the Spirit of Rationalism in Europe.* London: Longman, Green, Longman, Roberts and Green, 1865, 2 vols.

—— *The Political Value of History.* London: Edward Arnold, 1892.

Lehmann, William C. *John Millar of Glasgow, 1735–1801: His Life and Thought and his Contributions to Sociological Analysis.* Cambridge: Cambridge University Press, 1960.

Lloyd, Seton. *Foundations in the Dust: The Story of Mesopotamian Exploration.* Revised edn. London: Thames and Hudson, 1980.

Lubbock, John. *Prehistoric Times: As Illustrated by Ancient Remains and the Manners and Customs of Modern Savages*. London: Williams and Norgate, 1865.

—— *The Origin of Civilization and the Primitive Condition of Man: Mental and Social Conditions of Savages*. London: Longman, Green, 1870.

Lurie, Edward. *Louis Agassiz: A Life in Science*. Chicago: University of Chicago Press, 1960.

Lyell, Charles. *Principles of Geology*. London, 1830–33, 3 vols; 7th edn. London: John Murray, 1847.

—— *Geological Evidences of the Antiquity of Man*. London: John Murray, 1863.

Macaulay, Thomas Babbington. *The History of England from the Accession of James the Second*. London: Longman, Brown, Green and Longman, 1850–61, 5 vols.

—— *Critical and Historical Essays*. New impression. London: Longman, Green, 1908.

MacBride, E. W. *A Textbook of Embryology: Invertebrates*. London, 1914.

MacDougall, Hugh A: *Racial Myth in English History: Trojans, Teutons, and Anglo-Saxons*. Montreal: Harvest House; Hanover, NH: University Press of New England, 1982.

Mackenzie, Norman and Jeanne. *The Time Traveller: The Life of H. G. Wells*. London: Weidenfeld and Nicolson, 1973.

McLennan, John Ferguson. *Studies in Ancient History: Comprising a Reprint of Primitive Marriage: An Inquiry into the Origin of the Form of Capture in Marriage Ceremonies*. London: Bernard Quaritsch, 1876.

McMaster, Graham. *Scott and Society*. Cambridge: Cambridge University Press, 1981.

Maine, Henry. *Ancient Law*. London: Everyman, 1917.

Mandelbaum, Maurice. *History, Man, and Reason: A Study in Nineteenth-Century Thought*. Baltimore: Johns Hopkins University Press, 1971.

Mantell, Gideon. 'The Geological Age of Reptiles'. *Edinburgh New Philosophical Journal* 11 (1831): 181–5.

—— *The Wonders of Geology: or A Familiar Exposition of Geological Phenomena*. 3rd edn. London, 1839, 2 vols.

Mill, James. *The History of British India*. 4th edn, with notes by H. H. Wilson. London: James Madden, 1848, 6 vols.

Mill, John Stuart. *Auguste Comte and Positivism*. London: Trübner, 1865.

—— *The Autobiography of John Stuart Mill*. New York: Columbia University Press, 1944.

—— *Collected Works of John Stuart Mill.* Toronto: University of Toronto Press; London: Routledge and Kegan Paul, 1981–6, 25 vols.

Miller, Hugh. *The Old Red Sandstone: Or New Walks in an Old Field.* Edinburgh, 1841; new edn Boston, 1858.

—— *Footprints of the Creator: Or the Asterolepis of Stromness.* 3rd edn. London: Johnston and Hunter, 1850.

Millhauser, Milton. *Just before Darwin: Robert Chambers and Vestiges.* Middletown, Conn.: Wesleyan University Press, 1959.

Mivart, St George J. *On the Genesis of Species.* London: Macmillan, 1871.

—— *Man and Apes: An Exposition of Structural Resemblances Bearing upon Questions of Affinity and Origin.* London: Robert Harwicke, 1873.

—— 'On the Possible Dual Origin of the Mammalia'. *Proceedings of the Royal Society of London* 43 (1887–8): 372–379.

—— 'On the Development of the Individual and of the Species'. *Proceedings of the Zoological Society of London* (1884): 462–74.

Monypenny, W. F. and Buckle, G. E. *The Life of Benjamin Disraeli.* Revised edn. London: John Murray, 1929, 2 vols.

Moore, James R. *The Post-Darwinian Controversies: A Study of the Protestant Struggle to Come to Terms with Darwin in Britain and America, 1870–1900.* Cambridge: Cambridge University Press, 1979.

—— 'Herbert Spencer's Henchmen: The Evolution of Protestant Liberals in Late-Nineteenth-Century America'. In John Durant (ed.), *Darwinism and Divinity*, 76–100. Oxford: Basil Blackwell, 1985.

—— (ed.). *History, Humanity, and Evolution: Essays in Honour of John C. Greene.* Cambridge: Cambridge University Press, forthcoming.

Morgan, Lewis Henry. *Ancient Society: or Researches in the Lines of Human Progress from Savagery through Barbarism to Civilization.* Ed. Leslie A. White. Cambridge, Mass.: Harvard University Press, 1964.

Morton, Peter. *The Vital Science: Biology and the Literary Imagination, 1860–1900.* London: Allen and Unwin, 1984.

Müller, F. Max. *Lectures on the Science of Language Delivered at the Royal Institution of Great Britain.* London: Longman, Green, Longman and Roberts, 1861.

—— *The Science of Thought.* London: Longman, Green, 1887.

—— *Biographies of Words and The Home of the Aryans.* London: Longman, Green, 1888.

Newman, John Henry. *Callista: A Tale of the Third Century.* New edn. London: Longman, Green, 1910.

Nisbet, Robert A. *Social Change and History: Aspects of the Western Theory of Development.* New York: Oxford University Press, 1969.

—— *History of the Idea of Progress.* London: Heinemann, 1980.

Nordau, Max. *Degeneration.* 2nd edn. London: Heinemann, 1895.

Ospovat, Dov. 'The Influence of Karl Ernst von Baer's Embryology, 1828–1859: A Reappraisal in Light of Richard Owen and William B. Carpenter's "Paleontological Application of von Baer's Law"'. *Journal of the History of Biology* 9 (1976): 1–28.

—— *The Development of Darwin's Theory: Natural History, Natural Theology and Natural Selection, 1838–1859.* Cambridge: Cambridge University Press, 1981.

Owen, Richard. 'Report on British Fossil Reptiles, Part 2'. *Report of the British Association for the Advancement of Science*, 1841, 60–204.

—— *On the Nature of Limbs.* London: van Voorst, 1849.

—— *On the Anatomy of the Vertebrates.* London: Longman, Green, 1866–8, 3 vols.

Palgrave, Francis. *Truths and Fictions of the Middle Ages: The Merchant and the Friar.* London, 1837.

Pallister, Anne. *Magna Carta: The Heritage of Liberty.* Oxford: Oxford University Press, 1971.

Palmer, J. Foster. 'The Saxon Invasion and its Influence on our Character as a Race'. *Transactions of the Royal Historical Society* 2nd series 2 (1885): 173–96.

Paradis, James G. *T. H. Huxley: Man's Place in Nature.* Lincoln: University of Nebraska Press, 1978.

Pater, Walter. *The Renaissance: Studies in Art and Poetry.* Ed. Donald L. Hill. Berkeley: University of California Press, 1980.

Peel, J. D. Y. *Herbert Spencer: The Evolution of a Sociologist.* London: Heinemann, 1971.

Penniman, T. K. *A Hundred Years of Anthropology.* 2nd edn. London: Duckworth, 1952.

Phillips, John. *Life on Earth: Its Origin and Succession.* Cambridge and London: Macmillan, 1860.

Philmus, Robert M., and Hughes, David Y. *H. G. Wells: Early Writings in Science and Science Fiction.* Berkeley: University of California Press, 1975.

Poliakov, L. *The Aryan Myth.* New York: Basic Books, 1970.

Pollard, Sydney. *The Idea of Progress: History and Society.* Harmondsworth: Penguin Books, 1971.

Powell, Baden. *Essays on the Inductive Philosophy, The Unity of Worlds, and the Philosophy of Creation.* London: 1855.

Prichard, James Cowles. *Research into the Physical History of Man.* London: John and Arthur Arch, 1813.

Reade, Winwood. *The Martyrdom of Man.* 14th edn. London: Kegan Paul, Trench, Trübner, 1892.

Reader, John. *Missing Links: The Hunt for Earliest Man.* London: Collins, 1981.

Reynolds, Graham. *Victorian Painting.* Revised edn. London: Herbert Press, 1987.

Richards, Evelleen. 'A Question of Property Rights: Richard Owen's Evolutionism Reassessed'. *British Journal for the History of Science* 20 (1987): 129–72.

Richards, Robert J. *Darwin and the Emergence of Evolutionary Theories of Mind and Behavior.* Chicago: University of Chicago Press, 1987.

Romanes, George John. *Mental Evolution in Animals.* London: Kegan Paul, Trench, 1883.

—— *Mental Evolution in Man: Origins of Human Faculty.* London: Kegan Paul, Trench, Trübner, 1888.

Rossi, Paolo. *The Dark Abyss of Time: The History of the Earth and the History of Nations from Hooke to Vico.* Chicago: University of Chicago Press, 1984.

Rowse, A. L. *Froude the Historian: Victorian Man of Letters.* Gloucester: Alan Sutton, 1988.

—— *Froude's Spanish Story of the Armada.* Gloucester: Alan Sutton, 1988.

Rudwick, M. J. S. *The Meaning of Fossils: Episodes in the History of Palaeontology.* New York: American Elsevier, 1972.

—— 'Caricature as a Source for the History of Science: De la Beche's Anti-Lyellian Sketches of 1831'. *Isis* 66 (1975): 534–60.

—— *The Great Devonian Controversy: The Shaping of Scientific Knowledge among Gentlemanly Specialists.* Chicago: University of Chicago Press, 1985.

Rupke, Nicolaas. *The Great Chain of History: William Buckland and the English School of Geology, 1814–1849.* Oxford: Clarendon Press, 1983.

Ruse, Michael. *The Darwinian Revolution: Science Red in Tooth and Claw.* Chicago: University of Chicago Press, 1979.

Ruskin, John. *Arata Pentelici: Seven Lectures on the Elements of Sculpture given before the University of Oxford in Michaelmas Term 1870.* Orpington and London: George Allen, 1890.

—— *Lectures on Architecture and Painting Delivered at Edinburgh in November 1858.* New edn. London: George Allen, 1891.

Sanders, Andrew. *The Victorian Historical Novel, 1840–1880.* London: Macmillan, 1978.

Schaafhausen, D. 'On the Crania of the Most Ancient Races of Man'. Trans. George Busk. *Natural History Review* 8 (1861): 155–72.

Schliemann, Henry. *Troy and its Remains: A Narrative of Researches and Discoveries Made on the Site of Ilium in the Trojan Plain.* Ed. Philip Smith. London: John Murray, 1875.

—— *Mycenae: A Narrative of Researches and Discoveries at Mycenae and Tiryns.* Preface by W. E. Gladstone. London: John Murray, 1878.

—— *Ilios: The City and Country of the Trojans.* London: John Murray: 1880.

—— *Troja: Results of the Latest Researches and Discoveries on the Site of Homer's Troy.* London: John Murray, 1884.

Schrempp, Gregory. 'The Re-education of Friedrich Max Müller: Intellectual Appropriations and Epistemological Antinomy in Mid-Victorian Evolutionary Thought'. *Man* 18 (1983): 90–110.

Schwalbe, G. 'The Descent of Man'. In A. C. Seward (ed.), *Darwin and Modern Science*, 112–36. Cambridge: Cambridge University Press, 1909.

Scott, Sir Walter. *The Melrose Edition of the Waverley Novels.* London: Caxton Publishing, n.d. 25 vols.

Searle, G. R. *Eugenics and Politics in Britain, 1900–1914.* Leiden: Noordhoff International, 1976.

Secord, James A. *Controversy in Victorian Geology: The Cambrian–Silurian Dispute.* Princeton: Princeton University Press, 1986.

—— 'Behind the Veil: Robert Chambers and the Genesis of the *Vestiges of Creation*'. In James R. Moore (ed.), *History, Humanity and Evolution.* Cambridge: Cambridge University Press, forthcoming.

Seeley, J. R. *The Expansion of England: Two Courses of Lectures.* London: Macmillan, 1902.

Slobodin, R. *W. H. R. Rivers.* New York: Columbia University Press, 1981.

Smith, Adam. *Lectures on Jurisprudence.* ed. R. L. Meek et al. Oxford: Clarendon Press, 1978.

Sollas, W. J. *Ancient Hunters and their Modern Representatives.* London: Macmillan, 1911: 3rd edn. London: Macmillan, 1924.

Spencer, Herbert. *Social Statics: or The Conditions Essential to Human Happiness Specified, and the First of them Developed.* London: John Chapman, 1851.

—— *First Principles of a New Philosophy.* London: Williams and Norgate, 1861.

—— *Principles of Biology.* London: Williams and Norgate, 1864, 2 vols.

—— *Principles of Psychology.* 2nd edn. London: Williams and Norgate, 1870–2, 2 vols.

—— *The Principles of Sociology.* London: Williams and Norgate, 1876–96, 3 vols.

—— *Essays Scientific, Political, and Speculative.* London: Williams and Norgate, 1883, 3 vols.

Spengler, Oswald. *The Decline of the West.* Reprinted New York: Knopf, 1939.

Stanton, William. *The Leopard's Spots: Scientific Attitudes toward Race in America, 1815–1859.* Chicago: Phoenix Books, 1966.

Stepan, Nancy. *The Idea of Race in Science: Great Britain, 1800–1960.* London: Macmillan, 1982.

Stocking, George W., Jr. *Race, Culture, and Evolution: Essays in the History of Anthropology.* New York: Free Press; London: Collier-Macmillan, 1968.

—— 'What's in a Name? The Origins of the Royal Anthropological Institute (1837–1871)'. *Man* 6 (1971): 369–90.

—— (ed.). *Functionalism Historicized: Essays on British Social Anthropology.* Madison: University of Wisconsin Press, 1984.

—— *Victorian Anthropology.* New York: Free Press, 1987.

Strong, Roy. *And When Did You Last See Your Father? The Victorian Painter and British History.* London: Thames and Hudson, 1978.

Stubbs, William. *The Constitutional History of England in its Origins and Development.* 6th edn. Oxford: Clarendon Press, 1897, 3 vols.

Sulloway, Frank. *Freud: Biologist of the Mind: Beyond the Psychoanalytic Legend.* London: Burnett Books, 1979.

Symonds, J. A. *Renaissance in Italy.* London: John Murray, 1914–20, 7 vols.

Taylor, Isaac. *The Origin of the Aryans: An Account of Prehistoric Ethnology and Civilization in Europe.* London: Walter Scott, 1889.

Temple, Frederick, et al. *Essays and Reviews.* London: John W. Parker, 1860.

Tennyson, Alfred. *In Memoriam.* Ed. R. H. Ross. New York: Norton, 1973.

Thorp, Margaret F. *Charles Kingsley, 1819–1875.* Princeton: Princeton University Press, 1937.

Thucydides. *The History of the Peloponnesian War . . . with Notes by Thomas Arnold.* Oxford: S. Collingwood, 1830–5, 3 vols.

Toulmin, S. and Goodfield, J. *The Discovery of Time.* Chicago: University of Chicago Press, 1965.

Trautmann, Thomas R. *Lewis Henry Morgan and the Invention of Kinship.* Berkeley: University of California Press, 1987.

Turner, Frank Miller. *Between Science and Religion: The Reaction to Scientific Naturalism in Late Victorian England.* New Haven: Yale University Press, 1974.

—— *The Greek Heritage in Victorian Britain.* New Haven: Yale University Press, 1981.

Turner, Sharon. *The History of the Anglo-Saxons: Comprising the History of England from the Earliest Period to the Norman Conquest.* London: Longman, Hunt, Rees, Orme & Browne, 1820, 3 vols.

Tylor, Edward B. *Researches into the Early History of Mankind and the Development of Civilization.* 2nd edn. London: John Murray, 1870.

—— *Anthropology: An Introduction to the Study of Man and Civilization.* London: Macmillan, 1881.

Urry, James. 'Englishmen, Celts and Iberians: The Ethnographic Survey of the United Kingdom, 1892–1899'. In George W. Stocking (ed.), *Functionalism Historicized.* 83–105. Madison: University of Wisconsin Press, 1984.

Vogt, Carl. *Lectures on Man: His Place in Creation and the History of the Earth.* Ed. James Hunt. London: Longman, Green, Longman & Roberts for the Anthropological Society, 1864.

Vorzimmer, Peter, J. *Charles Darwin: The Years of Controversy.* Philadelphia: Temple University Press, 1970.

Wallace, Alfred Russel. *Darwinism: An Exposition of the Theory of Natural Selection.* London: Macmillan, 1889.

—— *Natural Selection and Tropical Nature.* New edn. London: Macmillan, 1895.

Waterfield, Gordon. *Layard of Nineveh.* London: John Murray, 1963.

Weiner, J. S. *The Piltdown Forgery.* London: Oxford University Press, 1955.

Whewell, William. *History of the Inductive Sciences.* 2nd edn. London, 1847, 3 vols.

—— *Philosophy of the Inductive Sciences.* 2nd edn. London, 1847, 2 vols.

White, A. D. *A History of the Warfare of Science with Theology in Christendom.* 1896; reprinted New York: Dover, 1960, 2 vols.

White, Haydon. *Metahistory: the Historical Imagination in Nineteenth-Century Europe.* Baltimore: Johns Hopkins University Press, 1973.

Willey, Basil. *Nineteenth-Century Studies: Coleridge to Matthew Arnold.* London: Chatto and Windus, 1949.

—— *More Nineteenth-Century Studies: A Group of Honest Doubters.* London: Chatto and Windus, 1956.

—— *Darwin and Butler: Two Versions of Evolution.* London: Chatto and Windus, 1960.

Wilson, Daniel. *The Archaeology and Prehistoric Annals of Scotland.* Edinburgh, 1851.

Wood, Christopher. *The Pre-Raphaelites.* London: Weidenfeld and Nicolson, 1981.

—— *Olympian Dreamers: Victorian Classical Painters, 1860–1914.* London: Constable, 1983.

Woodward, Arthur Smith. 'President's Address, Geological Section'. *Report of the British Association for the Advancement of Science.* 1909, 462–71.

—— *A Guide to the Fossil Remains of Man.* London: British Museum (Natural History), 1915.

—— *The Earliest Englishman.* London: Watts, 1948.

Wormell, Deborah. *Sir John Seeley and the Uses of History.* Cambridge: Cambridge University Press, 1980.

Worsaae, J. J. A. *The Primeval Antiquities of Denmark.* Trans. W. J. Thomas. London: J. H. Parker, 1849.

—— *The Pre-History of the North based on Contemporary Memorials.* Trans. H. F. Marland Simpson. London: Trübner, 1886.

Young, Robert M. *Darwin's Metaphor: Nature's Place in Victorian Culture.* Cambridge: Cambridge University Press, 1985.

Index

Note: Page references in *italics* indicate figures or illustrations.

Index compiled by Meg Davies